QUICK & EASY
MENU COOKBOOK

QUICK & EASY
MENU COOKBOOK

Weight Watchers

Ann Page-Wood

NEW ENGLISH LIBRARY

For information about the Weight Watchers classes, contact:
Weight Watchers UK Ltd, Kidwells Park House,
Kidwells Park Drive, Maidenhead, Berks SL6 8YT.
Telephone: (0628) 777077

Art Director: Roger Judd
Photography: Simon Smith at Barry Bullough Studios
assisted by Thierry Guinovart
Home Economist: Ann Page-Wood
Styling: Kathy Man

British Library Cataloguing in Publication Data

Page-Wood, Ann
  The quick and easy menu cookbook
  I. Title   II. Weight Watchers
  641.5'635

  ISBN 0-450-50999-0

First published in Great Britain 1989

Published by New English Library,
a hardcover imprint of Hodder and Stoughton,
a division of Hodder and Stoughton Ltd,
Mill Road, Dunton Green, Sevenoaks, Kent TN13 2YA
Editorial Office: 47 Bedford Square, London WC1B 3DP

Photoset by Rowland Phototypesetting Ltd,
Bury St Edmunds, Suffolk

Printed in Great Britain by
BPCC Hazell Books Ltd, Member of BPCC Ltd, Aylesbury, Bucks.

CONTENTS

Quick & Easy

HOW TO USE THIS BOOK

There are many books available which offer advice on losing weight and a tremendous number of them include recipes, but this book goes a great deal further. It not only gives every recipe as part of a whole day's eating plan but includes weekly menus which are based on the Weight Watchers Quick Success Programme.

The Weight Watchers Programme comprises five weekly food plans. Week 1 has a fairly limited choice of foods and is based on approximately 950 Calories each day. The amount of hard cheese, eggs and red meats is limited but, as the weeks progress, more foods are introduced and the calorie intake increases to a maximum of 1350 Calories per day by Week 5. Although the amount of red meats allowed is still restricted by Week 5, 12oz (360g) may be eaten in that week. Other luxuries which can be enjoyed by Week 5 include wines, spirits, cream, chocolate and croissants but it is essential to weigh food accurately to ensure a healthy well-balanced diet. The Week 5 food plan should be continued until your goal weight has been reached; then, when you reach your target, gradually introduce other foods until you are able to maintain that weight.

Following this introduction is a selection of notes on ingredients but to understand this diet and simplify the Menu Plan the book is divided into three sections.

The First Section

This contains a day's menu with a single recipe on every page, so there are seven recipes with the complete allowances for Week 1 through to Week 5. As Week 5 should be followed until your goal weight has been attained two complete menu plans with recipes are given. If you are a vegetarian, and therefore do not eat meat or fish, a smaller section is devoted to your diet, but as you will see many recipes in the book can be made and enjoyed by vegetarians as well as non-vegetarians.

The Second Section

The 'Weeks at a Glance' plans may be used as an alternative to those given in the first section, though it must be noted that a single day from, for example, Week 1 must not be substituted for a single day from the Week 1 in the Weekly Menu Plans. Use either the first or the second section plan every week. This is essential as some foods are restricted and these foods, such as red meats, cheese and eggs are calculated on a weekly basis. There are five weekly plans each for non-vegetarians and vegetarians but to avoid confusion the vegetarian section of recipes is followed by the Weeks at a Glance menu plans.

At least one recipe is included in every day's menu plan and these recipes can be found in the last part of the book.

The Third Section

This recipe collection includes starters, snacks, main courses and desserts. They may be used in the Weeks at a Glance plans or you may use them to design your own weekly diet. Every recipe has printed beside it a daily menu and gives the week the recipe and menu may be used. The recipes may be used from the week indicated and on all subsequent weeks. Therefore, if you particularly enjoy a recipe which is given as a Week 3 recipe it can also be enjoyed on Weeks 4 and 5. By making use of this recipe section you can continue your own Week 5 food plans. However, restrict yourself to no more than seven eggs, 12oz (360g) red meats, 4oz (120g) hard cheese and a total of 12oz (360g) peas, parsnips and broad beans per week until your goal weight has been attained. Do not include recipes which are only for vegetarians, which are indicated by . If you are a vegetarian read the notes at the beginning of the vegetarian section.

All the recipes and menus have been designed for women. Men or teenagers must add additional foods to their daily allowances. Teenagers must have an extra half pint (300ml) of skimmed milk and men as well as teenagers must have an additional 2oz (60g) of protein such as fish or poultry or 6oz (180g) of tofu (bean curd). Before commencing this, or any other diet, it is advisable to consult your doctor.

POINTS TO NOTE

To ensure success when following any recipe it is essential to use top quality fresh ingredients. All the recipes in this book have been tested and the following points should be noted when preparing the ingredients:

Bread

Any type of bread may be eaten. A slice of bread always refers to 1oz (30g), but if using reduced-calorie bread then allow up to 40 Calories per slice.

Eggs

Unless otherwise stated, always use size 3 eggs.

Meat

Buy the leanest meat possible: if a recipe requires minced meat I prefer to buy the meat and mince it myself, but if this is not possible ask your butcher for extra lean mince or, if shopping in a supermarket, look for a label indicating 'extra lean mince' or 'low-fat mince'. Meat and poultry skin must be removed before eating, preferably before cooking, but this does not always suit the recipe; for example, if you are roasting a chicken it is obviously more convenient and sensible to remove the skin afterwards. Never roast meat or poultry in a pan where it will rest in hot fat, stand the meat on a rack in a baking tin. Do not use the fat in gravy or accompanying sauces, skim it off and use the meat juices to make the gravy.

All meats except veal, offal and poultry should either be grilled or roasted on a rack for a short while before cooking until the fat has stopped dripping from the meat. When using minced meat shape it into small patties and turn the patties over to allow the fat to drip away but not cook the meat. Alternatively, place the meat in a little cold water, bring to the boil and simmer for a short while. Then cool rapidly and skim the fat from the surface.

The weights listed in the recipe ingredients are for uncooked but trimmed meat so allow for the discarding of all visible fat when buying meat. As meat shrinks during cooking a rough guide to help calculate the final cooked weight is that 4oz (120g) uncooked meat will yield 3oz (90g) cooked meat. It is the cooked weight which is counted in the restricted red meats mentioned earlier.

Fish

Use really fresh fish which is unblemished, shiny and bright-eyed. The weight of whole fish, fish steaks and cutlets can be deceptive so always weigh the cooked fish to check the weight. Fish, like meat, loses weight during cooking and a rough guide would be to allow about ½oz (15g) for the bone in a cutlet or fish steak and approximately a 1oz (30g) weight loss for every 4oz (120g) of fish flesh.

Tofu

At one time tofu was regarded purely as a vegetarian food, but it is becoming more easily available and can be enjoyed by everybody in sweet or savoury recipes. Tofu is a curd made from the soya bean and is low in calories. Three ounces (90g) of tofu may be used to replace 1oz (30g) hard cheese, cooked meat, fish or one egg. There are many different forms of tofu, some more easily available than others. The basic plain tofu is sold as a soft or firm curd, the soft tofu can be liquidised or used to make a spread, but the firm tofu is essential for stir-fries and bakes. Fresh or long-life tofu is sold smoked, marinated or even braised and canned. Always follow the packaging directions for preparation and storage.

Cheese

There is an extremely wide range of cheeses available and to control calorie intake and make the choice and inclusion of cheese as simple as possible it is divided into two categories: low-fat cheeses which contain no more than 50 Calories per ounce (up to 180 Calories per 100g) and hard cheese, soft cheese and cheese spreads which contain more than 50 but less than 120 Calories per ounce (30g). The low-fat group includes quark, cottage and the majority of curd cheeses, but always check to see if the calorie count is shown on the labelling. This category of cheese is not restricted and includes the low and 8% fat fromage frais. It is therefore suitable as a substitute for other protein foods. Two ounces of this category of cheese may be used in place of 1oz (30g) hard cheese, cooked meat, fish or one egg or 3oz (90g) tofu. You may choose which variety of fromage frais to use. I prefer the very low-fat for savoury dishes and the higher fat variety for use in desserts or as topping for fresh fruit.

The higher calorie hard cheeses and cheese spreads include Cheddar, Brie, Edam, Double Gloucester and many more, but avoid Blue Stilton and Norwegian Giest as these are too high in calories. This category of cheese is limited so do not use them to substitute for other protein foods. The non-vegetarian may have up to 4oz (120g) and the vegetarian up to 6oz (180g) of this group per week.

Cream cheese is introduced in Week 5. It is very high in calories and must be measured by the tablespoon as it is not considered an important protein food. It is always included in the recipe calorie count.

Milk

Always use fresh or long life skimmed milk, or reconstituted skimmed milk powder. Recipes and menu instructions indicate when it is essential to use fresh skimmed milk, for example when making junket. Buttermilk may be used in place of skimmed milk when it is listed as a snack or used to make a drink. The same quantity of buttermilk should be used in place of skimmed milk.

Fats and Oils

Margarine and fats must be those high in polyunsaturates (although butter is introduced in Week 5 it is calorie-counted and not included in this category). When a recipe lists 'vegetable oil' it is advisable to use a specific oil, for example, safflower, soya, or corn as oils sold as 'vegetable oils' contain many different blends. Some oils, such as sesame or olive, have strong distinct flavours and they are specifically mentioned in some recipes. Olive oil is not a wise choice for some methods of cooking like stir-frying over a high heat as it burns at a lower temperature than many others. As margarines which are high in polyunsaturates are very soft it is worthwhile freezing small quantities for use in 'rubbing in' recipes such as pastry or crumble.

To reduce the amount of fat and consequently the number of calories, line baking sheets and tins with non-stick baking parchment instead of greasing them; this also makes washing up easier!

If you prefer the flavour of low-fat spreads to margarine, two teaspoons of low-fat spread may be substituted for one teaspoon of margarine as a spread or topping on corn on the cob or a jacket potato. However, as low-fat spreads have a high water content do not use them in place of margarine in recipes.

Fruit

Unless specified, fresh fruit has been used throughout the book, but many fruits are seasonal and it may be necessary to substitute frozen or drained, canned fruit preserved in natural fruit juice, not syrup. Always weigh frozen fruit while still frozen. When canned or frozen fruits are used the consistency of the recipe may be affected. If a fruit is listed in the Menu Plan which you do not like, substitute it with one of the following: 4fl oz (120ml) orange or grapefruit juice, half a medium grapefruit, one medium orange or two medium satsumas or mandarins.

Vegetables

Unless otherwise indicated, fresh vegetables have been used, but frozen or canned (without additional sugar) may be substituted. However, this alteration may affect the recipe. If a vegetable accompaniment is listed which you do not like either substitute it with a salad without salad dressing, or carrots or any green vegetable except peas. Peas, parsnips, and broad beans are restricted to a maximum of 12oz (360g) per week and are not introduced until the latter weeks of the plan. It is worth noting when buying fresh peas that almost half the weight consists of the pods which are discarded. Therefore, if a recipe lists 6oz (180g) peas, buy 12oz (360g) of the peas in their pods.

Seasonings

A recipe can be transformed from a tasteless, unappetising collection of vegetables to a delicious tasty dish by the use of seasonings. Soy, pepper and Worcestershire sauces may be used to give additional flavour to recipes and drinks such as tomato juice. Capers, curry powder, spices, herbs and stock cubes should also be used to add interest. The herbs used in recipes are dried unless otherwise indicated. If possible use fresh herbs and then garnish the completed dish with more. Approximately three times the quantity of fresh herbs will give a similar flavour as its dried equivalent. A few recipes include a bouquet garni, these may be bought dried or you can make your own by tying a bay leaf, celery leaf, sprig of thyme and 2 or 3 sprigs of parsley together.

Dried herbs and spices lose their flavour during storage so always store in airtight containers in a cool dark cupboard and never keep them longer than a year.

Whenever pepper is listed in the ingredients I recommend black pepper with the exception of seasoning white sauces when black pepper looks unattractive. However, if you prefer, substitute white pepper.

Sweeteners

Many recipes are sweetened by sugar or honey, but if you prefer a sweeter taste add an artificial sweetener. Study the labelling of sweeteners carefully as some are not suitable for cooking. Also sweeten additional drinks with artificial sweeteners as these will not have been included in the day's calorie count.

Drinks

Herbal, and the more common teas, and coffee may be drunk as desired, but if you like milk in your tea or coffee always use the milk listed under 'Snacks'.

Vegetarians

Refer to the introduction at the beginning of the Vegetarian Menu Plan as alternate forms of protein as well as other foods are offered to you from Week 1. Recipes with the vegetarian symbol ▶ may only be eaten by vegetarians.

Weighing

Accuracy is vital to achieve good results when cooking and to control your own weight. Measure all ingredients carefully and use either the imperial or the metric system. Never mix the two. Teaspoon and tablespoon measures are always level. One teaspoon is equivalent to 5ml and one tablespoon equals 15ml or ½fl oz. Low-fat natural yogurt may be measured by the tablespoon or in a measuring jug. If a recipe requires 2½fl oz (75ml) it is worth remembering this is the same as five tablespoons as it may prove a more convenient method of measuring.

Shopping and Cooking Preparation Hints

Before setting out on a shopping expedition, read through the list of ingredients given for each recipe and in the day's Menu Plan. Don't be put off if a recipe calls for half a medium banana or half a red pepper; the remaining half of the banana can be stored for a day or two by first coating the cut section with lemon juice, leaving the skin on, and storing in the refrigerator. Similarly with peppers or other salad ingredients, store in a loose plastic bag in the refrigerator. As the amount of waste varies from one product to another, the prepared weight is usually listed in the ingredients.

Make a detailed shopping list before leaving home with the exact weight of meat, cheese etc. you require. It is so easy to be tempted to buy extra ingredients. The self-service sections of supermarkets and some greengrocers can be particularly useful as you can pick out, for example, 3oz (90g) grapes instead of having to buy a 'small bunch' which can weigh twice as much. If a recipe requires broccoli or cauliflower florets these are often sold in sealed packages, but it may be more economical to purchase a whole cauliflower, or the florets and stems of the broccoli, and freeze the excess. Alternatively use as a vegetable the following day or for making soup.

I have always found the local family butcher and fishmonger extremely helpful and they will cut small quantities of meat or fish. They will also give you advice to help calculate the approximate weight of bones etc. Supermarkets print the weight on prepared meat and fish so you can sort through and find the particular cut and weight required. Prepared meats and fish, such as boneless chicken breasts and trout fillets, can be expensive and it is more economical to buy a chicken breast with skin and bone or a whole trout and prepare it yourself. With practice, this only takes a short while and you will soon recognise the size of chicken breast or fish to buy to suit your needs.

Healthy Cooking Techniques

Eating good quality fresh ingredients is important, but no matter how nutritious the food is when purchased, if stored, prepared or cooked badly, it will not only taste less good but it will lose essential nutrients. Always look for the 'sell by' or 'best before' dates and, if possible, take an insulated bag or box to carry frozen or chilled food home. Store dry ingredients such as flour in an airtight container or fold over the packaging and place in a cool cupboard. Never leave opened foods in the can; transfer them to a bowl, cover with clingfilm and place in the refrigerator.

Oven Cooking

Oven cooking is suitable for meat, fish, fruit, vegetables and starchy ingredients. The oven is used for roasting, baking, casseroling and braising.

Casseroling, cooking in an oven brick, or 'en papillote' allows food to cook in its own juices and remain full of flavour. When cooking 'en papillote' it is very important to fold the baking parchment or foil securely so no moisture escapes.

Microwaving

Microwave ovens have become increasingly popular during the last few years, particularly for cooking single portions, defrosting and reheating food. Combination microwave ovens cook by microwaves and convected heat. Although there are no recipes specifically for cooking in a microwave oven in this book, many preparation tasks can be carried out quickly in a microwave; for example melting margarine and heating a small quantity of liquid. It is also an ideal method for cooking vegetables. Always use containers and materials which are 'microwave safe'. Do not use metallic containers, bone china or good quality glassware. It is important to remember foods such as potatoes, apples and eggs require special treatment or they will explode. Prick or score the skins of potatoes and place on kitchen paper, do the same with apples and place on a microwave-safe plate or dish. Never cook an egg in its shell or a whole egg, always prick the egg yolk to split the membrane which encases the yolk and never use a microwave to warm alcohol. If the alcohol becomes hot it can burst into flames. Remember to allow 'standing time' after microwaving as this completes the cooking process.

Pressure Cooking

Pressure cookers are particularly useful for cooking dried beans and pulses after their initial soaking. Pressure cooking raises the temperature of liquid much higher than boiling point so it is not only time-saving but also retains many nutrients. The pressure cooker can be used for milk puddings, steamed puddings and cooking fruit, vegetables, soups and meat.

Slow Cooking

A slow cooker is extremely useful to anyone with a busy life who wants a hot meal ready when returning home. A meal can be prepared in the morning and left to cook slowly throughout the day. Some models have automatic timers but the food should not be prepared and left for more than one or two hours before the slow cooker starts to heat up.

Steaming

There are a large number of steamers on sale, ranging from the traditional bamboo steamers to the modern electric models. No matter which is used the method is the same. The food is suspended in a covered pan of simmering water, so the steam penetrates and the temperature is maintained. A particularly useful steamer is a compact metal basket, but you can always improvise by placing a colander over the pan. Steaming vegetables retains their colour, texture and flavour and is recommended by many nutritionists, but the cooking time is usually a little longer than traditional boiling. Steaming is also used for cooking other foods such as couscous and fish.

Poaching

Poaching is a method of cooking suitable for foods which cook at low temperatures such as eggs and fish. Poaching eggs in water that is barely simmering requires practice or the white spreads out and sets in strands. There are two ways of helping keep the egg white remain compact: either add a little vinegar to the cooking water, about one tablespoon per pint (600ml), or about one tablespoon of salt per pint (600ml) of water. The vinegar tends to give the food a slight flavour but it creates a chemical reaction which hastens the coagulation of the egg. The salt raises the temperature of the water and the eggs have a slightly salty flavour. Whichever method you choose always slide the egg into just simmering water, never boiling. When poaching fish, the stock or seasoned water should be just simmering and come about halfway up the fish. Spoon the liquid over the fish during cooking.

Stir-Frying

Stir-frying is a traditional Asian method of cooking in a wok. Very little oil is required but the cook has to constantly stir the food to prevent burning. Electric free-standing woks are now available, but a saucepan may be used; do not use a frying pan or the ingredients will spill over the sides. A round-bottomed wok is designed for use on a gas hob and a flat-bottomed one for use on an electric hob.

WEEK 1

Day 1

Breakfast:

1 medium apple
1oz (30g) cereal
¼ pint (150ml) skimmed milk

Lunch: Pepper Omelette

Beat together 2 eggs, 2 tablespoons water, salt and pepper. Measure 1½ teaspoons margarine, place half the margarine in a small omelette pan and stir-fry 1 finely chopped green or red pepper for about 4 minutes until soft, remove the pepper from the pan and add the remaining margarine. Pour in the egg mixture and cook over a gentle heat, drawing the mixture from the edge towards the centre. When the underside is golden, spoon the pepper over half the omelette, cook for a further minute and fold over. Serve with 1oz (30g) slice of bread spread with 1 teaspoon margarine.

Dinner: ✴ Salmon with Yogurt Tarragon Sauce ✴

Mixed Salad – radicchio, sliced peppers, cucumber, radishes and chopped celery.

2 inch (5cm) wedge of honeydew melon

Snacks:

2½fl oz (75ml) low-fat natural yogurt
7½fl oz (225ml) skimmed milk

SALMON WITH YOGURT TARRAGON SAUCE

Serves 2
275 Calories per serving

2 × 4½oz (135g) salmon fillets

1 teaspoon olive oil

4 slices onion

2 slices lemon

2 sprigs tarragon

salt and pepper

For the sauce:
2½fl oz (75ml) low-fat natural yogurt

¼ teaspoon lemon juice

1 tablespoon chopped tarragon

1. Remove the skin from the salmon fillets.
2. Brush a piece of foil generously with oil, lay the onion slices on top and arrange the salmon fillets over the onion.
3. Lay the lemon slices and tarragon over the salmon and sprinkle with a little salt and pepper. Fold over the foil to make a secure package.
4. Transfer the salmon to a baking sheet and bake at 375°F/190°C/Gas Mark 5 for 12–15 minutes. Remove it from the oven and leave to cool.
5. Mix the yogurt, lemon juice and tarragon together. When the salmon is cool, add sufficient juices from the salmon to flavour the sauce. Serve chilled.

Exchanges per serving: Fat ½, Milk ¼, Protein 3

Salmon with Yogurt Tarragon Sauce
and salad; wedge of honeydew melon

WEEK 1

Day 2

Breakfast:

4fl oz (120ml) orange juice
1oz (30g) cereal
¼ pint (150ml) skimmed milk

Lunch: ✳ Curried Prawn Salad ✳

Served with 1oz (30g) French bread spread with 1 teaspoon margarine.

2oz (60g) drained, canned pineapple pieces stirred into 2½fl oz (75ml) low-fat natural yogurt and sprinkled with a little ground allspice.

Dinner: Roast Turkey with Vegetables

3oz (90g) roast turkey
Steamed or boiled carrots, cauliflower and cabbage.

4oz (120g) drained, canned grapefruit segments served with 2 tablespoons of the natural juice.

Snacks:

¼ pint (150ml) skimmed milk

CURRIED PRAWN SALAD

Serves 2
175 Calories per serving

4oz (120g) peeled prawns
4 spring onions
1½ inch (4cm) chunk of cucumber
½ red pepper, seeded
1 medium peach, or 2 canned peach halves, drained
2½fl oz (75ml) low-fat natural yogurt
½ teaspoon curry powder
4 teaspoons mayonnaise
1 teaspoon lemon juice
a few lettuce leaves

1. Place the prawns in a bowl.
2. Thickly slice the spring onions, dice the cucumber and chop the red pepper.
3. Cut round the peach, twist the two halves in opposite directions, scoop out the stone and chop up the fruit.
4. Stir the prawns, prepared vegetables and peach together.
5. In a small bowl mix the yogurt, curry powder, mayonnaise and lemon juice together.
6. Stir the curried dressing into the prawn mixture.
7. Line the base of two serving dishes with the lettuce leaves, pile the Curried Prawn Salad on top and serve.

Exchanges per serving: Fat 2, Fruit ½, Milk ¼, Protein 2, Vegetable 1½

WEEK 1

Day 3

Breakfast:

½ medium grapefruit
1oz (30g) slice of bread toasted with
1 teaspoon low-fat spread and
1 tablespoon marmalade.

Lunch: Cottage Cheese and Egg Salad

Mash 1 hard-boiled egg, 2oz (60g) cottage cheese, 1 tablespoon chopped chives and 1 teaspoon low-calorie mayonnaise together, season with salt and pepper. Mix together some shredded lettuce, sliced radishes, cucumber and diced green pepper. Arrange the salad on a plate and serve with the egg and cottage cheese mixture.

Pineapple Froth – place 4oz (120g) drained, canned pineapple pieces in a blender with ¼ pint (150ml) buttermilk and 1 teaspoon sugar. Process until frothy. Serve immediately.

Dinner: ✳ Poulet En Papillote ✳

4oz (120g) drained, canned mandarins served with 2 tablespoons of the natural juice and 2½fl oz (75ml) low-fat natural yogurt.

Snacks:

½ pint (300ml) skimmed milk

Optional Calories 70

POULET EN PAPILLOTE

Serves 1
330 Calories per serving

2 teaspoons safflower oil
1 leek
1 carrot
4oz (120g) chicken fillet, skinned
1 small clove garlic, chopped
1 tablespoon finely chopped spring onion
1½oz (45g) mushrooms, finely chopped
1oz (30g) fresh breadcrumbs
good pinch of mixed herbs
salt and pepper
2 tablespoons chicken stock

1. Brush a piece of foil about 8 inches (20cm) square with a little of the oil.
2. Thinly slice the leek and carrot and place in the centre of the foil.
3. Cut almost halfway through the chicken breast fillet lengthwise.
4. Heat the remaining oil in a small saucepan, add the garlic and stir-fry for 1 minute. Add the spring onion and mushrooms and cook for a further 3 minutes until soft.
5. Stir the breadcrumbs and herbs into the mushroom mixture and season with salt and pepper.
6. Spoon the mushroom stuffing into the chicken fillet, place on top of the carrots and leeks, pour over the stock and fold over the foil to seal. Bake at 375°F/190°C/Gas Mark 5 for 35 minutes.

Exchanges per serving: Bread 1, Fat 2, Protein 3, Vegetable 3½

WEEK 1

Day 4

Breakfast:

4fl oz (120ml) grapefruit juice
Toast a 1oz (30g) slice of bread,
sprinkle 1oz (30g) grated Cheddar
cheese over one side and grill until
bubbling. Serve with 1 sliced tomato.

Lunch: Egg Salad

Cut 1 hard-boiled egg into wedges
and serve with shredded lettuce,
sliced cucumber, radish, celery and
grated carrot, tossed in 2 teaspoons
low-calorie salad dressing. Serve with
1oz (30g) slice of bread spread with
1 teaspoon margarine.

2oz (60g) drained, canned fruit salad
stirred into 5fl oz (150ml) low-fat
natural yogurt.

Dinner: Grilled Liver with Vegetables

Place 4oz (120g) sliced lamb's or
calf's livers on the rack of a grill pan,
brush with ½ teaspoon oil and grill
for 4 minutes under a moderate heat,
turn and brush with 1 teaspoon
vegetable oil, continue grilling until
cooked. Serve with a grilled tomato,
steamed or boiled courgettes and
baby onions.

✻ Saint Clements Special ✻

Snacks:

7½fl oz (225ml) skimmed milk

Optional Calories 20

Saint Clements Special

Serves 2
110 Calories per serving

8fl oz (240ml) orange juice
2 teaspoons caster sugar
2 teaspoons gelatine
½ lemon, zest and juice
2½fl oz (75ml) low-fat natural yogurt
4oz (120g) drained, canned mandarin segments

1. Place 3 tablespoons orange juice in a cup or small basin and chill the remaining juice.
2. Sprinkle the caster sugar and gelatine into the cup or basin containing the 3 tablespoons orange juice, place in a saucepan of simmering water and leave until the sugar and gelatine have dissolved.
3. Finely grate the zest from the lemon. Stir the zest and the lemon juice into the chilled orange juice.
4. Mix the dissolved gelatine into the orange and lemon juices, pour into two ¼ pint (150ml) moulds and chill until set.
5. Dip the moulds into hot water and invert on to two serving plates.
6. Spoon the yogurt round each jelly and arrange the mandarin segments on top of the yogurt.

Exchanges per serving: Fruit 1½, Milk ¼, Optional Calories 20

Saint Clements Special; grilled liver
with vegetables

WEEK 1

Day 5

Breakfast:

½ medium grapefruit
1oz (30g) slice of bread, toasted,
spread with 1 teaspoon margarine
and topped with 1 poached egg.

Lunch: Cottage Cheese and Salad Sandwich

Spread 2 slices of reduced-calorie
bread with 2 teaspoons margarine.
Arrange lettuce leaves over one slice
of bread and top with a few slices of
cucumber. Spread 2oz (60g) cottage
cheese or low-fat soft cheese on top,
season with salt and pepper and
sprinkle with mustard and cress.
Sandwich together with the other
slice of bread, serve with 1 tomato.

1 medium orange

Dinner: ✳ Economical Casserole ✳

5fl oz (150ml) low-fat natural yogurt

Snacks:

½ pint (300ml) skimmed milk

Optional Calories 20

ECONOMICAL CASSEROLE

Serves 2
240 Calories per serving

1 large or 2 medium leeks

4oz (120g) carrots

8oz (240g) shin of beef, trimmed of all visible fat

½oz (15g) flour

12fl oz (360ml) vegetable or beef stock

2 teaspoons vinegar

3oz (90g) mushrooms

good pinch of mixed herbs

salt and pepper

1. Cut the leeks and carrots into thick slices and put to one side.
2. Place the beef on the rack of a grill pan. Cook under a moderate heat, turning once, until the fat stops dripping from the meat. Allow to cool a little.
3. Cut the beef into cubes and place in a casserole dish. Sprinkle the flour over the meat and stir it round to cover the meat. Gradually add the stock and vinegar.
4. If the mushrooms are small leave them whole, but cut large mushrooms in halves or quarters and add all the vegetables to the casserole.
5. Stir the herbs, salt and pepper into the casserole, cover and place in a preheated oven at 325°F/160°C/Gas Mark 3 for 3 hours.

Exchanges per serving: Protein 3, Vegetable 2, Optional Calories 20

WEEK 1

Day 6

Breakfast:

4fl oz (120ml) orange juice
1oz (30g) cereal
¼ pint (150ml) skimmed milk

Lunch: Tuna Sandwich with Mixed Salad

Spread 2 slices of reduced-calorie bread with 2 teaspoons margarine. Mash 2oz (60g) drained, canned tuna with 1 teaspoon chopped chives, lemon juice and salt and pepper to taste. Arrange thin slices of 1 tomato over one slice of the bread, spread the tuna mixture on top and sandwich it together with the other slice of bread. Serve with a mixed salad of chicory, sliced red pepper, cucumber and radishes.

1 medium pear

Dinner: Grilled Haddock with Vegetables

Brush a 4oz (120g) skinless haddock fillet with ½ teaspoon vegetable oil. Grill for 5 minutes, turn, brush with ½ teaspoon vegetable oil and grill until cooked. Serve with boiled or steamed green beans, carrots and leeks.

✳ Strawberry Steps ✳

Snacks:

½ pint (300ml) skimmed milk

Optional Calories 30

STRAWBERRY STEPS

Serves 1
185 Calories per serving

5oz (150g) strawberries

2oz (60g) Quark or curd cheese

1½ teaspoons set honey

¼–½ teaspoon orange flower water

2½fl oz (75ml) low-fat natural yogurt

1. Mash or purée 2oz (60g) of the strawberries, slice the remainder and put to one side.
2. Mix the puréed strawberries and cheese together until smooth. Add the honey and orange flower water and mix well.
3. Reserve a few slices of strawberries for decoration.
4. Place about a third of the sliced strawberries in the base of a glass, top with a third of the strawberry cheese and spoon over a third of the yogurt to just cover the strawberry mixture.
5. Continue layering the fruit, strawberry cheese and yogurt, ending with a layer of yogurt. Decorate with the reserved strawberry slices and chill until ready to serve.

Exchanges per serving: Fruit 1, Milk ½, Protein 1, Optional Calories 30

WEEK 1

Day 7

Breakfast:

4fl oz (120ml) grapefruit juice
1 slice of reduced-calorie bread
spread with 1 teaspoon margarine
and served with 1 boiled egg.

Lunch: Open Cheese Sandwich

Spread 1 slice of reduced-calorie
bread with 1 teaspoon margarine and
1 teaspoon mayonnaise. Top with
slices of cucumber, tomato and
shredded lettuce and 1oz (30g) thinly
sliced Edam or 1oz (30g) crumbled
Danish Blue cheese.

1 medium pear

Dinner: * Crispy-Topped Haddock *

Steamed or boiled carrots and
spinach.

5fl oz (150ml) low-fat natural yogurt
served with ½ teaspoon honey.

Snacks:

¼ pint (150ml) skimmed milk

Optional Calories 10

CRISPY-TOPPED HADDOCK

Serves 1
270 Calories per serving

3oz (90g) leeks, finely chopped
3oz (90g) skinless haddock fillet
2 teaspoons chopped parsley
¼ pint (150ml) skimmed milk
salt and pepper
¼oz (10g) cornflour
1½oz (45g) mushrooms, thinly sliced
¾oz (20g) fresh breadcrumbs
½oz (15g) cheese, finely grated
pinch of powdered mustard

1. Place the leeks, haddock, parsley and milk in a saucepan and season with salt and pepper. Cover and simmer gently for 7–8 minutes until the haddock is cooked. Allow it to cool a little.
2. Remove the haddock from the saucepan and flake into large pieces.
3. Blend a little of the milk with the cornflour to form a smooth paste and put it to one side.
4. Add the mushrooms to the remaining milk and leeks and simmer for 2–3 minutes. Mix in the cornflour paste and bring to the boil, stirring all the time. Add the haddock and stir over a low heat until heated through.
5. Spoon the haddock sauce into a warm 4½ inch (11cm) soufflé dish.
6. Mix the breadcrumbs, cheese and mustard together and sprinkle over the top of the haddock mixture. Place under a preheated, moderate grill and cook until golden.

Exchanges per serving: Bread 1, Milk ½, Protein 3, Vegetable 1½

WEEK 2

Day 1

Breakfast:

1 kiwi fruit
1oz (30g) cereal
¼ pint (150ml) skimmed milk

Lunch: Stuffed Egg

Hard-boil 1 egg, shell and cut in half
lengthways. Scoop out the yolk and
mash with 2oz (60g) cottage cheese.
Add 1 teaspoon of mayonnaise, salt
and pepper and pile back into the
egg-white halves.
Mixed Salad – shredded lettuce,
endive, chicory, sliced cucumber,
tomato and mushrooms.
Crispbread up to 80 Calories, spread
with 2 teaspoons low-fat spread.

Dinner: ✳ Spinach-Cod Roll ✳

Steamed or boiled peas, carrots and
courgettes.
3oz (90g) boiled potatoes

Banana Froth – 1 banana blended
with ¼ pint (150ml) buttermilk and
1 teaspoon of sugar. Serve
immediately in a tall glass.

Snacks:

½ pint (300ml) skimmed milk

Optional Calories 40

SPINACH-COD ROLL

Serves 1
260 Calories per serving

3oz (90g) fresh spinach, coarse stalks removed

2oz (60g) curd cheese

salt and pepper

freshly grated nutmeg

2 teaspoons grated Parmesan cheese

4oz (120g) tail-end of cod, skin removed

1 teaspoon margarine

1. Wash the spinach well, shake off the excess water, place in a
   saucepan over a low to moderate heat and cook for 5–10
   minutes until tender.
2. Drain the spinach well and transfer to a blender. Add the
   curd cheese and process until smooth. Season to taste with
   salt, pepper and nutmeg, and stir in the Parmesan cheese.
3. Lay the cod flat with the side which had the skin attached
   facing upwards.
4. Spread the spinach and cheese mixture along the length of
   the cod. Loosely roll up like a Swiss roll.
5. Grease a piece of foil with half the margarine. Place the rolled
   cod on the greased foil and dot with the remaining
   margarine. Wrap the foil over the cod, place on a baking
   sheet and bake at 375°F/190°C/Gas Mark 5 for 30 minutes.
6. Serve the Spinach-Cod Roll with the juices poured round it.

**Exchanges per serving: Fat 1, Protein 4, Vegetable 1,
Optional Calories 20**

WEEK 2

Day 2

Breakfast:

½ medium grapefruit
1 boiled egg
1oz (30g) slice of wholemeal bread
1 teaspoon low-fat spread

Lunch: Cheese and Ham Salad

1oz (30g) hard cheese, grated,
1oz (30g) cooked ham, sliced, served
with 2 sticks celery, chopped and
mixed with 1 grated carrot,
2 chopped spring onions and
2 teaspoons low-calorie mayonnaise.
Tomato and Cucumber Salad –
1 tomato thinly sliced and mixed with
thin slices of cucumber, sprinkled
with 1 teaspoon of chopped chives.

5oz (150g) drained, canned
raspberries served with a little of the
natural unsweetened juice.

Dinner: ✳ Crunchy Coated Chicken ✳

Steamed or boiled asparagus, carrots
and leeks.
3oz (90g) boiled potato

5fl oz (150ml) low-fat natural yogurt.

Snacks:

½ pint (300ml) skimmed milk

Optional Calories 5

CRUNCHY COATED CHICKEN

Serves 2
280 Calories per serving

½oz (15g) flour
salt and pepper
1 tablespoon skimmed milk
1½oz (45g) fresh breadcrumbs
1½ teaspoons tarragon
2 × 4oz (120g) skinned and boned chicken breasts
1 tablespoon vegetable oil

1. Season the flour with a little salt and pepper, sprinkle on to a plate and put to one side.
2. Measure the milk on to a plate and mix the breadcrumbs and tarragon together on a third plate.
3. Turn the chicken breasts in the flour, then the milk and lastly the tarragon breadcrumbs. If not completely covered turn in the remaining milk and breadcrumbs.
4. Place the breadcrumb-coated chicken on the rack of a grill pan. Drizzle half the oil over the chicken and cook under a moderate heat for 5–7 minutes until golden.
5. Turn the chicken breasts over, drizzle the remaining oil evenly over the breadcrumbs and continue cooking under a moderate heat until cooked through.

Exchanges per serving: Bread 1, Fat 1½, Protein 3, Optional Calories 5

WEEK 2

Day 3

Breakfast:

4fl oz (120ml) orange juice
1oz (30g) cereal
¼ pint (150ml) skimmed milk

Lunch: Prawn Salad

2½oz (75g) peeled prawns mixed in
2 teaspoons low-calorie mayonnaise
seasoned with a large pinch of curry
powder.
Mixed Salad – shredded lettuce,
chopped celery, bean sprouts and
strips of red pepper.

Dinner: Grilled Plaice with Vegetables

Lay 5oz (150g) plaice fillet skin side
up on a pan, dot with ½ teaspoon
margarine, grill 3–4 minutes. Turn
and dot with ½ teaspoon margarine,
grill until cooked.
3oz (90g) boiled potato
3oz (90g) boiled or steamed
cauliflower and carrots

✳ Peach Pancakes ✳

Served with 2½ tablespoons low-fat
natural yogurt.

Snacks:

½ pint (300ml) skimmed milk

PEACH PANCAKES

Serves 2
310 Calories per serving

2oz (60g) plain flour

pinch of salt

1 egg

¼ pint (150ml) skimmed milk

2 teaspoons vegetable oil

1lb (480g) drained, canned sliced peaches, with juice reserved

large pinch of allspice

1. Sieve the flour and salt into a bowl, make a well in the centre, add the egg and gradually beat in the milk.
2. Sprinkle a 7 inch (18cm) frying pan with salt, heat gently, tip out the salt then wipe thoroughly with kitchen paper. Heat a little oil in the frying pan and wipe out again with kitchen paper.
3. Heat a few drops of oil in the frying pan and pour a little batter into the pan, turning so the base is completely covered. Cook over a moderate heat until the underside is golden. Toss or turn over and cook the other side.
4. Slide the cooked pancake on to a plate, cover and keep warm in a low oven while repeating the procedure to make eight pancakes.
5. Heat the peaches in their juice with the allspice. Drain the peaches, divide them between the pancakes and roll up. Serve with 2–3 tablespoons of the hot peach juice poured over.

Exchanges per serving: Bread 1, Fat 1, Fruit 2, Milk ¼, Protein ½

WEEK 2

Day 4

Breakfast:

4fl oz (120ml) orange juice
1oz (30g) cereal
¼ pint (150ml) skimmed milk

Lunch: Turkey Salad

2oz (60g) cooked turkey, sliced, served with a mixed salad of shredded lettuce, sliced peppers, chopped spring onions and celery, tossed in 2 teaspoons salad dressing.

5oz (150g) watermelon chunks

Dinner: ✳ Saucy Tagliatelle ✳

5oz (150g) gooseberries stewed in a little water and sweetened to taste with artificial sweetener, served with 2½fl oz (75ml) low-fat natural yogurt.

Snacks:

¼ pint (150ml) skimmed milk

Optional Calories 20

SAUCY TAGLIATELLE

Serves 1
595 Calories per serving

1oz (30g) tagliatelle
salt
8oz (240g) mixture of carrot and calabrese broccoli
2 teaspoons sesame oil
1 clove garlic, chopped (optional)
2 spring onions, chopped
2oz (60g) cooked ham, cut in thin strips
2 eggs
¼ pint (150ml) skimmed milk
dash of pepper sauce
2 teaspoons grated Parmesan cheese

1. Boil the tagliatelle according to the packaging instructions in salted water.
2. Cut the carrot and broccoli into small lengths. Divide the broccoli heads into florets. Boil in salted water for 3 minutes, drain.
3. Heat the oil, add the garlic and spring onion and stir-fry for 2–3 minutes. Add the ham and other vegetables and stir-fry for a further 1–2 minutes.
4. Beat together the eggs and milk, and season with the pepper sauce.
5. Add the hot drained tagliatelle and egg mixture to the hot vegetables. Stir over a very low heat until the sauce thickens.
6. Transfer the mixture to a warm serving plate. Sprinkle with the Parmesan cheese and serve.

Exchanges per serving: Bread 1, Fat 2, Milk ½, Protein 4, Vegetable 3, Optional Calories 20

Saucy Tagliatelle; gooseberries with yogurt

WEEK 2

Day 5

Breakfast:

2 inch (5cm) wedge honeydew melon
1 boiled or poached egg
1oz (30g) slice of bread, toasted
1 teaspoon margarine

Lunch: Sardine Open Sandwich

Spread a 1oz (30g) slice of rye bread with 1 teaspoon margarine. Top with shredded lettuce and 1 tomato, sliced. Lay 2oz (60g) drained, canned sardines over the salad and garnish with a twist of lemon.

1 medium apple

Dinner: ✳ Veal Kebabs ✳

Tossed Mixed Salad – endive, chicory, sliced mushrooms and cucumber tossed in 2 teaspoons low-calorie French dressing.

Junket – heat ¼ pint (150ml) fresh skimmed milk (*not* long life) until warm, add 2–3 drops of vanilla essence, 1 teaspoon of sugar or honey and 1 teaspoon essence of rennet. Pour into a serving dish and leave in the warm for 15–20 minutes until set.

Snacks:

¾ pint (450ml) skimmed milk

Optional Calories 20

VEAL KEBABS

Serves 2
225 Calories per serving

8oz (240g) veal escalopes

4oz (120g) drained, canned pineapple cubes, juice reserved

½ red pepper, seeded

½ green pepper, seeded

For the marinade:
3 tablespoons reserved pineapple juice

3 tablespoons lemon juice

2 tablespoons soy sauce

½ teaspoon finely chopped fresh root ginger

2 teaspoons sesame oil

1 clove garlic, crushed

1. Cut the veal into cubes, place in a bowl with the pineapple cubes.
2. Cut the pepper halves into even-sized cubes, add to the veal and pineapple.
3. Mix all the marinade ingredients together, pour over the veal etc. and leave to marinate for 2–3 hours, turning occasionally.
4. Thread the veal, pineapple and peppers on to skewers and place on a grill rack under a moderate grill, basting frequently with the marinade and turning until evenly cooked.

Exchanges per serving: Fat 1, Fruit ½, Protein 3, Vegetable ½

WEEK 2

Day 6

Breakfast:

½ medium grapefruit
1oz (30g) bagel
1 teaspoon margarine
2 teaspoons strawberry or black cherry jam

Lunch: Salad Filled Pitta

1oz (30g) pitta filled with 2oz (60g) shredded cooked chicken, grated carrot, 2–3 chopped spring onions and shredded lettuce with 2 teaspoons French dressing drizzled over.

4oz (120g) pineapple

Dinner: ✳ Liver Casserole ✳

Steamed or boiled broccoli and carrots.

2oz (60g) drained, canned fruit salad stirred into 5fl oz (150ml) low-fat natural yogurt.

Snacks:

½ pint (300ml) skimmed milk

Optional Calories 50

LIVER CASSEROLE

Serves 2
320 Calories per serving

8oz (240g) lamb's liver, sliced

1 tablespoon flour

large pinch of powdered mustard

salt and pepper

2 teaspoons vegetable oil

1 medium onion, thinly sliced

1 medium cooking apple, peeled, cored and sliced

1 red pepper, seeded and sliced

6fl oz (180ml) vegetable stock

1. Rinse the liver under cold water and pat dry with kitchen paper.
2. Mix the flour, mustard, salt and pepper together on a plate.
3. Turn the liver in the seasoned flour and put to one side.
4. Heat the oil in a small flameproof casserole, quickly turn the liver in the oil, just enough to brown, remove and repeat with all the slices of liver.
5. Remove the casserole dish from the heat, lay a few slices of liver over the base, cover with some of the onion, apple and pepper, continue until all the ingredients are in the casserole.
6. Pour over the stock, cover and bake at 350°F/180°C/Gas Mark 4 for 40 minutes.

Exchanges per serving: Fat 1, Fruit ½, Protein 3, Vegetable 1½, Optional Calories 15

WEEK 2

Day 7

Breakfast:

1 medium apple
1oz (30g) porridge oats simmered in
¼ pint (150ml) skimmed milk.

Lunch: Cottage Cheese and Tuna Salad

2oz (60g) cottage cheese mixed with
1oz (30g) drained and flaked, canned
tuna, 2 teaspoons low-calorie
mayonnaise and a pinch of curry
powder.
3oz (90g) baked jacket potato with
1 teaspoon margarine, 1 sliced
tomato, a few lettuce leaves, sprigs of
watercress, grated carrot and bean
sprouts.

Dinner: ✳ Blue Cheese Pear ✳

Steak with Vegetables

4oz (120g) rump or fillet steak
brushed with ½ teaspoon of oil,
grilled, turned and brushed with
½ teaspoon of oil and grilled until
cooked.
Steamed or boiled calabrese broccoli,
cauliflower and leeks.

5oz (150g) strawberries sprinkled
with 1 teaspoon caster sugar served
with 2½fl oz (75ml) low-fat natural
yogurt.

Snacks:

½ pint (300ml) skimmed milk

Optional Calories 20

Blue Cheese Pear; grilled steak with
vegetables; strawberries with yogurt

BLUE CHEESE PEAR

Serves 2
115 Calories per serving

| 1 medium pear |
| lemon juice |
| 1oz (30g) Danish Blue cheese |
| 2oz (60g) fromage frais |
| few lettuce leaves |
| 1 teaspoon chopped chives |
| 2 chive flowers (optional) |

1. Cut the pear in half lengthways, scoop out the core with a teaspoon and remove the stringy strands which attach the centre core to the stalk. Brush each cut half with lemon juice.
2. Crumble the Danish Blue cheese into a bowl, mash well. Gradually add the fromage frais.
3. Transfer the cheese mixture to a piping bag fitted with a ½ inch (1.5 cm) fluted nozzle.
4. Lay the lettuce leaves on each serving plate, sprinkle over the chives and lay each pear half on top.
5. Pipe the cheese mixture into the cavity left by the core and down towards the stalk end.
6. Garnish each pear half with a chive flower, and serve.

Exchanges per serving: Fruit ½, Protein 1, Vegetable ¼

WEEK 3

Day 1

Breakfast:

1 medium pear, chopped
1oz (30g) cereal
¼ pint (150ml) skimmed milk

Lunch: Cottage Cheese and Corned Beef Salad

3oz (90g) cottage cheese and 1oz (30g) corned beef, sliced.
Green Salad – shredded lettuce, chicory, endive, white cabbage, alfalfa sprouts and slices of cucumber tossed in 1 tablespoon French dressing.
Tomato and Onion Salad – 1 tomato, thinly sliced, sprinkled with 2 finely chopped spring onions.

1 medium nectarine

Dinner: ✳ Fish Risotto ✳

Steamed asparagus and carrots.

4oz (120g) pineapple chopped and mixed into 5fl oz (150ml) low-fat natural yogurt, sprinkled with a little ground ginger.

Snacks:

¼ pint (150ml) skimmed milk

Optional Calories 20

FISH RISOTTO

Serves 2
360 Calories per serving

1 tablespoon margarine
3oz (90g) long-grain rice
1 stick celery, chopped
3 tomatoes, peeled and roughly chopped
½ teaspoon basil
1 teaspoon chopped parsley
¼ pint (150ml) vegetable stock
5oz (150g) skinned cod or monkfish fillet
salt and pepper
3oz (90g) peeled prawns
4 teaspoons grated Parmesan cheese

1. Melt the margarine in a saucepan, add the rice and stir round for 3–4 minutes until the fat has been absorbed. Remove from the heat.
2. Stir in the celery, tomatoes, basil, parsley and stock.
3. Cut the cod or monkfish into chunks, about 2 inches (5cm) in size and add to the saucepan.
4. Bring to the boil over a moderate heat, season with a little salt and pepper, reduce the heat, cover and simmer for 12 minutes, stirring occasionally.
5. Add the prawns and stir well, cook for a further 2–3 minutes. Adjust the seasoning if necessary. Serve each portion with 2 teaspoons grated Parmesan cheese sprinkled over the top.

Exchanges per serving: Bread 1½, Fat 1½, Protein 3½, Vegetable 1½, Optional Calories 20

WEEK 3

Day 2

Breakfast:

4fl oz (120ml) orange juice
Toast a 1oz (30g) slice of bread, sprinkle 1oz (30g) grated Cheddar cheese over one side and grill until bubbling. Serve with 1 tomato.

Lunch: ✳ Smoked Tofu Stir-Fry ✳

Strawberry Froth – place 5oz (150g) strawberries, ¼ pint (150ml) buttermilk and 2 teaspoons sugar in a blender. Blend until smooth and frothy. Serve immediately.

Dinner: Prawn Omelette with Tomatoes

Beat together 2 eggs, 2 tablespoons water, salt and pepper. Heat 1 teaspoon margarine in a small omelette pan, pour in the egg mixture and cook over a gentle heat drawing the mixture from the edge towards the centre. When the underside is golden brown sprinkle 2 teaspoons chopped chives and 1oz (30g) peeled prawns over one half of the omelette, cook for a further minute, fold over and serve. Halve two tomatoes and grill until hot.

1 medium apple

Snacks:

2½fl oz (75ml) low-fat natural yogurt
1 digestive biscuit
½ pint (300ml) skimmed milk

Optional Calories 45

SMOKED TOFU STIR-FRY

Serves 2
220 Calories per serving

2oz (60g) carrot
½ green pepper, seeded
2oz (60g) courgettes
12oz (360g) smoked tofu
4 teaspoons sesame seed oil
1 clove garlic, chopped
1 teaspoon finely chopped fresh root ginger
3 spring onions, cut in 1 inch (2.5cm) pieces
3oz (90g) cauliflower florets
1 tablespoon tomato purée
5 tablespoons water
3oz (90g) bean sprouts
2–3 teaspoons soy sauce
salt and pepper

1. Cut the carrot, pepper and courgettes into thin strips.
2. Cut the smoked tofu into 1 inch (2.5cm) cubes.
3. Heat the oil in a large saucepan, add the garlic and ginger and stir-fry for 1 minute. Add the spring onions, cauliflower and tofu. Remove from the heat.
4. Mix the tomato purée and water together.
5. Stir the vegetables and tofu gently over a low heat, pour in the tomato purée and water, mix well. Cover the saucepan and leave to simmer 5–10 minutes stirring occasionally.
6. Add the bean sprouts and stir for 2 minutes. Season to taste with soy sauce, salt and pepper, serve.

Exchanges per serving: Fat 2, Protein 2, Vegetable 2, Optional Calories 5

WEEK 3

Day 3

Breakfast:

4fl oz (120ml) orange juice
1oz (30g) slice of bread, toasted and spread with 1 tablespoon smooth or crunchy peanut butter.

Lunch: Cheese on Toast

Toast 2 slices of reduced-calorie bread, sprinkle 2oz (60g) grated Cheddar cheese over one side of each slice and grill until bubbling. Tomato and Onion Salad –
2 tomatoes sliced, mixed with 1 small, thinly sliced onion.

Peach Froth – place 1 stoned medium peach or 2 drained, canned peach halves into a blender, add ¼ pint (150ml) buttermilk and 1 teaspoon sugar. Blend until smooth and frothy. Serve immediately.

Dinner: ✳ Smoked Haddock Soufflé ✳

Steamed green beans and carrots.

4oz (120g) stewed apple and blackberries. Serve with 2½fl oz (75ml) low-fat natural yogurt.

Snacks:

7½fl oz (225ml) skimmed milk

Optional Calories 30

SMOKED HADDOCK SOUFFLÉ

Serves 2
310 Calories per serving

4 teaspoons margarine

4oz (120g) smoked haddock

7fl oz (210ml) skimmed milk

2 tablespoons chopped chives

1 tablespoon chopped parsley

1oz (30g) flour

3 eggs, separated

salt and pepper

1. Use ¼–½ teaspoon margarine to grease a very deep, 6 inch (15cm) soufflé dish, capacity approximately 2 pints (1.2 litres).
2. Lay the smoked haddock in a pan, pour in the milk and add the chives and parsley. Place over a low to moderate heat and poach for about 8 minutes. Remove the fish, discard the skin and flake the flesh.
3. Heat the remaining margarine in a large saucepan, add the flour and mix well. Remove from the heat and gradually blend in the hot milk and herbs. Bring to the boil, stirring continuously and boil for 2 minutes. Remove from the heat and allow to cool a little.
4. Stir the flaked fish and the egg yolks into the sauce. Season with salt and pepper.
5. Whisk the egg whites with a pinch of salt until peaking. Using a metal spoon lightly fold the egg whites into the sauce.
6. Transfer the mixture to the soufflé dish and bake at 350°F/180°C/Gas Mark 4 for 35–40 minutes until well risen and golden brown. Serve immediately.

Exchanges per serving: Bread ½, Fat 2, Milk ¼, Protein 3, Optional Calories 10

Smoked Haddock Soufflé with carrots and green beans; stewed apples and blackberries with yogurt

WEEK 3

Day 4

Breakfast:

½ medium grapefruit
1oz (30g) slice of bread, toasted, spread with 1 teaspoon margarine and topped with 1 poached egg.

Lunch: * Spicy Lentil Soup *

4oz (120g) drained, canned mandarins, stirred into 5fl oz (150ml) low-fat natural yogurt.

Dinner: Roast Turkey and Salad

3oz (90g) roast turkey
6oz (180g) baked jacket potato
Large Mixed Salad – shredded endive, chicory, lettuce, sliced red and yellow peppers and radishes.
Beetroot and Orange Salad –
3oz (90g) beetroot sliced very thinly and mixed with 1 thinly sliced medium orange, 1 tablespoon French dressing and 1 teaspoon chopped chives.

Junket – heat ¼ pint (150ml) fresh skimmed milk (*not* long life) until warm, add 2–3 drops of vanilla essence, artificial sweetener equivalent to 1 teaspoon sugar and 1 teaspoon of essence of rennet. Pour into serving dish and leave in the warm for 15–20 minutes until set.

Snacks:

¼ pint (150ml) skimmed milk

SPICY LENTIL SOUP

Serves 3
195 Calories per serving

1½ teaspoons vegetable oil
½ teaspoon chopped fresh root ginger
1 clove garlic, chopped
1 onion, chopped
½ teaspoon ground coriander
½ teaspoon ground cumin
½ teaspoon turmeric
good pinch of chilli powder
3 tomatoes, peeled, seeded and chopped
¾ pint (450ml) vegetable stock
4oz (120g) split red lentils, rinsed
salt and pepper
2oz (60g) cooked ham, chopped

1. Heat the oil in a saucepan. Add the ginger and garlic and stir-fry for 1 minute. Add the onion and stir-fry for a further 3–4 minutes.
2. Mix all the spices into the onion, stir over a low heat for 1 minute.
3. Add the tomatoes, stock and lentils to the saucepan. Bring to the boil and boil rapidly for 10 minutes. Reduce the heat, cover and simmer until the lentils are cooked.
4. Pour the soup into a food processor or blender and blend until smooth. Return it to the saucepan. Season to taste with salt and pepper.
5. Add the ham and reheat. Pour into warm soup bowls and serve.

Exchanges per serving: Fat ½, Protein 2, Vegetable 1

WEEK 3

Day 5

Breakfast:

1 medium apple
1oz (30g) cereal
¼ pint (150ml) skimmed milk

Lunch: Rollmop Salad

3oz (90g) rollmop with a tossed
mixed salad of shredded lettuce,
sliced cucumber, celery, red pepper,
chopped spring onions and
2 teaspoons of French dressing.
1 rice cake spread with ½ teaspoon
margarine.

1 medium tangerine stirred into
2½fl oz (75ml) low-fat natural yogurt.

Dinner: Chicken Salad

2oz (60g) roast chicken
Potato Salad – 3oz (90g) cooked,
diced potatoes mixed with
1 tablespoon low-calorie mayonnaise
and 2 teaspoons chopped chives.
Green Salad – shredded lettuce,
endive, chicory, chopped celery,
cucumber, spring onions and
1 tomato cut in thin wedges.

✳ Strawberry Creme ✳

Snacks:

1 medium nectarine
7½fl oz (225ml) skimmed milk

Optional Calories 40

STRAWBERRY CREME

Serves 2
150 Calories per serving

5oz (150g) strawberries, sliced

1 teaspoon caster sugar

For the topping:
½oz (15g) cornflour

¼ pint (150ml) skimmed milk

2 or 3 drops vanilla or almond essence

1 egg, separated

pinch of cream of tartar

1 tablespoon caster sugar

1. Reserve a few slices of strawberries for decoration. Divide the remainder between two dishes and sprinkle evenly with the sugar. Put to one side.
2. Mix the cornflour to a smooth paste with a little of the milk.
3. Heat the remaining milk until steaming, pour on to the cornflour paste and return to the saucepan. Bring to the boil stirring all the time.
4. Remove the saucepan from the heat and stir in the vanilla or almond essence. Allow to cool a little then stir in the egg yolk.
5. Pour the sauce into a bowl, cover with clingfilm and leave until cold.
6. Whisk the egg white with the cream of tartar until peaking, add the sugar and whisk again until stiff.
7. Carefully fold the egg white into the cold sauce, then spoon over the sweetened strawberries. Decorate with the reserved sliced strawberries and serve.

Exchanges per serving: Bread ¼, Fruit ½, Milk ¼, Protein ½, Optional Calories 40

WEEK 3

Day 6

Breakfast:

1oz (30g) cereal
½ medium banana, sliced
¼ pint (150ml) skimmed milk

Lunch: Ham and Curd Cheese Salad

Mix together 1oz (30g) cooked ham, chopped finely with 2oz (60g) curd cheese, 1 tablespoon low-calorie mayonnaise, a dash of pepper sauce and 1 teaspoon chopped chives. Mixed Salad – shredded lettuce, sliced tomato, radishes and beetroot.

5oz (150g) gooseberries stewed in a little water and sweetened with artificial sweetener, served with 2½fl oz (75ml) low-fat natural yogurt.

Dinner: ✳ Chilli Con Carne ✳

Green Salad – shredded lettuce, sliced cucumber, celery, green pepper and sprigs of watercress.

4oz (120g) fruit salad

Snacks:

½ pint (300ml) skimmed milk

Optional Calories 15

CHILLI CON CARNE

Serves 2
470 Calories per serving

9oz (270g) lean minced beef
1 tablespoon vegetable oil
1 clove garlic, chopped
1 onion, chopped
1 small red or green pepper or ½ each, seeded and chopped
½ teaspoon chilli powder
1 teaspoon ground cumin
1 tablespoon flour
1 small (8oz/227g) can chopped tomatoes
9oz (270g) drained, canned kidney beans
7fl oz (210ml) beef stock
salt

1. Form the minced beef into patties, place on the rack of a grill pan and grill under a moderate heat, turning once until the fat has stopped dripping from the meat. Remove from the heat.
2. Heat the oil in a saucepan, add the garlic and stir-fry for 1 minute. Add the onion and pepper and stir-fry over a moderate heat for 4 minutes.
3. Stir the chilli powder, cumin and flour into the saucepan, mix well and remove from the heat.
4. Gradually stir in the chopped tomatoes, beans and stock. Crumble in the meat patties and bring to the boil over a moderate heat. Cover and simmer gently for 30 minutes.
5. Season to taste with salt and serve immediately.

Exchanges per serving: Bread 1½, Fat 1½, Protein 3½, Vegetable 1½, Optional Calories 15

Chilli Con Carne with salad; fruit salad

WEEK 3

Day 7

Breakfast:

½ medium grapefruit
1oz (30g) slice of wholemeal bread
spread with 1 teaspoon margarine.
1 boiled egg

Lunch: Salmon Salad

2oz (60g) drained and flaked, canned
salmon sprinkled with a little lemon
juice and served with a salad of
shredded lettuce, sliced tomato,
cucumber, chopped spring onion and
sprigs of watercress.

5oz (150g) drained, canned
blackberries served with
2 tablespoons of the juice and
2½fl oz (75ml) low-fat natural yogurt.

Dinner: Grilled Liver with Vegetables

4oz (120g) lamb's or calf's liver
brushed with ½ teaspoon vegetable
oil and grilled.
Steamed or boiled broccoli, leeks and
carrots.
4½oz (135g) baked jacket potato

✳ Apple Pie ✳

Served with 3 tablespoons frozen
whipped dessert topping.

Snacks:

¾ pint (450ml) skimmed milk

Optional Calories 110

APPLE PIE

Serves 4
210 Calories per serving

For the pastry:
2oz (60g) plain flour
pinch of salt
2 tablespoons margarine
Approximately 2 teaspoons ice-cold water
For the base:
1lb (480g) cored, peeled and sliced cooking apples
4 tablespoons sugar
2–3 tablespoons water
good pinch of cinnamon

1. Reserve 1 tablespoon flour and sieve the remainder into a bowl with the salt. Rub in the margarine (if possible margarine which has been stored in a freezer) until the mixture resembles fresh breadcrumbs.
2. Gradually add the water and mix to form a dough with a round-bladed knife. Cover with clingfilm and refrigerate.
3. Place all the base ingredients in a saucepan, cover and simmer gently to soften the slices of apple. Allow to cool and spoon into a 1 pint (600ml) pie dish.
4. Sprinkle a rolling pin and work surface with the reserved flour, roll out the pastry a little larger than the pie dish and cut a strip from the edge. Dampen the lip of the pie dish and press on the pastry strip, brush with cold water and cover with the pastry lid.
5. Trim the pastry edge, press to seal with a fork or decorate by flaking with the back of a knife.
6. Bake at 400°F/200°C/Gas Mark 6 for 15 minutes then at 350°F/180°C/Gas Mark 4 for a further 15 minutes.

Exchanges per serving: Bread ½, Fat 1½, Fruit 1, Optional Calories 60

WEEK 4

Day 1

Breakfast:

4fl oz (120ml) orange juice
Toast a 1oz (30g) slice of bread,
sprinkle 1oz (30g) grated Cheddar
cheese over it and grill until
bubbling. Serve with 1 tomato.

Lunch: Liver Sausage Sandwich

Spread 2 slices of reduced-calorie
bread with 2 teaspoons low-fat
spread. Top one slice with two
lettuce leaves, 1½oz (45g) liver
sausage, sliced, and 1 tomato, sliced.
Spread the other slice of bread with a
little mustard then place on top of the
filling.
Fennel and Pepper Salad – thinly
sliced fennel mixed with thinly sliced
mixed peppers.

3 medium apricots chopped and
stirred into 5fl oz (150ml) low-fat
natural yogurt.

Dinner: Grilled Plaice with Vegetables

4oz (120g) fillet of plaice brushed
with ½ teaspoon vegetable oil grilled,
turned, brushed with ½ teaspoon
vegetable oil and grilled until cooked.
Steamed or boiled asparagus, carrots
and leeks.

✳ Fluffy Strawberry Flan ✳

Snacks:

½ pint (300ml) skimmed milk

Optional Calories 40

FLUFFY STRAWBERRY FLAN

Serves 6
195 Calories per serving

6 large digestive biscuits

2 tablespoons margarine

15oz (450g) strawberries

4 tablespoons caster sugar

2 tablespoons water

4 teaspoons gelatine

6oz (180g) fromage frais

1. Place the biscuits in a plastic bag and, using a rolling pin, crush to form crumbs.
2. Melt the margarine and mix into the biscuit crumbs. Press into a 7 inch (18cm) springform tin.
3. Reserve a few strawberries for decoration. Blend the remaining strawberries and sugar together, pour into a bowl and stir well until the sugar has dissolved.
4. Pour the water into a cup or small basin and sprinkle in the gelatine. Stand the cup in a saucepan of simmering water until dissolved. Stir into the strawberry purée.
5. Leave the strawberry purée until beginning to set. Fold the fromage frais into the setting purée. Spoon the mixture over the biscuit base and refrigerate until set.
6. To serve; remove the Fluffy Strawberry Flan from the tin, transfer to a serving plate and decorate with the reserved strawberries.

Exchanges per serving: Bread 1, Fat 1, Fruit ½, Protein ½, Optional Calories 40

WEEK 4

Day 2

Breakfast:

1oz (30g) dried apricots, chopped
1oz (30g) cereal
¼ pint (150ml) skimmed milk

Lunch: Prawn Salad

2oz (60g) peeled prawns mixed with
1 tablespoon seafood sauce.
Shredded lettuce, grated carrot,
1 sliced tomato and chopped spring
onions topped with 2 teaspoons low-
calorie mayonnaise.
1 oatcake spread with 1 teaspoon
margarine.

3oz (90g) grapes

Dinner: Roast Turkey with Vegetables

3oz (90g) roast turkey
Steamed or boiled carrots,
cauliflower and Brussels sprouts.
1 medium corn on the cob, boiled,
served with 1 teaspoon margarine,
salt and pepper.

✳ Layered Fruit Sundae ✳

Snacks:

12½fl oz (375ml) skimmed milk

Optional Calories 60

LAYERED FRUIT SUNDAE

Serves 4
120 Calories per serving

1 medium mango

½ medium banana

juice of ½ a lime

2 teaspoons clear honey

4oz (120g) curd cheese

5fl oz (150ml) low-fat natural yogurt

5oz (150g) strawberries

1. Cut the mango lengthways down the broadside of the fruit about ½ inch (1.25cm) away from the centre. Cut through the other side about the same distance from the centre. Scrape the flesh from each half and from round the stone into a blender.
2. Add the banana, lime juice, 1 teaspoon honey and curd cheese to the blender. Blend until smooth.
3. Mix the remaining honey and yogurt together, put to one side.
4. Reserve four strawberries for decoration and slice the remaining strawberries.
5. Layer the strawberries, yogurt and mango purée in tall narrow glasses. Start with a layer of strawberries, spoon over a little of the yogurt mixture then a little of the mango purée. Repeat the layers and decorate each glass with the reserved strawberries.

Exchanges per serving: Fruit 1, Milk ¼, Protein ½, Optional Calories 10

Layered Fruit Sundae; roast turkey
with vegetables; corn on the cob

WEEK 4

Day 3

Breakfast:

3 medium prunes
1oz (30g) cereal
¼ pint (150ml) skimmed milk

Lunch: Tongue Open Sandwich

Spread 1oz (30g) slice of wholemeal
bread with 1 teaspoon margarine
and top with slices of cucumber,
tomato and 1 teaspoon mayonnaise.
Roll up 2 × 1oz (30g) slices of
tongue and lay on top.

5oz (150g) strawberries served with
5fl oz (150ml) low-fat natural yogurt.

Dinner: * Ratatouille-Style Chicken *

3oz (90g) boiled potato

4oz (120g) fresh fruit salad served
with 2 tablespoons single cream.

Snacks:

¼ pint (150ml) skimmed milk

Optional Calories 60

RATATOUILLE-STYLE CHICKEN

Serves 2
254 Calories per serving

6oz (180g) aubergine
salt
2 teaspoons olive oil
1 large clove garlic, chopped
1 large onion, chopped
1 red pepper, seeded, and cut into strips
6oz (180g) courgettes, cut in chunks
1 small (8oz/227g) can chopped tomatoes
½ teaspoon basil
½ teaspoon oregano
2 × 4oz (120g) skinned and boned chicken breasts
pepper

1. Cut the aubergine into cubes, sprinkle liberally with the salt and leave to drain for 20–30 minutes. Then rinse well and pat dry.
2. Heat the oil in a flameproof casserole. Add the garlic, onion and red pepper and sauté for 2–3 minutes.
3. Mix the aubergine, courgettes, tomatoes, herbs and chicken in the casserole. Season with a little salt and pepper.
4. Bring to the boil, stirring all the time. Remove from the heat, cover the casserole and place in a preheated oven 350°F/180°C/Gas Mark 4 for 1 hour.

Exchanges per serving: Fat 1, Protein 3, Vegetable 4½

WEEK 4
Day 4

Breakfast:
1 medium apple
1oz (30g) cereal
¼ pint (150ml) skimmed milk

Lunch:
4fl oz (120ml) tomato or vegetable juice

✳ Potatoes in a Green Dressing ✳
Mixed Salad – shredded lettuce, sliced peppers, fennel and tomato tossed in 2 teaspoons French dressing.

1 medium orange

Dinner: Smoked Fish with Vegetables
4oz (120g) smoked cod or haddock poached in a little water.
Steamed or boiled carrots, courgettes and Brussels sprouts.

Junket – heat ¼ pint (150ml) fresh skimmed milk (not long life) until warm, add 2–3 drops of vanilla essence, 1 teaspoon of sugar or honey and 1 teaspoon essence of rennet. Pour into a serving dish and leave in the warm for 15–20 minutes until set.

Snacks:
7½fl oz (225ml) skimmed milk

Optional Calories 20

POTATOES IN A GREEN DRESSING
Serves 2
340 Calories per serving

2 eggs

12oz (360g) new potatoes, scraped

1oz (30g) lean Parma ham

For the dressing:
2½fl oz (75ml) low-fat natural yogurt

2oz (60g) fromage frais

3oz (90g) watercress

1 small clove garlic, peeled

1 small spring onion, roughly chopped

4 teaspoons low-calorie mayonnaise

salt and pepper

cayenne pepper to garnish

1. Place the eggs in a saucepan of cold water, bring to the boil and simmer for 10–12 minutes. Plunge into cold water and remove the shells.
2. While the eggs are cooking, boil or steam the potatoes.
3. Roughly chop the eggs, cut the potatoes into chunks and the ham into strips.
4. Place all the dressing ingredients into a blender, process until smooth.
5. Pour the watercress dressing over the eggs, ham and potatoes, toss well to coat.
6. Spoon the salad into a bowl and dust well with cayenne pepper before serving.

Exchanges per serving: Bread 2, Fat 1, Milk ¼, Protein 2, Vegetable ½

WEEK 4

Day 5

Breakfast:

4fl oz (120ml) orange juice
1oz (30g) bap
1 teaspoon margarine
1 tablespoon jam or marmalade

Lunch: Cottage Cheese Salad

4oz (120g) cottage cheese mixed with
1 tablespoon chopped red pepper.
Green Salad – shredded lettuce,
chopped spring onion and celery
mixed with sliced cucumber.
Tomato Salad – 1 tomato thinly
sliced, drizzled with 1 teaspoon
French dressing mixed with
1 teaspoon chopped chives.

Banana Froth – ½ medium banana
blended with 2½fl oz (75ml) low-fat
natural yogurt, ¼ pint (150ml)
buttermilk and 1 teaspoon of sugar.
Serve immediately in a tall glass.

Dinner: ✳ Lamb Hot Pot ✳

Steamed or boiled green beans.

4oz (120g) drained, canned, or
fresh cherries served with 2½fl oz
(75ml) low-fat natural yogurt.

Snacks:

2oz (60g) ice-cream
¼ pint (150ml) skimmed milk

Optional Calories 170

LAMB HOT POT

Serves 2
480 Calories per serving

| 8oz (240g) lean boneless chump chops |
| 2 leeks, thickly sliced |
| 2 carrots, sliced |
| 4oz (120g) parsnips, cubed |
| 4oz (120g) swede, cubed |
| 1oz (30g) pearl barley |
| ½ pint (300ml) vegetable stock |
| salt and pepper |
| 9oz (270g) potato |
| 1 tablespoon margarine |

1. Place the chump chops on the rack of a grill pan and cook under a moderate heat, turning once, until the fat has stopped dripping from the meat. Remove from the heat.
2. Cut the meat into large cubes, and place the meat, prepared vegetables, pearl barley and stock into a flameproof casserole. Bring to the boil stirring all the time.
3. Season the meat with a little salt and pepper. Thinly slice the potato and arrange over the top of the hot pot.
4. Melt the margarine and brush over the potato slices.
5. Bake at 325°F/160°C/Gas Mark 3 for 1½ hours until the potatoes are turning golden brown. If necessary brown under a hot grill for 2–3 minutes.

Exchanges per serving: Bread 2, Fat 1½, Protein 3, Vegetables 3

Lamb Hot Pot with green beans;
cherries with yogurt

WEEK 4

Day 6

Breakfast:

½ medium grapefruit
Toast a 1oz (30g) slice of bread,
spread with 1 teaspoon margarine
and top with 3oz (90g) baked beans.

Lunch: Mushroom Omelette

Beat together 2 eggs, 2 tablespoons
water, salt and pepper. Heat
1 teaspoon margarine in a small
omelette pan, stir-fry 3oz (90g) sliced
mushrooms for 3–4 minutes, remove.
Heat another 1 teaspoon margarine in
the pan, add the egg mixture and
cook over a gentle heat drawing the
mixture from the edge towards the
centre. When the underside is golden
spoon the mushrooms over half the
omelette, cook for a further minute,
fold over and serve.

4oz (120g) pineapple

Dinner: ✳ Melon Cocktail ✳

Ham with Vegetables

3oz (90g) cooked ham, sliced
3oz (90g) baby corn, boiled
Steamed or boiled mange-tout and
carrots.

5fl oz (150ml) low-fat natural yogurt

Snacks:

½ pint (300ml) skimmed milk

MELON COCKTAIL

Serves 3
60 Calories per serving

½ medium charentais melon
½ medium galia melon
5oz (150g) wedge of watermelon
3oz (90g) fromage frais
2–3 teaspoons chopped mint
1–2 teaspoons lemon juice
few endive leaves
lemon slices and/or sprigs of mint to garnish

1. Scoop out and discard the seeds of the charentais and galia
   melons. Using a melon baller or teaspoon scoop out the flesh
   in the shape of balls, place in a bowl. Reserve the skins and
   any juices which escape while making the melon balls.
2. Remove as many black seeds as possible from the
   watermelon and using the same method, form into balls and
   mix with the other melon balls. Discard the skin, but add any
   juices to the reserved melon juice.
3. Squeeze the reserved melon skins to extract as much
   remaining juice as possible. Gradually stir the fromage frais
   into the melon juice. Add mint and lemon juice to taste.
4. Arrange the endive leaves round the edge of three serving
   plates or glasses.
5. Pour the melon and fromage frais dressing over the melon
   balls, spoon into the centre of the endive leaves and decorate
   with slices of lemon and/or sprigs of mint.

Exchanges per serving: Fruit 1, Protein ½

WEEK 4

Day 7

Breakfast:

4fl oz (120ml) grape juice
1 medium crumpet, toasted and spread with 2 teaspoons low-fat spread.

Lunch: Cottage Cheese Open Sandwich

Spread 1oz (30g) slice of rye bread with 1 teaspoon margarine and top with lettuce or chicory. Pile 4oz (120g) cottage cheese in the centre of the lettuce. Arrange slices of tomato and cucumber round the cheese. Mixed Salad – radicchio, sliced radishes, peppers, fennel and grated carrot.

5fl oz (150ml) low-fat natural yogurt

Dinner: ✳ Fruity Mackerel Salad ✳

5oz (150g) gooseberries, stewed in a little water and sweetened with artificial sweetener, topped with 2 tablespoons frozen whipped topping.

Snacks:

½ pint (300ml) skimmed milk

Optional Calories 40

FRUITY MACKEREL SALAD

Serves 3
355 Calories per serving

10oz (300g) smoked peppered mackerel fillets
¼ medium galia melon
1 medium apple
1 tablespoon lemon juice
2 inch (5cm) wedge cucumber, diced
2 tablespoons chopped spring onions
6 stuffed olives, sliced
2 tomatoes, cut in wedges
shredded lettuce
3 lemon wedges
3 × 1oz (30g) pieces French bread
1 tablespoon margarine

1. Remove the skin from the mackerel fillets and flake the fish into large pieces.
2. Discard the melon seeds and thinly peel away the skin. Cut the melon widthways into thin slices.
3. Quarter the apple, remove the core and slice the apple, toss in the lemon juice.
4. Mix the peppered mackerel, melon, apple, cucumber, spring onions, stuffed olives and tomatoes together.
5. Arrange the shredded lettuce round the edge of the serving dish or bowl, pile the salad in the centre and garnish with the lemon wedges.
6. Spread each piece of French bread with a teaspoon of margarine and serve with the salad.

Exchanges per serving: Bread 1, Fat 1, Fruit ½, Protein 3, Vegetable 1, Optional Calories 10

WEEK 5

Day 1

Breakfast:

1 medium mandarin
1oz (30g) cereal
¼ pint (150ml) skimmed milk

Lunch: Beans on Toast

Toast 2 × 1oz (30g) slices of bread,
spread with 2 teaspoons margarine
and top with 6oz (180g) baked beans.

Gooseberries and Yogurt – top and
tail 5oz (150g) gooseberries and stew
in a little water, sweeten to taste with
artificial sweetener and serve with
2½fl oz (75ml) low-fat natural yogurt.

Dinner: Grilled Plaice with Vegetables

Place 5oz (150g) plaice fillet on
the rack of a grill pan, brush with
1 teaspoon of melted margarine. Grill
until cooked. Serve with a wedge of
lemon.
Steamed or boiled fennel, and grilled
tomatoes.

* Pears in Chocolate Sauce *

Snacks:

½ pint (300ml) skimmed milk

Optional Calories 105

PEARS IN CHOCOLATE SAUCE

Serves 2
165 Calories per serving

| 1 medium orange, zest and juice |
| 1 tablespoon water |
| 1 tablespoon caster sugar |
| 2 medium firm pears |
| 1oz (30g) plain chocolate |

1. Remove the zest from the orange with a zester, or use a potato peeler and then cut the zest into very thin strips.
2. Squeeze the juice from the orange and place in a saucepan with the water, caster sugar and orange zest.
3. Peel the pears, cut in half lengthways, scoop out the core with a teaspoon and cut away the strands connecting the main core to the stalk.
4. Gently heat the orange juice and sugar, add the pear halves, cover and simmer over a very low heat for about 15 minutes until just cooked, but not mushy.
5. Remove the pear halves and place on a cooling rack over a plate. Strain the syrup and reserve the zest.
6. Return the syrup to the saucepan and boil rapidly for 1 minute until reduced. Remove from the heat. Grate the chocolate and stir into the syrup. Allow to cool.
7. To serve; place two pear halves in 2 serving dishes and, just before serving, pour over the chocolate sauce and the reserved orange zest.

Exchanges per serving: Fruit 1½, Optional Calories 105

Pears in Chocolate Sauce; grilled
plaice with vegetables

WEEK 5

Day 2

Breakfast: * Swiss Muesli *

Lunch: Sardine Salad

2oz (60g) well-drained, canned sardines, served with a mixed salad of shredded lettuce, sliced cucumber, red pepper, celery, radish and chopped spring onion, tossed in 2 teaspoons French dressing.
1oz (30g) French bread spread with 1 teaspoon margarine.
4fl oz (120ml) grapefruit juice

Dinner: Grilled Halibut with Vegetables

5oz (150g) halibut steak brushed with ½ teaspoon margarine and grilled for 4 minutes, turned, brushed with ½ teaspoon margarine and grilled until cooked.
3oz (90g) boiled potatoes
Steamed or boiled broccoli, carrots and leeks.

Junket and Peaches – heat ¼ pint (150ml) fresh skimmed milk (*not* long life) until warm, add 2–3 drops vanilla essence, 1 teaspoon of sugar or honey and 1 teaspoon essence of rennet. Pour into a serving dish and leave in the warm for 15–20 minutes until set. Just before serving top with 2oz (60g) drained, canned sliced peaches.

Snacks:

½ pint (300ml) skimmed milk

Optional Calories 40

SWISS MUESLI

Serves 4
235 Calories per serving

1oz (30g) barley flakes
1oz (30g) rye flakes
1oz (30g) millet flakes
1oz (30g) jumbo oats
1½oz (45g) mixed dried fruit e.g. apple rings, apricots
½oz (15g) sultanas
2 teaspoons wheatgerm
1 teaspoon sesame seeds
2 teaspoons sunflower seeds
8fl oz (240ml) orange juice
To serve: 10fl oz (300ml) low-fat natural yogurt
1 medium peach, stoned and diced
4oz (120g) drained, canned pineapple pieces

1. Mix together the barley, rye and millet flakes and jumbo oats.
2. Chop the dried apple rings, apricots etc. and stir into the barley mixture with the sultanas, wheatgerm, sesame and sunflower seeds.
3. Place the muesli in a non-metallic bowl and stir in the orange juice, cover and leave overnight.
4. To serve; stir in the low-fat natural yogurt, peach and pineapple to form a wet mixture, divide between 4 bowls. If only two people require muesli, divide the dry mixture in half, add 4fl oz (120ml) orange juice, soak overnight, then add 5fl oz (150ml) natural yogurt. The orange-soaked muesli may be kept for a further day. Refrigerate if only one serving is required.

Exchanges per serving: Bread 1, Fruit 1½, Milk ½, Optional Calories 20

WEEK 5

Day 3

Breakfast:

4fl oz (120ml) orange juice
1oz (30g) lean back bacon, grilled, served with 2 grilled tomatoes and 1oz (30g) slice of bread, toasted.

Lunch: Peanut Butter Sandwich

2 × 1oz (30g) slices of bread, spread one slice with 1 teaspoon low-fat spread. Spread the other slice of bread with 1 tablespoon peanut butter. Sandwich together with the other slice.
Green Salad – shredded lettuce, sliced cucumber, green pepper, celery and spring onions.

Dinner: ✳ Meaty Mango Kebabs ✳

Steamed or boiled spinach and cauliflower.

5fl oz (150ml) low-fat natural yogurt

Snacks:

½ pint (300ml) skimmed milk

MEATY MANGO KEBABS

Serves 1
280 Calories per serving

1 tablespoon lemon juice
1½ teaspoons sunflower oil
½ teaspoon very finely chopped root ginger
4oz (120g) skinned chicken or turkey fillets
½ red pepper, seeded
½ medium mango
4–6 bulbous spring onions

1. Mix the lemon juice, oil and ginger together in a small non-metallic bowl.
2. Cut the chicken or turkey into cubes. Cut the pepper into 1 inch (2.5cm) dice.
3. Stir the poultry and pepper into the lemon marinade.
4. Cut the mango into large dice – this is easily prepared by making cuts through the mango flesh almost to the stone in one direction then making cuts at right angles to the first cuts. Lastly turn the skin under the fruit so the cubes rise up and separate, cut the cubes of mango from the skin and stir into the marinade.
5. Cover the basin and leave to marinate for about 3 hours, stirring occasionally.
6. Thread the chicken or turkey, pepper, spring onions and mango on to two skewers. Place under a preheated grill, brushing with the marinade and turning from time to time.

Exchanges per serving: Fat 1½, Fruit 1, Protein 3, Vegetable ½

WEEK 5

Day 4

Breakfast:

½ medium grapefruit
Toast a 1oz (30g) slice of bread and spread with 1 tablespoon peanut butter.

Lunch: Liver Sausage Salad

2oz (60g) liver sausage, sliced, shredded lettuce, 2 stuffed olives, sliced and mixed with chopped peppers, fennel and celery.
1 slice reduced-calorie bread, spread with 1 teaspoon margarine.

8oz (240g) rhubarb sweetened with artificial sweetener, served with 2½fl oz (75ml) low-fat natural yogurt.

Dinner: ✳ Creamy Lemon Chicken ✳

Steamed or boiled mange-tout and carrots.

Pineapple Froth – place 4oz (120g) drained, canned pineapple pieces in a blender with ¼ pint (150ml) buttermilk and 1 teaspoon caster sugar, process until smooth. Serve immediately.

Snacks:

½ pint (300ml) skimmed milk

Optional Calories 100

Creamy Lemon Chicken with mange-tout and carrots; Pineapple Froth

CREAMY LEMON CHICKEN

Serves 4
395 Calories per serving

For the chicken:
1 teaspoon margarine

few slices of onion

4 × 4oz (120g) boned and skinned chicken breasts

1 lemon

6 tablespoons vegetable or chicken stock

1 tablespoon cornflour

6 tablespoons single cream

salt and pepper

For the rice:
a few strands of saffron

1 tablespoon vegetable oil

1 red pepper, seeded and chopped

6 spring onions

6oz (180g) long grain rice

8 black olives, pitted and halved

1. Place a large piece of foil over a baking sheet, grease with the margarine. Arrange the onion rings and chicken along the length of the foil. Finely grate the lemon zest over the chicken and pour over the stock. Fold the foil over securely and transfer to a preheated oven 350°F/180°C/Gas Mark 4 for 30–35 minutes.
2. While the chicken is cooking prepare the rice. Soak the saffron in 2 tablespoons warm water for 20 minutes. Heat the oil and add the red pepper, stir-fry for 2–3 minutes. Cut the spring onion into 1 inch (2.5cm) diagonal lengths, chop a little of the green part and reserve.
3. Add the spring onion and rice to the oil and stir-fry for 1–2 minutes, add the olives, saffron and the saffron water together with the amount of water recommended on the packaging instructions. Boil for the recommended time.
4. Remove the chicken pieces from the oven, keep warm. Discard the onion and drain off the stock.
5. Blend the stock and chicken juices into the cornflour, bring to the boil stirring all the time, stir in the cream, 2 teaspoons of lemon juice, salt and pepper. Simmer gently until thickened.
6. Arrange the rice on a warm serving plate, place the chicken on top, pour over the sauce and sprinkle with the chopped spring onions.

Exchanges per serving: Bread 1½, Protein 3, Fat 1, Vegetable ½, Optional Calories 70

WEEK 5

Day 5

Breakfast:

Raspberry Froth – place 5oz (150g) raspberries, ¼ pint (150ml) buttermilk and 1½ teaspoons caster sugar in a blender. Process until frothy. Serve immediately.
Toast a 1oz (30g) slice of bread, spread with 1 tablespoon peanut butter.

Lunch: Salmon Salad

2oz (60g) drained and flaked, canned salmon with 1 teaspoon chopped chives and lemon juice to taste. Served with a mixed salad of shredded lettuce, sliced pepper, tomato, cucumber and celery tossed in 2 teaspoons French dressing.

1 medium pear

Dinner: ✳ Mexican Tacos ✳

Steamed or boiled peas and cauliflower.

4oz (120g) drained, canned mandarins served with 2½fl oz (75ml) low-fat natural yogurt.

Snacks:

7½fl oz (225ml) skimmed milk

Optional Calories 40

MEXICAN TACOS

Serves 2
360 Calories per serving

8oz (240g) minced pork
1 clove garlic, finely chopped
1–1½ teaspoons hot chilli powder
2 tablespoons vinegar
½ teaspoon oregano
good pinch of cinnamon
2 teaspoons vegetable oil
1 small onion, finely chopped
½ green pepper, seeded and chopped
2 tablespoons tomato purée
salt
4 taco shells
shredded lettuce
2½fl oz (75ml) low-fat natural yogurt

1. Mix the pork, garlic, chilli powder, vinegar, oregano and cinnamon together in a small non-metallic bowl, cover and refrigerate overnight.
2. The next day form the pork mixture into four patties, place on a grill rack and cook, turning once until the fat has stopped dripping from them. Allow to cool.
3. Heat the oil in a saucepan, add the onion and pepper and stir-fry for about 4 minutes. Crumble in the minced pork patties and stir in the tomato purée, season to taste with the salt. Stir over a moderate heat for about 5 minutes.
4. While the minced pork is cooking, heat the taco shells according to the packaging instructions.
5. Place a little shredded lettuce in the base of each taco shell, spoon the mixture over the lettuce and top with the yogurt. Serve immediately.

Exchanges per serving: Bread 2, Fat 1, Milk ¼, Protein 3, Vegetable 1, Optional Calories 10

Week 5

Day 6

Breakfast:

½ medium grapefruit
1oz (30g) slice of bread toasted,
spread with 1 teaspoon margarine
and topped with 1 poached egg.

Lunch: Toasted Cheese

Toast 2 × 1oz (30g) slices of bread,
sprinkle 2oz (60g) grated cheese on
top and grill until bubbling.
Mixed Salad – endive, sliced pepper,
cucumber, and sprigs of watercress,
served with 1 teaspoon mayonnaise.

1 medium orange

Dinner: ✳ Kidneys in Sherry Sauce ✳

Steamed or boiled swede, carrots and
parsnips.

Papaya Yogurt – scoop out the seeds
from ½ medium papaya, chop the
flesh and stir into 5fl oz (150ml) low-
fat natural yogurt with 1 teaspoon
clear honey.

Snacks:

½ pint (300ml) skimmed milk

Optional Calories 80

KIDNEYS IN SHERRY SAUCE

Serves 2
200 Calories per serving

6oz (180g) lamb's kidneys

1 tablespoon flour

pinch of powdered mustard

salt and pepper

2 teaspoons vegetable oil

1 small clove garlic, finely chopped

2 tablespoons chopped spring onions

6 tablespoons medium or dry sherry

1 teaspoon chopped parsley

1. Remove the outer skin from the kidneys, cut each kidney in half lengthways and remove the central core. Wash the kidney halves well and dab dry on kitchen paper.
2. Season the flour with the mustard, salt and pepper. Turn each kidney half in the flour, reserve the remaining flour.
3. Heat the oil in a small saucepan, add the garlic and stir-fry for 1 minute. Turn the kidneys in the hot oil until browned all over.
4. Stir the spring onions and remaining flour into the saucepan. Add the sherry and simmer gently for 6–7 minutes until the kidneys are cooked.
5. Transfer the kidneys and sherry sauce to a warm serving dish, sprinkle with chopped parsley and serve.

Exchanges per serving: Fat 1, Protein 2, Optional Calories 60

WEEK 5

Day 7

Breakfast:

1 kiwi fruit, chopped
1oz (30g) cereal
¼ pint (150ml) skimmed milk

Lunch: Cheese Omelette with Grilled Tomatoes

Beat together 2 eggs, 2 tablespoons water, salt and pepper. Heat 1 teaspoon margarine in a small omelette pan, add the egg mixture and cook over a gentle heat, drawing the mixture from the edge towards the centre. When the underside is golden, sprinkle with ½oz (15g) grated mature Cheddar cheese, fold over and serve with grilled tomatoes.

3oz (90g) grapes

Dinner: ✻ Steak in Peppercorn Sauce ✻

6oz (180g) baked jacket potato served with ½ teaspoon margarine.
Steamed or boiled carrots and courgettes.

1 medium orange

Snacks:

5fl oz (150ml) low-fat natural yogurt
1 teaspoon honey
¼ pint (150ml) skimmed milk

Optional Calories 100

STEAK IN PEPPERCORN SAUCE

Serves 2
305 Calories per serving

1 tablespoon green peppercorns in brine, drained

3 tablespoons Marsala

2 × 4oz (120g) rump or fillet steaks

1 tablespoon safflower oil

2 tablespoons finely chopped onion

4 teaspoons single cream

1. Rinse the peppercorns. Crush half the corns using a pestle and mortar or the back of a spoon.
2. Mix the crushed peppercorns and Marsala together.
3. Place the steaks in a non-metallic dish and pour over the Marsala mixture. Leave to marinate for at least 2 hours.
4. Transfer the steaks from the marinade to the rack of a grill pan, reserve the marinade.
5. Place the steaks under a moderate grill for 7–10 minutes, turning once.
6. While the steaks are cooking heat the oil in a saucepan. Add the chopped onion and the remaining whole green peppercorns and stir-fry for 3–4 minutes until the onion is cooked. Add the marinade and boil for 1–2 minutes. Remove from the heat and stir in the cream.
7. Arrange the steaks on a warm serving plate and pour over the peppercorn sauce.

Exchanges per serving: Fat 1½, Protein 3, Vegetable ¼, Optional Calories 80

WEEK 5

Day 1

Breakfast:

4fl oz (120ml) grapefruit juice
1 croissant
1 teaspoon margarine

Lunch: Open Sandwich

Spread 1 slice of reduced-calorie bread with 1 teaspoon low-fat spread. Arrange 2 lettuce leaves on top and place a 2–3oz (60–90g) rollmop in the centre. Cut a tomato into thin wedges and arrange round the rollmop with 2 sliced, stuffed olives. Green Salad – endive, chicory, chopped spring onions, celery, sliced cucumber and green pepper.

1 medium pear

Dinner: ✳ Oriental Stir-Fry ✳

3oz (90g) cooked rice

1 persimmon, chopped and stirred into 5fl oz (150ml) low-fat natural yogurt.

Snacks:

½ pint (300ml) skimmed milk

Optional Calories 130

ORIENTAL STIR-FRY

Serves 2
215 Calories per serving

4oz (120g) carrots, cut in thin strips

3oz (90g) mange-tout

1 tablespoon sesame oil

¾ inch (4cm) piece of fresh root ginger, finely chopped

1 clove garlic, chopped

3 spring onions, cut in 1 inch (2.5cm) diagonal lengths

½ red pepper, seeded and cut into strips

1 stick celery, sliced

4½oz (135g) water chestnuts, sliced

1 tablespoon soy sauce

6oz (180g) peeled prawns

2oz (60g) bean sprouts

2 teaspoons chopped coriander

lemon wedges

1. Plunge the prepared carrots in boiling water, boil for 1 minute then add the mange-tout and boil for a further 2 minutes.
2. Heat the oil in a wok or saucepan, add the ginger and garlic, stir-fry for 1 minute. Add the spring onion, red pepper and celery and stir-fry for a further 4–5 minutes.
3. Add the carrots, mange-tout, water chestnuts, soy sauce, prawns and bean sprouts and stir-fry for a further 4–5 minutes.
4. Divide the Oriental Stir-Fry between two warm serving dishes, sprinkle with the chopped coriander and serve with lemon wedges.

Exchanges per serving: Bread ½, Fat 1½, Protein 3, Vegetable 2½, Optional Calories 20

WEEK 5

Day 2

Breakfast:

1 kiwi fruit
1oz (30g) cereal
¼ pint (150ml) skimmed milk

Lunch: Ham Salad

2oz (60g) cooked ham, sliced,
1 tomato sliced and mixed with a few
slices of cucumber tossed in
2 teaspoons French dressing mixed
with 1 teaspoon chopped chives.
Served with 3oz (90g) diced beetroot
and shredded lettuce.

Dinner: Grilled Liver with Vegetables

4oz (120g) lamb's or calf's liver
brushed with ½ teaspoon vegetable
oil, grilled for 4–5 minutes, turned
and brushed with ½ teaspoon
vegetable oil, then grilled until
cooked.
Steamed or boiled marrow, mange-
tout and cauliflower.
1 medium corn on the cob, served
with 1 teaspoon margarine.

✳ Tropical Dream ✳

Snacks:

1 digestive biscuit
¾ pint (450ml) skimmed milk

Optional Calories 35

TROPICAL DREAM

Serves 2
155 Calories per serving

1 medium papaya
1 medium banana
2 teaspoons lemon juice
2 teaspoons honey
4oz (120g) fromage frais
1 egg white
pinch of cream of tartar
1 teaspoon desiccated coconut, toasted

1. Cut the papaya in half. Scoop out and discard the seeds. Scoop out all the flesh and place in a blender.
2. Roughly chop the banana and add to the blender with the lemon juice and honey. Process until smooth.
3. Add the fromage frais to the blender and process once again. Transfer the purée to a bowl.
4. Whisk the egg white with the cream of tartar until peaking. Using a metal spoon carefully fold the egg white through the fruit purée.
5. Spoon the mixture into two glass dishes, sprinkle with the desiccated coconut and serve, or chill and serve within 40 minutes.

Exchanges per serving: Fruit 2, Protein 1, Optional Calories 35

WEEK 5

Day 3

Breakfast:

4fl oz (120ml) orange juice
Toast a 1oz (30g) slice of bread, sprinkle 1oz (30g) grated cheese over one side and grill until bubbling.

Lunch: Pepper Omelette

Beat together 2 eggs, 2 tablespoons water, salt and pepper. Measure 1½ teaspoons margarine. Place half the margarine in a small omelette pan and stir-fry ½ a finely chopped green or red pepper for about 4 minutes until soft, remove the pepper from the pan and add the remaining margarine. Add the egg mixture and cook over a gentle heat, drawing the mixture from the edge towards the centre. When the underside is golden, spoon the cooked pepper over half the omelette, cook for a further minute, fold over and serve with a 1oz (30g) slice of bread, spread with 1 teaspoon low-fat spread.
Green Salad – shredded lettuce, chopped celery, spring onion and sliced cucumber.

3oz (90g) grapes

Dinner: ✳ Individual Fish Pie ✳

2oz (60g) drained, canned fruit salad stirred into 5fl oz (150ml) low-fat natural yogurt.

Snacks:

½ pint (300ml) skimmed milk

Optional Calories 15

INDIVIDUAL FISH PIE

Serves 1
305 Calories per serving

4fl oz (120ml) tomato and vegetable juice
2 tablespoons water
good pinch of mixed herbs
3oz (90g) skinned cod or haddock fillet
salt and pepper
3oz (90g) potato
1 teaspoon vegetable oil
½ medium onion, finely chopped
1 teaspoon flour
2oz (60g) okra, sliced
2 teaspoons skimmed milk
½oz (15g) Parmesan or mature Cheddar cheese, finely grated
good pinch of powdered mustard

1. Place the tomato and vegetable juice, water, mixed herbs and fish in a saucepan. Season with a little salt and pepper, cover and simmer for 7–8 minutes until the fish is cooked.
2. While the fish is cooking boil or steam the potato.
3. Remove the fish from the liquor and flake into large pieces.
4. Heat the oil in a saucepan, add the onion and stir-fry for 3–4 minutes. Stir in the flour, mix well then gradually add the tomato and vegetable juice and okra. Bring to the boil, reduce the heat and simmer for 6–7 minutes, stirring occasionally to prevent sticking. Add the flaked fish and cook for a further minute.
5. Mash the potato, milk, cheese and mustard together, season with salt and pepper.
6. Spoon the fish mixture into a warm 4½ inch (11cm) soufflé dish, cover with the mashed potato and place under a preheated grill until beginning to brown.

Exchanges per serving: Bread 1, Fat 1, Fruit ½, Protein 3, Vegetable 1, Optional Calories 15

WEEK 5

Day 4
Breakfast:

8fl oz (240ml) vegetable juice
Toast a 1oz (30g) slice of bread,
spread with 1 tablespoon peanut
butter.

Lunch: Salmon Open Sandwich

Spread a 1oz (30g) slice of bread with
1 teaspoon margarine, top with
endive or lettuce and slices of radish.
Flake 2oz (60g) drained, canned
salmon and mix with 1 teaspoon
mayonnaise, 1 teaspoon chopped
chives and lemon juice to taste, pile
on top of the lettuce etc. Serve with
slices of tomato and sprigs of
watercress.

4oz (120g) drained, canned fruit
salad served with a little of the
natural juice and 2½fl oz (75ml) low-
fat natural yogurt.

Dinner: ✱ Farmhouse Casserole ✱

Coffee Junket with Mandarins – heat
¼ pint (150ml) fresh skimmed milk
(*not* long life) with a little instant
coffee powder until warm and the
coffee has dissolved, stir in
1 teaspoon caster sugar and
1 teaspoon essence of rennet. Pour
into a serving dish and leave in the
warm for 15–20 minutes until set.
Serve with 4oz (120g) drained,
canned mandarin segments.

Snacks:

½ pint (300ml) skimmed milk

Optional Calories 50

FARMHOUSE CASSEROLE

Serves 4
330 Calories per serving

1lb (480g) shin of beef
½oz (15g) flour
½ pint (300ml) beer
2 tablespoons tomato purée
6oz (180g) potato
9oz (270g) mixture of swede, parsnip and turnip
3oz (90g) carrot
2 leeks
4½oz (135g) baby corn on the cob
4fl oz (120ml) strong beef stock
½ teaspoon mixed herbs
salt and pepper

1. Place the beef on the rack of a grill pan, grill under a
   moderate heat, turning once until the fat has stopped
   dripping. Allow to cool then cut into chunks.
2. Transfer the beef to a casserole dish, add the flour and stir
   well. Mix in the beer and tomato purée.
3. Cut the potato, swede, parsnip and turnip into large chunks.
   Thickly slice the carrot and leeks.
4. Stir all the vegetables, stock, herbs, salt and pepper into the
   casserole.
5. Place the casserole in a preheated oven 325°F/160°C/Gas
   Mark 3 for 2¾–3 hours.

**Exchanges per serving: Bread 1, Protein 3,
Vegetable 1¾, Optional Calories 30**

Farmhouse Casserole; coffee junket
with mandarins

WEEK 5

Day 5

Breakfast:

½oz (15g) sultanas
1oz (30g) cereal
¼ pint (150ml) skimmed milk

Lunch: Beans on Toast

2 slices of reduced-calorie bread,
toasted and spread with 2 teaspoons
low-fat spread.
6oz (180g) baked beans
3oz (90g) mushrooms, stir-fried in
1 teaspoon margarine.
3oz (90g) tomatoes, grilled.

1 medium orange

Dinner: ✱ Hawaiian Lamb ✱

3oz (90g) baked jacket potato served
with 1 teaspoon margarine.
Steamed or boiled Brussels sprouts
and carrots.

Junket – heat ¼ pint (150ml) fresh
skimmed milk (*not* long life) until
warm, add 2–3 drops of vanilla
essence, 1 teaspoon of sugar or
honey and 1 teaspoon essence of
rennet. Pour into a serving dish and
leave in the warm for 15–20 minutes
until set.

Snacks:

1 medium apple
½ pint (300ml) skimmed milk

Optional Calories 25

HAWAIIAN LAMB

Serves 4
200 Calories per serving

1lb (480g) minced lamb
½ teaspoon mixed herbs
large pinch of chilli powder
2oz (60g) drained, canned pineapple rings
6fl oz (180ml) pineapple juice
approximately 1 tablespoon lemon juice
½ teaspoon sugar
dash of soy sauce
1½ teaspoons cornflour
salt and pepper

1. Mix the lamb, herbs and chilli powder together in a bowl.
2. Cut each pineapple ring into six pieces.
3. Using damp hands form the lamb into twelve balls, flatten a little and shape each ball round one piece of pineapple. Repeat with all the lamb and pineapple.
4. Place the lamb balls on a grill rack, cook under a preheated grill for about 15 minutes, turning occasionally until beginning to brown.
5. Place the pineapple and lemon juice in a large saucepan, add the lamb balls to the saucepan, cover and simmer for 12–15 minutes.
6. Remove the lamb balls, cover and keep warm. Add the sugar and soy sauce to the saucepan.
7. Blend the cornflour to a smooth paste with a little water and stir into the sauce. Bring to the boil, stirring all the time, adjust the seasoning, pour over the meatballs and serve.

Exchanges per serving: Fruit ½, Protein 3, Optional Calories 5

WEEK 5

Day 6

Breakfast:

½ medium banana, sliced
1oz (30g) cereal
¼ pint (150ml) skimmed milk

Lunch: Cottage Cheese and Tuna Salad

2oz (60g) cottage cheese mixed with
1oz (30g) drained and flaked, canned
tuna, 2 teaspoons low-calorie
mayonnaise and a pinch of curry
powder.
Green Salad – shredded lettuce,
sliced cucumber, green pepper and
spring onion.
1oz (30g) French bread spread with
1 teaspoon margarine.
4fl oz (120ml) pineapple juice

5fl oz (150ml) low-fat natural yogurt

Dinner: Roast Chicken and Vegetables

3oz (90g) roast chicken
3oz (90g) baby corn boiled and
topped with 1 teaspoon margarine.
Steamed or boiled carrots and
asparagus.

✳ Chocolate Mousse ✳

Snacks:

½ medium ogen melon
¼ pint (150ml) skimmed milk

Optional Calories 155

CHOCOLATE MOUSSE

Serves 6
230 Calories per serving

3 eggs, separated, plus 1 extra egg white

6 tablespoons caster sugar

½ teaspoon instant coffee dissolved in 2 tablespoons boiling water

2 tablespoons hot water

2 teaspoons gelatine

2½oz (75g) plain chocolate, melted

4 teaspoons rum

pinch of cream of tartar

6oz (180g) fromage frais

3 tablespoons double cream

1. Secure a double band of greaseproof paper around a 6 inch (15cm) soufflé dish.
2. Place the egg yolks, sugar and coffee in a bowl standing over a saucepan of simmering water. Whisk until the mixture begins to thicken (about 10 minutes). Remove from the heat and continue whisking until cool.
3. Pour the hot water into a cup, sprinkle in the gelatine and 2oz (60g) of the chocolate. Stand in a saucepan of simmering water until dissolved.
4. Spread the remaining chocolate on a sheet of greaseproof paper. When set cut into six triangles or other shapes.
5. Stir the dissolved chocolate with the rum and gelatine into the whisked mixture, leave until setting.
6. Whisk the egg whites and cream of tartar until peaking. Fold the fromage frais into the setting mixture then carefully fold in the egg whites. Transfer to the soufflé dish.
7. Whisk the double cream until stiff, spoon into a piping bag.
8. To serve; remove the paper band from the set mousse. Pipe the cream on top and decorate with the chocolate shapes.

**Exchanges per serving: Protein 1,
Optional Calories 155**

WEEK 5

Day 7

Breakfast:

½ medium grapefruit
1oz (30g) slice of bread toasted and
spread with 1 teaspoon low-fat spread
and topped with 1 poached egg.

Lunch: Frankfurter Salad

2oz (60g) frankfurters
Mixed Salad – lettuce, sliced peppers,
radish, cucumber and celery mixed
with chopped spring onions.
2oz (60g) bread roll spread with
2 teaspoons low-fat spread.

4oz (120g) drained, canned apricots
stirred into 5fl oz (150ml) low-fat
natural yogurt.

Dinner: Grilled Salmon

5oz (150g) salmon steak. Brush with
½ teaspoon vegetable oil, grill for
5 minutes, turn and brush with
1 teaspoon vegetable oil. Grill until
cooked.
Mixed Salad – young spinach leaves,
shredded radicchio, endive and
lettuce.

✳ Four-Berry Treat ✳

Snacks:

½ pint (300ml) skimmed milk

Optional Calories 65

FOUR-BERRY TREAT

Serves 4
105 Calories per serving

5oz (150g) raspberries
5oz (150g) tayberries
5oz (150g) strawberries
5oz (150g) blueberries
1 tablespoon caster sugar
4 tablespoons sweet white wine
3 tablespoons double cream

1. Reserve a few berries of your choice for decoration, place the remainder in a blender. Process until smooth.
2. Add the sugar and wine to the blender and process once again.
3. Pour the fruit purée into four glasses and chill for 2–3 hours until thick.
4. Whisk the double cream until thick. Spoon the cream into a piping bag fitted with a ½ inch (1.25cm) fluted nozzle.
5. Pipe a swirl of cream on top of each fruit purée and decorate with the reserved fruit. Keep in the refrigerator until ready to serve.

Exchanges per serving: Fruit 1, Optional Calories 65

Four-Berry Treat; grilled salmon with
salad

WEEKS AT A GLANCE
WEEK – 1

Get off to a flying start by following the first week's daily Menu Plans. To add interest to meals choose from a range of unsweetened cereals and sometimes have wholemeal bread, other times eat rye or granary bread. Always weigh food accurately and prepare it following the directions given. Tea, coffee and water may be drunk as desired. It is essential to include ½ pint (300ml) skimmed milk in every day's menu. This is in addition to the milk already listed. You may like to enjoy the milk as a hot or chilled drink, or add it to your cups of tea and coffee throughout the day.

Day 1

Breakfast:
1 medium tangerine
1oz (30g) cereal
¼ pint (150ml) skimmed milk
Tea or coffee

Lunch:
Tuna Salad
2oz (60g) drained, canned tuna
1 teaspoon mayonnaise
wedge of lemon

Red Cabbage Salad (page 112)

Tomato and Cucumber Salad –
1 tomato, sliced mixed with a
1½ inch (4cm) wedge of
cucumber, sliced and
2 teaspoons chopped chives.
1oz (30g) pitta bread
1 teaspoon low-fat spread
Tea, coffee or mineral water

Dinner:
Orange Pork (page 153)

6oz (180g) broccoli
4oz (120g) celery
4oz (120g) drained, canned
fruit salad
2½fl oz (75ml) low-fat natural
yogurt
Tea or coffee

Optional Calories: 15

Day 2

Breakfast:
4fl oz (120ml) orange juice
2oz (60g) low-fat soft cheese
1oz (30g) bread, toasted
1 teaspoon margarine
1 tomato, sliced
Tea or coffee

Lunch:
Mackerel Salad
1½oz (45g) smoked mackerel
fillet
Mixed Salad – shredded
endive, chopped red pepper,
celery, spring onions, sliced
tomato and cucumber.
1 teaspoon mayonnaise
1oz (30g) roll
1 teaspoon margarine
Tea, coffee or mineral water

Dinner:
Roast Turkey with Vegetables
2oz (60g) roast turkey
3oz (90g) carrots
6oz (180g) cauliflower
1 medium apple, stewed

Baked Egg Custard (page 190)
Tea or coffee

Snacks:
¼ pint (150ml) buttermilk

Optional Calories: 35

Day 3

Breakfast:
1 medium pear
1oz (30g) Cheddar cheese,
grated
1oz (30g) bread, toasted
1 tomato, sliced
Tea or coffee

Lunch:
Turkey Salad
1½oz (45g) roast turkey
2oz (60g) carrot, grated and
mixed with 2oz (60g)
courgette, grated and
2 teaspoons chopped spring
onions.
Mixed Salad – shredded
lettuce, sliced radish,
cucumber and pepper.
1 teaspoon mayonnaise
1oz (30g) bread
1 teaspoon margarine
Tea, coffee or mineral water

Dinner:
Smoked Haddock Ring
(page 162)

Green Salad – shredded
lettuce, sliced cucumber, green
pepper, celery and spring onion.
2 teaspoons low-calorie French
dressing
5oz (150g) strawberries
2½ tablespoons low-fat natural
yogurt
Tea or coffee

Snacks:

¼ pint (150ml) skimmed milk

Optional Calories: 5

Day 4

Breakfast:

1 medium apple
1oz (30g) cereal
¼ pint (150ml) skimmed milk
Tea or coffee

Lunch:

Cheese and Tomato Sandwich
2 slices reduced-calorie bread
2 teaspoons margarine
3oz (90g) cottage cheese
1 tomato, sliced
Green Salad – shredded
lettuce, sliced cucumber,
celery, spring onion and green
pepper.
2 teaspoons low-calorie French
dressing
1 medium orange
Tea, coffee or mineral water

Dinner:

Grilled Lamb with Vegetables
5oz (150g) lamb chop
4oz (120g) Brussels sprouts
3oz (90g) carrots

Honeycomb Mould (page 189)

Tea or coffee

Optional Calories: 40

Day 5

Breakfast:

4fl oz (120ml) orange juice
1oz (30g) cereal
¼ pint (150ml) skimmed milk
Tea or coffee

Lunch:

Liver Sausage Salad
2oz (60g) liver sausage
Mixed Salad – shredded
lettuce, sliced cucumber,
tomato, pepper, celery and
spring onion.
¾oz (20g) French bread
1 teaspoon margarine
Tea, coffee or mineral water

Dinner:

Blue Cheese Soufflé (page 145)

4oz (120g) spinach
6oz (180g) cauliflower
4oz (120g) pineapple
2½ tablespoons low-fat natural
yogurt
Tea or coffee

Day 6

Breakfast:

4fl oz (120ml) grapefruit juice
2oz (60g) low-fat soft cheese
1oz (30g) bread, toasted
1 teaspoon margarine
1 tomato, sliced
Tea or coffee

Lunch:

Poached Egg on Toast
1oz (30g) bread, toasted
1 teaspoon margarine
1 egg, poached
5fl oz (150ml) low-fat natural
yogurt
Tea, coffee or mineral water

Dinner:

Mexican Fish (page 165)

3oz (90g) green beans
6oz (180g) courgettes
1 medium peach
Tea or coffee

Optional Calories: 5

Day 7

Breakfast:

2 inch (5cm) wedge of
honeydew melon
1oz (30g) cereal
¼ pint (150ml) skimmed milk
Tea or coffee

Lunch:

Cheese and Egg Salad
1 egg, hard-boiled
1oz (30g) Cheddar cheese,
grated
Green Salad – shredded
lettuce, sliced cucumber,
celery, pepper and spring
onion.
2 teaspoons low-calorie French
dressing
1oz (30g) bread, toasted
1 teaspoon margarine
Tea, coffee or mineral water

Dinner:

Peppered Frittata (page 177)

3oz (90g) carrots
4oz (120g) marrow

Spicy Fruit Salad (page 194)

2½fl oz (75ml) low-fat natural
yogurt
Tea or coffee

Optional Calories: 30

Total Optional Calories for
Week 1: 130

WEEKS AT A GLANCE
WEEK – 2

The range of foods has increased this week as well as the number of Optional Calories allowed. Pasta, rice, potatoes and crumpets are included as well as lean ham, asparagus, bean sprouts, watermelon, bananas, gooseberries, raspberries and peanut butter! Continue to add ½ pint (300ml) skimmed milk to every day's menu.

Day 1

Breakfast:
4fl oz (120ml) orange juice
1oz (30g) cereal
¼ pint (150ml) skimmed milk
Tea or coffee

Lunch:
Peach and Cottage Cheese Platter (page 129)

1oz (30g) French bread
1 teaspoon margarine
Tea, coffee or mineral water

Dinner:
Chicken and Ham Bake (page 160)

4oz (120g) asparagus
5oz (150g) gooseberries, stewed
2½fl oz (75ml) low-fat natural yogurt
Tea or coffee

Day 2

Breakfast:
4fl oz (120ml) grapefruit juice
1 tablespoon peanut butter
1 slice reduced-calorie bread, toasted
Tea or coffee

Lunch:
Stuffed Egg Salad
1 hard-boiled egg, halved and the yolk mashed with 1oz (30g) low-fat soft cheese,
2 teaspoons low-calorie

mayonnaise and 2 teaspoons chopped chives, seasoned with a dash of pepper sauce.
Green Salad – shredded lettuce, sliced cucumber, green pepper, celery and spring onion.
1 tomato, sliced
5oz (150g) watermelon chunks
Tea, coffee or mineral water

Dinner:
Grilled Liver with Vegetables
4oz (120g) lamb's or calf's liver, brushed with ½ teaspoon vegetable oil and grilled.
6oz (180g) baked jacket potato
1 teaspoon low-fat spread
3oz (90g) cabbage
3oz (90g) green beans
5fl oz (150ml) low-fat natural yogurt
Tea or coffee

Snacks:
1 medium orange

Day 3

Breakfast:
4fl oz (120ml) grapefruit juice
1oz (30g) slice of bread, toasted
1 egg, poached
Tea or coffee

Lunch:
Cottage Cheese Salad
3oz (90g) cottage cheese, mixed with 1 tablespoon chopped red pepper,

2 teaspoons chopped chives and 1 teaspoon low-calorie mayonnaise.
Mixed Salad – shredded lettuce, sliced green and yellow pepper, tomato and cucumber.
1 tablespoon low-calorie French dressing
5fl oz (150ml) low-fat natural yogurt
Tea, coffee or mineral water

Dinner:
Creole Swordfish (page 167)

4oz (120g) courgettes
6oz (180g) cauliflower

Gooseberry Charlotte (page 192)
Tea or coffee

Snacks:
1 medium orange
Optional Calories: 30

Day 4

Breakfast:
2 inch (5cm) wedge of honeydew melon
1oz (30g) cereal
¼ pint (150ml) skimmed milk
Tea or coffee

Lunch:
Salmon Salad
2oz (60g) drained, canned salmon
1 teaspoon mayonnaise
wedge lemon
Mixed Salad – shredded

lettuce, bean sprouts, grated carrot, sliced red pepper, radish and cucumber. 4 teaspoons low-calorie French dressing
4oz (120g) drained, canned fruit salad
2½fl oz (75ml) low-fat natural yogurt
Tea, coffee or mineral water

Dinner:
Spaghetti Bolognaise (page 157)

Green Salad – shredded endive, sliced celery, spring onion and green pepper. 2 teaspoons low-calorie French dressing

Raspberry Bonanza (page 193)

Tea or coffee

Optional Calories: 85

Day 5
Breakfast:
1 medium apple
2oz (60g) curd cheese
1 medium crumpet
1 tomato, sliced
few sprigs watercress
Tea or coffee

Lunch:
Rolled Ham Salad
1oz (30g) lean cooked ham, spread with 2oz (60g) cottage cheese and 2 teaspoons chopped chives and rolled up Swiss roll style.
Mixed Salad – sliced red and green pepper, cucumber, tomato, mushrooms and spring onion.
1 tablespoon low-calorie French dressing
2oz (60g) cold curried rice (cooked weight)

½ medium banana, sliced and stirred into 2½ tablespoons low-fat natural yogurt.
Tea, coffee or mineral water

Dinner:
Cheese and Spinach Soufflé (page 145)

1 tomato, halved and grilled
3oz (90g) leeks
3oz (90g) carrots

Simple Milk Pudding (page 217)

Tea or coffee

Snacks:
1 medium orange

Optional Calories: 40

Day 6
Breakfast:
½ medium grapefruit
1 tablespoon peanut butter
1 slice reduced-calorie bread, toasted
Tea or coffee

Lunch:
Cottage Cheese Open Sandwich
1 slice reduced-calorie bread spread with 1 teaspoon margarine, topped with alternate slices of tomato and cucumber, with 3oz (90g) cottage cheese piled on top and sprinkled with 1 tablespoon chopped chives.
Green Salad – shredded endive, sliced celery, green pepper and sprigs of watercress.
2 teaspoons French dressing
Tea, coffee or mineral water

Dinner:
Tuna and Pasta Mix (page 166)

6oz (180g) broccoli
5oz (150g) drained, canned raspberries with 2 tablespoons natural juice.
2½ tablespoons low-fat natural yogurt
Tea or coffee

Snacks:
¼ pint (150ml) skimmed milk

Optional Calories: 25

Day 7
Breakfast:
½ medium grapefruit
1 egg, boiled or poached
1 slice reduced-calorie bread, toasted
1 teaspoon margarine
Tea or coffee

Lunch:
Smoked Mackerel Salad
Flake 1½oz (45g) smoked mackerel and mix with ½ red pepper chopped, 1½oz (45g) bean sprouts, a 1 inch (2.5cm) wedge of cucumber, sliced and a few radicchio leaves, toss in 1 tablespoon low-calorie French dressing.
1 slice reduced-calorie bread
1 teaspoon low-fat spread
Tea, coffee or mineral water

Dinner:
Cottager's Pie (page 146)

4oz (120g) Brussels sprouts
4oz (120g) pineapple
5fl oz (150ml) low-fat natural yogurt
Tea or coffee

Snacks:
1 medium orange

Optional Calories: 10

Total Optional Calories for Week 2: 190

WEEKS AT A GLANCE
WEEK – 3

This week the number of Optional Calories has increased by 100 and beans, peas and lentils, as well as aubergines, are introduced to enable baked beans, Crispy Topped Beans, Moussaka and Aubergine Purée to be enjoyed. Grapes and blackberries give added variety to salads and desserts. In addition to the recipes given for Weeks 1 and 2, this week's menus list a wider selection. Remember to add ½ pint (300ml) skimmed milk to every day's eating plan.

Day 1

Breakfast:
½ medium banana, sliced
1oz (30g) cereal
¼ pint (150ml) skimmed milk
Tea or coffee

Lunch:
Cottage Cheese Salad
2oz (60g) cottage cheese mixed with 2oz (60g) curd cheese, 1 tablespoon chopped red pepper and dash of pepper sauce.

Red Cabbage Salad (page 112)

Green Salad – shredded lettuce, sliced cucumber, celery and green pepper.
1 medium tangerine
Tea, coffee or mineral water

Dinner:
Veal Stew (page 156)

3oz (90g) rice (cooked weight)
3oz (90g) green beans

Flapjack Pudding (page 196)

2½fl oz (75ml) low-fat natural yogurt
Tea or coffee

Snacks:
1 teaspoon cocoa

Optional Calories: 85

Day 2

Breakfast:
4fl oz (120ml) orange juice
1oz (30g) bread, toasted
1 teaspoon margarine
1 tablespoon marmalade
Tea or coffee

Lunch:
Peach and Cottage Cheese Platter (page 129)

5fl oz (150ml) low-fat natural yogurt
Tea, coffee or mineral water

Dinner:
Mexican Fish (page 165)

3oz (90g) rice (cooked weight)
4oz (120g) drained, canned pears served with
2 tablespoons natural juice and 2oz (60g) fromage frais.
Tea or coffee

Snacks:
1 digestive biscuit

Optional Calories: 55

Day 3

Breakfast:
1 medium apple
1oz (30g) cereal
¼ pint (150ml) skimmed milk
Tea or coffee

Lunch:
Bean Salad (page 121) (half of recipe)

Sally's Special Salad (page 113)

1 medium tangerine
Tea, coffee or mineral water

Dinner:
Moussaka (page 148)

6oz (180g) baked jacket potato
½ teaspoon margarine
4oz (120g) carrots
5oz (150g) chunks of honeydew melon
Tea or coffee

Optional Calories: 30

Day 4

Breakfast:
3oz (90g) grapes
3oz (90g) baked beans
1oz (30g) bread, toasted
1 teaspoon margarine
Tea or coffee

Lunch:
Green Pea Soup (page 110)

2oz (60g) liver sausage
Mixed Salad – chopped red and green pepper, celery, spring onion, sliced tomato and cucumber.
1 cream cracker

1 teaspoon margarine
4oz (120g) pineapple
2½ tablespoons low-fat natural yogurt
Tea, coffee or mineral water

Dinner:
Trout Pudding with Parsley Sauce (page 164)

3oz (90g) asparagus
6oz (180g) cauliflower

Raspberry Bonanza (page 193)
Tea or coffee

Optional Calories: 55

Day 5

Breakfast:
4fl oz (120ml) orange juice
1oz (30g) cereal
¼ pint (150ml) skimmed milk
Tea or coffee

Lunch:
Smoked Haddock Ring (page 162)

Savoury Fruit Salad (page 114)

Tomato and Cucumber Salad –
1 tomato sliced, mixed with
1½ inch (4cm) wedge of cucumber, sliced, 2 teaspoons chopped chives and
2 teaspoons low-calorie French dressing.
Tea, coffee or mineral water

Dinner:
Stuffed Marrow (page 178)

4½oz (135g) baked jacket potato
1 teaspoon margarine
4oz (120g) carrots
3oz (90g) leeks
5oz (150g) blackberries, stewed

2½ tablespoons low-fat natural yogurt
Tea or coffee

Optional Calories: 30

Day 6

Breakfast:
½ medium grapefruit
1oz (30g) bread, toasted
1 tablespoon peanut butter
Tea or coffee

Lunch:
Stuffed Egg Salad
1 hard-boiled egg, halved and the yolk mashed with
1 teaspoon low-calorie mayonnaise, 1oz (30g) cottage cheese and 2 teaspoons chopped chives.

Beetroot Salad (page 116)

Green Salad – shredded lettuce, sliced cucumber, green pepper, spring onion, celery and sprigs of watercress.
1 medium orange
Tea, coffee or mineral water

Dinner:
Mixed Vegetable Stew (page 186)

Aubergine Purée (page 125)
(⅓ of recipe)

2oz (60g) chopped pineapple stirred into 2½fl oz (75ml) low-fat natural yogurt and sprinkled with ground ginger.
Tea or coffee

Snacks:
1 medium crumpet
1 teaspoon low-fat spread
¼ pint (150ml) skimmed milk

Optional Calories: 30

Day 7

Breakfast:
4fl oz (120ml) orange juice
1oz (30g) bread, toasted
1oz (30g) Cheddar cheese
1 tomato, sliced
Tea or coffee

Lunch:
Ham and Cheese Salad (page 131)

1oz (30g) bread
1 teaspoon low-fat spread
Tea, coffee or mineral water

Dinner:
Crispy-Topped Beans (page 182)

6oz (180g) broccoli
1 medium apple, stewed
2½fl oz (75ml) low-fat natural yogurt
Tea or coffee

Snacks:
¼ pint (150ml) skimmed milk

Optional Calories: 5

Total Optional Calories for Week 3: 290

WEEKS AT A GLANCE
WEEK – 4

The weekly Optional Calories have risen to 400 and, with the range of food, it seems hard to believe this week's plan is designed especially for the weight conscious. More exotic fruits are included in recipes such as Sweet-Topped Fruit and Blueberry Mousse and the addition of swede, parsnip and turnip make the Layered Vegetable Pâté and Braised Beef ideal for a dinner party. In addition to the food listed it is still important to incorporate an extra ½ pint (300ml) skimmed milk every day.

Day 1

Breakfast:
1 medium apple
1oz (30g) cereal
¼ pint (150ml) skimmed milk
Tea or coffee

Lunch:
Filled Potato and Salad
6 oz (180g) baked jacket potato
6oz (180g) baked beans
Green Salad – shredded lettuce, sliced fennel, celery, green pepper.
2 teaspoons low-calorie mayonnaise
Tomato and Cucumber Salad –
1 tomato sliced and mixed with a 1½ inch (4cm) wedge of cucumber sliced, 2 teaspoons French dressing and
2 teaspoons chopped chives.
4oz (120g) pineapple, chopped
2½fl oz (75ml) low-fat natural yogurt
Tea, coffee or mineral water

Dinner:
Braised Beef (page 150)

4oz (120g) green beans

Blueberry Mousse (page 201)

Tea or coffee

Optional Calories: 85

Day 2

Breakfast:
1 medium apple
1oz (30g) bread, toasted
1oz (30g) Cheddar cheese
1 tomato, sliced
Tea or coffee

Lunch:
4oz (120g) low-fat soft cheese

Red Cabbage Salad (page 112)

Green Salad – shredded lettuce, sliced fennel, cucumber, celery and sprigs of watercress.
1oz (30g) French bread
1 teaspoon margarine
Tea, coffee or mineral water

Dinner:
Vegetable Curry (page 179)

3oz (90g) rice (cooked weight)
1 kiwi fruit, sliced
Tea or coffee

Snacks:
5fl oz (150ml) low-fat natural yogurt

Day 3

Breakfast:
1 medium pear
1oz (30g) cereal
¼ pint (150ml) skimmed milk
Tea or coffee

Lunch:
Smoked Trout Pâté (page 172)

Mixed Salad – shredded endive, sliced fennel, cucumber, tomato and yellow or red pepper.
2 teaspoons French dressing
1oz (30g) roll
1 teaspoon margarine
Tea, coffee or mineral water

Dinner:
1 medium corn on the cob
1 teaspoon margarine

Roast Chicken with Vegetables
2oz (60g) roast chicken
3oz (90g) mange-tout
3oz (90g) carrots

Aubergine Purée (page 125)
(⅓ of recipe)

5oz (150g) gooseberries, stewed
2½ tablespoons low-fat natural yogurt
Tea or coffee

Snacks:
5oz (150g) strawberries
½ teaspoon caster sugar

Optional Calories: 20

Day 4

Breakfast:
4fl oz (120ml) grape juice

1oz (30g) bread, toasted
1 tablespoon peanut butter
Tea or coffee

Lunch:

Baked Beans on Toast
2 slices reduced-calorie bread
2 teaspoons margarine
6oz (180g) baked beans
½ medium ogen melon
Tea, coffee or mineral water

Dinner:

Green Pea Soup (page 110)

3oz (90g) peppered smoked
mackerel fillet

Russian Salad (page 117)

Green Salad – shredded
lettuce, sliced cucumber,
fennel and spring onion.
1 medium tangerine
Tea or coffee

Snacks:

2oz (60g) cherries stirred into
2½ tablespoons low-fat natural
yogurt with 1 teaspoon honey.

Optional Calories: 20

Day 5

Breakfast:

½ medium mango
1oz (30g) cereal
¼ pint (150ml) skimmed milk
Tea or coffee

Lunch:

Ploughman's Lunch
1oz (30g) French bread
1 teaspoon low-fat spread
2oz (60g) hard cheese
1 tablespoon pickle
1 tomato
2–3 sticks celery
4oz (120g) drained, canned
mandarins, stirred in

2½ tablespoons low-fat natural
yogurt.
Tea, coffee or mineral water

Dinner:

Plaice Florentine (page 169)

3oz (90g) fennel
3oz (90g) carrots

Pineapple Cheesecake
(page 198)
Tea or coffee

Optional Calories: 115

Day 6

Breakfast:

4oz (120g) pineapple
1oz (30g) bread
1 teaspoon margarine
3oz (90g) cottage cheese
Tea or coffee

Lunch:

Melon Soup (page 111)

3oz (90g) smoked tofu, cubed
1 tomato, sliced
Green Salad – shredded
lettuce, sliced fennel,
cucumber, spring onion.
5fl oz (150ml) low-fat natural
yogurt
Tea, coffee or mineral water

Dinner:

Somerset Casserole (page 149)

6oz (180g) baked jacket potato
1 teaspoon margarine
6oz (180g) broccoli
1 medium orange
Tea or coffee

Snacks:

2 medium apricots

Optional Calories: 100

Day 7

Breakfast:

3 medium prunes
1oz (30g) cereal
¼ pint (150ml) skimmed milk
Tea or coffee

Lunch:

Tuna and Cheese Salad
2oz (60g) drained, canned tuna
mixed with 1oz (30g) cottage
cheese, good pinch of curry
powder and 1 teaspoon
mayonnaise.
1oz (30g) bread
1 teaspoon margarine
½ medium mango, cubed
2½fl oz (75ml) low-fat natural
yogurt
Tea, coffee or mineral water

Dinner:

Liver in Pepper Sauce
(page 161)

3oz (90g) cabbage
3oz (90g) carrots

Sweet-Topped Fruit (page 200)

Tea or coffee

Snacks:

1 digestive biscuit

Optional Calories: 50

Total Optional Calories for
Week 4: 390

WEEKS AT A GLANCE
WEEK – 5

This is the last of the five weekly Menu Plans. By now you should have lost some weight and you must continue following the Programme, not eating more than 500 Optional Calories until you reach your goal. Then gradually introduce additional foods so you are able to find out how much you can eat without putting on any weight. This week's plan includes another selection of new foods such as olives, game and spirits. You will find many more Week 5 menus throughout the recipe section of the book. Continue to add ½ pint (300ml) skimmed milk to each day's allowance.

Day 1

Breakfast:
1oz (30g) ready-to-eat dried apricots, chopped
1oz (30g) cereal
¼ pint (150ml) skimmed milk
Tea or coffee

Lunch:
Greek Feta Salad (page 120)

1oz (30g) bread
2 teaspoons margarine
Tea, coffee or mineral water

Dinner:
Melon Appetiser with Raspberry Sauce (page 142)

Roast Pheasant with Vegetables
3oz (90g) roast pheasant
3oz (90g) carrots
3oz (90g) courgettes
3oz (90g) leeks
½ medium papaya, sprinkled with lime juice
2½ tablespoons low-fat natural yogurt
Tea or coffee

Snacks:
1 digestive biscuit
Optional Calories: 40

Day 2

Breakfast:
4fl oz (120ml) tomato juice
1oz (30g) muffin
1 teaspoon margarine
2 teaspoons marmalade
Tea or coffee

Lunch:
Tuna and Cottage Cheese Salad
3oz (90g) cottage cheese mixed with 1oz (30g) drained, canned tuna
2 teaspoons chopped chives
Tomato and Cucumber Salad –
1 tomato, sliced mixed with a 1½ inch (4cm) wedge of cucumber, sliced and
1 tablespoon chopped spring onion.
2oz (60g) grated carrot
1oz (30g) roll
1 teaspoon low-fat spread
Tea, coffee or mineral water

Dinner:
Curried Chicken Salad (page 158)

Green Salad – shredded lettuce, sliced fennel, green pepper, cucumber and spring onion.
1 tablespoon low-calorie French dressing

Mixed Fruit Flambé (page 210)
Tea or coffee

Snacks:
½ pint (300ml) buttermilk

Optional Calories: 120

Day 3

Breakfast:
½ medium banana, sliced
1 tablespoon peanut butter
1oz (30g) bread, toasted
Tea or coffee

Lunch:
Turkey Salad
1½oz (45g) turkey
Mixed Salad – shredded endive, sliced fennel, cucumber, red pepper, radish and sprigs of watercress.
1 tablespoon low-calorie French dressing
1 tomato, sliced
1 slice reduced-calorie bread
1 teaspoon low-fat spread
1 medium tangerine
Tea, coffee or mineral water

Dinner:
Curried Fish (page 174)

3oz (90g) rice (cooked weight)

Scottish Cream (page 208)

Tea or coffee

Snacks:
3oz (90g) grapes
¼ pint (150ml) buttermilk

Optional Calories: 70

Day 4

Breakfast:
½oz (15g) sultanas
1oz (30g) cereal
¼ pint (150ml) skimmed milk
Tea or coffee

Lunch:
Salmon and Cucumber
Sandwich
2 slices reduced-calorie bread,
2 teaspoons low-fat spread,
2oz (60g) drained, canned
salmon mixed with
2 teaspoons mayonnaise, a
squeeze of lemon, 2 teaspoons
chopped chives, and a 1½ inch
(4cm) wedge of cucumber,
sliced.
1 tomato
1 medium orange
Tea, coffee or mineral water

Dinner:
Kipper Salad (page 175)

Green Salad – shredded
lettuce, sliced green pepper,
celery and spring onion.

Plum Mousse (page 216)

Tea or coffee

Snacks:
1 digestive biscuit

Optional Calories: 70

Day 5

Breakfast:
4fl oz (120ml) orange juice
1oz (30g) bread
1 teaspoon margarine
3oz (90g) cottage cheese
1 tomato, sliced
Tea or coffee

Lunch:
Filled Potato and Salad
6oz (180g) baked jacket potato
4½oz (135g) baked beans
Mixed Salad – chopped red
and green pepper, spring
onion, sliced fennel and
cucumber.
4 teaspoons low-calorie French
dressing
4oz (120g) cherries
Tea, coffee or mineral water

Dinner:
Savoury Squash (page 180)

4oz (120g) green beans
5oz (150g) loganberries
1 teaspoon caster sugar
5fl oz (150ml) low-fat natural
yogurt
Tea or coffee

Optional Calories: 50

Day 6

Breakfast:
4fl oz (120ml) apple juice
1 slice reduced-calorie bread,
toasted
1 tablespoon peanut butter
Tea or coffee

Lunch:
Filled Potato and Salad
6oz (180g) baked jacket potato
1½oz (45g) hard cheese,
grated
Tomato and Cucumber Salad –
1 tomato, sliced with a
1½ inch (4cm) wedge of
cucumber, sliced and mixed
with 2 teaspoons chopped
chives.
2 or 3 sticks celery
1 medium orange, chopped
5fl oz (150ml) low-fat natural
yogurt
Tea, coffee or mineral water

Dinner:
Grilled Liver with Vegetables
4oz (120g) lamb's or calf's liver
brushed with ½ teaspoon
vegetable oil and grilled.

Stir-Fried Vegetables
(page 137)

Caribbean Choice (page 212)

Tea or coffee

Optional Calories: 55

Day 7

Breakfast:
1 medium persimmon
1oz (30g) cereal
¼ pint (150ml) skimmed milk
Tea or coffee

Lunch:
Salad Niçoise (page 118)

1oz (30g) bread
1 teaspoon margarine
1 medium pear, chopped and
stirred into
2oz (60g) fromage frais.
Tea, coffee or mineral water

Dinner:
Squid and Prawn Gumbo
(page 176)

6oz (180g) broccoli
3oz (90g) carrots
4oz (120g) drained, canned
mandarins
2½fl oz (75ml) low-fat natural
yogurt
Tea or coffee

Snacks:
1 digestive biscuit

Optional Calories: 45

Total Optional Calories for
Week 5: 450

THE VEGETARIAN MENU PLAN

As a vegetarian you have chosen not to eat meat or fish and therefore this section is written specifically for you. The recipes given in the first section of weekly plans follow the outline explained in the introduction. Some of the recipes in the Weeks at a Glance section include gelatine which is an animal product therefore substitute the gelatine with agar agar, 2 teaspoons of agar agar is approximately equivalent to 1½ teaspoons gelatine, but always follow the packaging instructions.

There are many recipes in the third section of the book which are suitable for you. If the Menu Plan includes rennet to make junket, substitute the rennet with non animal rennet and, if you prefer, eat vegetarian cheese in place of other hard cheeses.

Unlike the people following the basic plan you may include nuts, beans and pulses in your diet from Week 1; you are also allowed rice and rice cakes earlier than the alternative food plan. The amount of hard cheese up to 120 Calories per ounce (30g) allowed every week is limited to 6oz (180g), but you may substitute the lower calorie category of cheese as described in the Points to Note as these are not restricted. Two ounces (60g) low-fat cheese may replace 3oz (90g) cooked kidney beans, baked beans or tofu.

This diet has been devised for a woman. However, if a teenager or man wishes to follow it, additional foods must be included. A teenager must have an extra ½ pint (300ml) skimmed milk and teenagers and men must include either 4oz (120g) low-fat soft cheese or 6oz (180g) cooked beans, pulses or tofu every day.

WEEK 1

Day 1

Breakfast:

1 medium tangerine
1oz (30g) cereal
¼ pint (150ml) skimmed milk

Lunch: Beans on Toast

1oz (30g) slice of bread, toasted and spread with 1 teaspoon margarine and topped with 6oz (180g) baked beans.
Green Salad – shredded endive, sliced cucumber, celery and green pepper with 1½ teaspoons mayonnaise.

1 medium peach

Dinner: ✳ Fruit and Vegetable Salad ✳

5fl oz (150ml) low-fat natural yogurt

Snacks:

¼ pint (150ml) skimmed milk

Optional Calories 20

FRUIT AND VEGETABLE SALAD

Serves 2
290 Calories per serving

4oz (120g) carrot

1 small courgette

2oz (60g) bean sprouts

1oz (30g) cashew nuts

6oz (180g) drained, canned or cooked kidney beans

6oz (180g) drained, canned or cooked flageolet beans

1 medium orange

1 head of chicory

For the dressing:
1 teaspoon finely chopped fresh root ginger

3 tablespoons lemon juice

2 teaspoons clear honey

1 tablespoon soy sauce

3–4 teaspoons chopped chives

1. Coarsely grate the carrot and courgette. Mix the carrot and courgette together with the bean sprouts, nuts and beans.
2. Using a sharp knife remove the peel and white pith from the orange. Cut in between each membrane to separate into segments, catching any juice which escapes. Stir the orange segments into the bean and carrot mixture.
3. Line two serving plates with the chicory leaves.
4. Mix together all the dressing ingredients, adding any juice from the orange.
5. Pour the dressing over the salad and toss well. Pile the salad on to the prepared plates and serve.

Exchanges per serving: Fat ½, Fruit ½, Protein 3, Vegetable 2, Optional Calories 20

WEEK 1

Day 2

Breakfast:

4fl oz (120ml) grapefruit juice
1oz (30g) cereal
¼ pint (150ml) skimmed milk

Lunch: Smoked Tofu and Cottage Cheese Salad

2oz (60g) cottage cheese served with 3oz (90g) smoked tofu, diced and a mixed salad of shredded lettuce, sliced cucumber, tomato, celery and yellow pepper.
2 rice cakes spread with 1 tablespoon low-fat spread.

Dinner: Plain Omelette

Beat together 2 eggs, 2 tablespoons water, salt and pepper. Heat
1 teaspoon margarine in a small omelette pan, add the egg mixture and cook over a gentle heat drawing the mixture from the edge towards the centre. When the underside is golden brown, sprinkle 2 teaspoons chopped chives over the top, fold in half and serve.
Steamed or boiled carrots and broccoli.

✱ Nutty Fruit Salad ✱

Served with 2½fl oz (75ml) low-fat natural yogurt.

Snacks:

½ pint (300ml) skimmed milk

Optional Calories 20

NUTTY FRUIT SALAD

Serves 3
130 Calories per serving

½ a lemon, zest and juice
6 tablespoons water
2 thin slices fresh root ginger
1½ inch (4cm) stick cinnamon, crumbled
1 tablespoon honey
1 medium pear
1 medium apple
1 medium orange
½oz (15g) pine nuts
½oz (15g) walnut pieces
½oz (15g) hazelnuts

1. Remove the zest from the lemon with a zester, or use a potato peeler and cut the lemon zest into thin strips.
2. Place the lemon zest, juice, water, ginger, cinnamon and honey in a saucepan, bring to the boil for 2–3 minutes. Remove from the heat and allow to cool.
3. Quarter the pear and apple, remove the cores and slice the fruit thinly. Peel the orange with a sharp knife removing the white pith, cut into thin slices then halve the slices.
4. Pour the cool syrup over the fruit and chill for 2–3 hours, turning occasionally.
5. Toast the nuts under a moderate grill or in a moderate oven, until golden.
6. Remove the ginger before serving and stir in the toasted nuts.

Exchanges per serving: Fat ½, Fruit 1, Protein 1, Optional Calories 20

WEEK 1

Day 3

Breakfast:

Pineapple Buttermilk Froth – place 4oz (120g) drained, canned pineapple pieces in a blender with ¼ pint (150ml) buttermilk and 1 teaspoon sugar or honey. Process until frothy, serve immediately. 1 slice of reduced-calorie bread, toasted and spread with 1 teaspoon low-fat spread.

Lunch: Cheese Salad

2oz (60g) curd cheese, mixed with 1 tablespoon chopped chives and served with shredded lettuce, sliced cucumber, tomato, celery, mustard and cress, tossed in 2 teaspoons French dressing.

1 medium orange

Dinner: * Spicy Rice and Lentils *

Slices of tomato and onion.

Junket – heat ¼ pint (150ml) fresh skimmed milk (*not* long life) until warm, add 2–3 drops of vanilla essence, 1 teaspoon sugar or honey and 1 teaspoon essence of rennet. Pour into a serving dish and leave in the warm for 15–20 minutes until set.

Snacks:

½ pint (300ml) skimmed milk

Optional Calories 40

SPICY RICE AND LENTILS

Serves 2
520 Calories per serving

5oz (150g) green lentils
2 teaspoons sesame oil
1 onion, chopped
1 clove garlic, chopped
½ green chilli, seeded and chopped
½ teaspoon ground coriander
¾ teaspoon cumin seeds
¼ teaspoon ground cinnamon
3oz (90g) long-grain rice
salt
3oz (90g) carrots, diced
2oz (60g) green beans, cut in 1 inch (2.5cm) lengths
2oz (60g) mushrooms, sliced
1oz (30g) pine nuts, toasted
1–2 teaspoons garam masala

1. Place the lentils in cold water, cover and simmer for about 30 minutes until soft.
2. Heat the oil in a saucepan, add the onion, garlic and chilli, stir-fry for 5 minutes.
3. Add the coriander, cumin, cinnamon, rice and the amount of water given on the rice packaging (this will vary from one variety to another), season well with salt, cover and bring to the boil.
4. Ten minutes before the end of the rice cooking time add the carrots, beans and mushrooms. Then 3–4 minutes before the rice should ̄e cooked add the hot drained lentils.
5. Remove from the heat and stir in the pine nuts and garam masala, season with additional salt if necessary.

Exchanges per serving: Bread 1½, Fat 1½, Protein 3½, Vegetable 1¾

WEEK 1

Day 4

Breakfast:

4fl oz (120ml) orange juice
Toast a 1oz (30g) slice of bread,
sprinkle 1oz (30g) grated Cheddar
cheese over one side and grill until
bubbling. Serve with 1 tomato, sliced.

Lunch: Cottage Cheese Salad

Mix 2oz (60g) cottage cheese with a
good pinch of curry powder and
1 teaspoon grated onion.
Mixed Salad – shredded lettuce,
chopped red pepper, spring onion,
celery and sliced cucumber tossed in
2 teaspoons French dressing.

Dinner:

2 inch (5cm) wedge of honeydew
melon

∗ Vegetable Crumble ∗

4oz (120g) pink fleshed or drained,
canned grapefruit segments
2½fl oz (75ml) low-fat natural yogurt

Snacks:

¾ pint (450ml) skimmed milk

VEGETABLE CRUMBLE

Serves 2
450 Calories per serving

1 small (8oz/227g) can chopped tomatoes

2 tablespoons soy sauce

1 leek, chopped

3oz (90g) carrots, sliced

½ green pepper, cut in strips

1 clove garlic, finely chopped

4oz (120g) caulifower florets

2oz (60g) mushrooms, sliced

6oz (180g) drained, canned or cooked chick peas

9oz (270g) firm tofu

For the crumble:
2oz (60g) wholemeal flour

4 teaspoons margarine

1oz (30g) mature Cheddar cheese

1. Mix the tomatoes and soy sauce together in a saucepan. Stir in the leek, carrots, pepper, garlic, cauliflower, mushrooms and chick peas.
2. Cut the tofu into ¾ inch (2cm) cubes, stir into the vegetable mixture. Bring to the boil, reduce the heat, cover and simmer for 12–14 minutes.
3. While the vegetables are cooking make the crumble topping. Place the flour in a bowl and rub in the margarine (if possible margarine which has been stored in the freezer). Finely grate the cheese and stir into the crumble.
4. Spoon the vegetable mixture into a deep ovenproof dish, about 5½ inches (14cm) in diameter, sprinkle over the crumble topping and bake in a preheated oven, 350°F/180°C/ Gas Mark 4 for about 20 minutes.

Exchanges per serving: Bread 1, Fat 2, Protein 3, Vegetable 3½

Vegetable Crumble; grapefruit with
yogurt; wedge of honeydew melon

WEEK 1

Day 5

Breakfast:

1 medium apple
1oz (30g) cereal
¼ pint (150ml) skimmed milk

Lunch: Cheese Salad

1oz (30g) hard cheese, grated and
served with 1 tomato cut in wedges,
sprigs of watercress and grated
carrot.
Crispbread up to 80 Calories spread
with 2 teaspoons margarine.

5fl oz (150ml) low-fat natural yogurt

Dinner:

2 inch (5cm) wedge of honeydew
melon

✳ Vegetable Bake ✳

Snacks:

¼ pint (150ml) skimmed milk

Optional Calories 50

VEGETABLE BAKE

Serves 1
480 Calories per serving

2oz (60g) green lentils
¼ pint (150ml) water
1 teaspoon safflower oil
1 clove garlic, chopped
1 onion, chopped
2 tomatoes
½ teaspoon ground coriander
½ teaspoon basil
3oz (90g) firm tofu, grated
salt and pepper
3oz (90g) courgettes, sliced
1 egg
3 tablespoons low-fat natural yogurt
2 teaspoons grated Parmesan cheese

1. Place the lentils in a saucepan, add the water, cover and
   simmer for about 30 minutes until soft.
2. Heat the oil, add the garlic and onion, stir round the pan and
   place over a very low heat to cook for 5 minutes.
3. Plunge the tomatoes in boiling water for 40–50 seconds,
   drain and slip off the skins and chop the tomatoes.
4. Stir the coriander and basil into the onion mixture, add the
   tomatoes, tofu and drained lentils. Bring to the boil, season
   to taste with salt and pepper. Transfer to a deep 5 inch
   (13cm) ovenproof dish.
5. Blanch the courgettes in boiling water for 3 minutes, drain
   well and arrange on top of the lentil and tofu mixture.
6. Beat the egg, yogurt and Parmesan cheese together, spoon
   over the courgettes. Bake at 375°F/190°C/Gas Mark 5 for
   25–30 minutes.

**Exchanges per serving: Fat 1, Protein 4, Vegetable 3½,
Optional Calories 50**

WEEK 1

Day 6

Breakfast:

4fl oz (120ml) orange juice
1oz (30g) cereal
¼ pint (150ml) skimmed milk

Lunch: Beans on Toast

Toast a 1oz (30g) slice of bread, spread with 1½ teaspoons low-fat spread and top with 6oz (180g) baked beans. Serve with 3oz (90g) grilled tomatoes and 3oz (90g) grilled mushrooms.

Dinner: ✳ Egg in a Nest ✳

Tossed Green Salad – shredded lettuce, sliced cucumber, green pepper, celery and sprigs of watercress tossed in 2 teaspoons mayonnaise.

4oz (120g) fruit salad served with 2½fl oz (75ml) low-fat natural yogurt.

Snacks:

½ pint (300ml) skimmed milk

EGG IN A NEST

Serves 1
270 Calories per serving

¼ teaspoon margarine
3oz (90g) smoked tofu
4 teaspoons finely chopped spring onion
1 egg
salt and pepper
1oz (30g) cheese, e.g. Cheddar
few slices of tomato

1. Grease a 3 inch (7.5cm) ramekin with the margarine and put to one side.
2. Dice the tofu into small cubes. Mix the spring onions and tofu together and spoon into the greased ramekin.
3. Make a dip in the centre of the tofu, break the egg into the dip. Season with a little salt and pepper.
4. Grate the cheese, sprinkle evenly over the top of the egg and tofu. Cover the ramekin with foil and transfer to a saucepan containing 1 inch (2.5cm) of simmering water. Cover the saucepan and simmer for 12–13 minutes.
5. Preheat the grill. Remove the foil and carefully transfer the ramekin from the saucepan to the grill. Grill for 1 minute, remove from the heat, arrange the tomato slices on top and return to the grill for a few seconds to warm the tomato. Serve immediately.

Exchanges per serving: Fat ¼, Protein 3, Vegetable ¼

WEEK 1

Day 7

Breakfast:

4fl oz (120ml) grapefruit juice
1oz (30g) slice of reduced-calorie
bread, toasted, spread with
1 teaspoon margarine and topped
with 1 poached egg.

Lunch: Cottage Cheese and Bean Salad

2oz (60g) cottage cheese served with
3oz (90g) drained, canned kidney
beans and mixed with 2 teaspoons
chopped chives and 2 teaspoons
French dressing and a salad of
shredded lettuce, sliced cucumber,
tomato and green pepper.

Junket – heat ¼ pint (150ml) fresh
skimmed milk (*not* long life) until
warm. Add 2–3 drops of vanilla
essence, 1 teaspoon essence of
rennet and 1 teaspoon sugar or
honey. Pour into a serving dish and
leave in the warm for 15–20 minutes
until set.

Dinner: ✳ Tofu Kedgeree ✳

Served with slices of tomato and
cucumber sprinkled with 1 teaspoon
chopped spring onion.

4oz (120g) fruit salad

Snacks:

12½fl oz (375ml) skimmed milk

Optional Calories 20

TOFU KEDGEREE

Serves 2
325 Calories per serving

3oz (90g) long-grain brown rice

salt

2 teaspoons vegetable oil

4–6 spring onions, sliced

½ red pepper, roughly chopped

½ green pepper, roughly chopped

9oz (270g) smoked tofu

1 hard-boiled egg, chopped

2½fl oz (75ml) low-fat natural yogurt

1 tablespoon chopped parsley

pepper

1. Boil the rice in salted water for 30–40 minutes following the
   packaging instructions.
2. Heat the oil, stir-fry the spring onions and peppers for
   4–5 minutes, remove from the heat until the rice is cooked.
3. Cut the smoked tofu into small dice.
4. Drain any excess water from the rice, reheat the spring
   onions and peppers, add the smoked tofu and stir round for
   2 minutes.
5. Add the hot rice, hard-boiled egg, yogurt and parsley. Stir
   over a low heat until heated through, adjust the seasoning
   adding more salt and pepper, serve.

**Exchanges per serving: Bread 1½, Fat 1, Milk ¼,
Protein 2, Vegetable 1**

Tofu Kedgeree with sliced tomato
and cucumber; fruit salad

WEEK 5

Day 1

Breakfast:

1oz (30g) sultanas
1oz (30g) cereal
¼ pint (150ml) skimmed milk

Lunch: Cheese and Tomato Sandwich

2 × 1oz (30g) slices of bread spread with 1½ teaspoons margarine and filled with 2oz (60g) hard cheese and 1 tomato, sliced.

4oz (120g) cherries

Dinner: ✳ Nut Roast with Tomato Sauce ✳

Steamed or boiled asparagus and cauliflower.
5fl oz (150ml) low-fat natural yogurt
1 teaspoon honey

Snacks:

5oz (150g) chunks of honeydew melon
¼ pint (150ml) skimmed milk

Optional Calories 70

NUT ROAST WITH TOMATO SAUCE

Serves 6
305 Calories per serving

2oz (60g) ground almonds
6oz (180g) hazelnuts, brazil nuts and walnuts, finely chopped
1½oz (45g) fresh breadcrumbs
2oz (60g) cheese, grated
1 teaspoon walnut oil
2 onions, finely chopped
2 eggs
2 tablespoons tomato purée
½ teaspoon yeast extract
½ teaspoon mixed herbs
1 medium (15oz/450g) can of chopped tomatoes
1 carrot, chopped
½ teaspoon basil
1 tablespoon cornflour
2 tablespoons water
salt and pepper

1. Line a 1lb (500g) loaf tin with non-stick baking parchment.
2. Mix together the nuts, breadcrumbs and cheese.
3. Heat the oil in a saucepan, add 1 chopped onion and stir-fry for 1 minute, stir into the nut mixture.
4. Beat the eggs, 1 tablespoon tomato purée, the yeast extract and mixed herbs together, stir into the nuts etc. Spoon the mixture into the prepared tin and bake at 350°F/180°C/Gas Mark 4 for 1 hour. Turn out and leave to stand a few minutes before slicing.
5. Meanwhile, place the remaining onion, tomato purée, chopped tomatoes, carrot and basil in a saucepan, cover and simmer for 20–25 minutes. Transfer to a blender or food processor and process for a few seconds.
6. Blend the cornflour with the water, stir into the tomato sauce and return to the saucepan. Bring to the boil, stirring all the time, boil for 1–2 minutes. Season to taste and serve with the nut roast.

Exchanges per serving: Fat 1½, Protein 3, Vegetable 1½, Optional Calories 50

WEEK 5

Day 2

Breakfast:

½ medium grapefruit
Toast 1 slice of reduced-calorie bread
spread with 1 teaspoon margarine
and top with a poached egg.

Lunch: Cottage Cheese Salad

4oz (120g) cottage cheese mixed with
1 tablespoon chopped chives and
served with 1 rice cake spread with
1 teaspoon margarine.
Mixed Salad – sliced red and green
pepper, tomato and spring onion
tossed in 1 teaspoon low-calorie
salad dressing.

4oz (120g) pineapple served with
2½fl oz (75ml) low-fat natural yogurt.

Dinner: ✳ Butter Bean Goulash ✳

Green Salad – shredded lettuce,
sliced cucumber, spring onion and
celery.

Junket and Fruit Salad – heat
¼ pint (150ml) skimmed milk
(*not* long life) until warm, add
1–2 teaspoons vanilla essence,
1 teaspoon sugar or honey and
1 teaspoon essence of rennet. Pour
into a serving dish and leave in the
warm for 15–20 minutes until set.
Serve with 2oz (60g) drained, canned
fruit salad.

Snacks:

1 digestive biscuit
7½fl oz (225ml) skimmed milk

Optional Calories 25

BUTTER BEAN GOULASH

Serves 4
325 Calories per serving

4oz (120g) split red lentils
12fl oz (360ml) water
1 tablespoon vegetable oil
2 onions, chopped
1 green pepper, seeded and chopped
4 teaspoons mild chilli powder
16fl oz (480ml) tomato juice
6oz (180g) tofu
1 tablespoon tomato purée
1lb 2oz (540g) drained, canned or cooked butter beans
2 tablespoons basil, chopped
5fl oz (150ml) low-fat natural yogurt

1. Place the lentils and water in a saucepan, cover and boil rapidly for 10 minutes, reduce the heat and simmer until tender and the water has been absorbed.
2. Meanwhile, heat the oil, add the onions and pepper and stir-fry for 5 minutes until soft. Stir in the chilli powder and remove from the heat.
3. Place the lentils, tomato juice, tofu and tomato purée in a blender or food processor, process until smooth.
4. Pour the tomato sauce into the onion and peppers, stir well and add the butter beans and basil. Cover and simmer gently for 20 minutes.
5. To serve; ladle into four serving bowls and spoon a quarter of the yogurt on top of each serving.

Exchanges per serving: Fat ¾, Fruit ½, Milk ¼, Protein 3, Vegetable 1, Optional Calories 5

WEEK 5

Day 3

Breakfast:

4fl oz (120ml) grape juice

* Breakfast Crunch *

Lunch: Beans on Toast

1oz (30g) slice of bread toasted, topped with 6oz (180g) baked beans. Mixed Salad – shredded lettuce, sliced red pepper, cucumber and tomato, tossed in 2 teaspoons low-calorie French dressing.

Dinner: Cheese Omelette

Beat together 2 eggs, 2 tablespoons water, salt and pepper. Heat 1 teaspoon margarine in a small omelette pan, add the egg mixture and cook over a gentle heat drawing the mixture from the edge towards the centre. When the underside is golden, sprinkle 1oz (30g) grated cheese and 2 teaspoons chopped chives over, cook for a further minute then fold over and serve.
3oz (90g) corn on the cob
Steamed or boiled fennel and carrots.

Tipsy Mango Froth – place ½ medium mango, ¼ pint (150ml) buttermilk, 2oz (60g) vanilla ice-cream and 1 tablespoon kirsch in a blender and process until frothy. Sprinkle with ground cinnamon. Serve immediately.

Snacks:

½ pint (300ml) skimmed milk

Optional Calories 185

Breakfast Crunch; grape juice; coffee

BREAKFAST CRUNCH

Serves 6
350 Calories per serving

3oz (90g) rye flakes
3oz (90g) jumbo oats
2 teaspoons wheatgerm
3oz (90g) hazelnuts, chopped
2 teaspoons sunflower seeds
2 teaspoons sesame seeds
½oz (15g) desiccated coconut
1 tablespoon vegetable oil
3 tablespoons honey
To serve per person: **1oz (30g) sultanas**
2½fl oz (75ml) low-fat natural yogurt

1. Mix the rye flakes, jumbo oats, wheatgerm, hazelnuts, seeds and coconut together in a bowl.
2. Heat the oil and honey together, pour over the dry ingredients and mix well to coat.
3. Spoon the mixture on to a large baking sheet and bake at 275°F/140°C/Gas Mark 1 for 45 minutes. Allow to cool and store in an airtight container. This recipe makes approximately 10oz (300g) of Breakfast Crunch.
4. To serve one person weigh 1½oz (45g) of Breakfast Crunch, place in a serving bowl, stir in the sultanas and yogurt and serve.

Exchanges per serving: Bread 1, Fat 1, Fruit 1, Milk ½, Protein 1, Optional Calories 50

WEEK 5

Day 4

Breakfast:

1 medium apple
1oz (30g) cereal
¼ pint (150ml) skimmed milk

Lunch: Beans on Toast

1oz (30g) slice of bread, toasted and
spread with 1 teaspoon margarine,
topped with 6oz (180g) baked beans.
Mixed Salad – shredded lettuce,
grated carrot, cucumber, celery and
chopped spring onion.

Strawberries and Cream – 5oz (150g)
strawberries, sprinkled with
1 teaspoon sugar and served with
1 tablespoon double cream.

Dinner: ✶ Tofu Frittata ✶

1oz (30g) French bread spread with
1 teaspoon margarine
Mixed Salad – shredded lettuce,
sliced tomato and yellow pepper.

Papaya and Yogurt – ½ medium
papaya, sliced and topped with
2½fl oz (75ml) low-fat natural yogurt.

Snacks:

½ pint (300ml) skimmed milk

Optional Calories 90

TOFU FRITTATA

Serves 1
310 Calories per serving

1 teaspoon vegetable oil

1 large spring onion, chopped

½ red pepper, seeded and chopped

2 eggs

2 tablespoons water

3oz (90g) smoked tofu

2 teaspoons grated Parmesan cheese

1 teaspoon chopped parsley

1. Heat the oil in a 7 inch (18cm) omelette pan, add the spring onion and red pepper, stir-fry for 3–4 minutes.
2. Beat the eggs and water together. Dice the smoked tofu and add to the eggs.
3. Pour the egg mixture into the omelette pan and place over a low heat for 10–15 minutes until golden underneath and just set on top.
4. Sprinkle over the Parmesan cheese and transfer to a hot grill for a minute.
5. Sprinkle the chopped parsley over the surface and serve.

Exchanges per serving: Fat 1, Protein 3, Vegetable ¾, Optional Calories 20

WEEK 5

Day 5

Breakfast:

4fl oz (120ml) grapefruit juice
Toast a 1oz (30g) slice of bread and
spread with 1 tablespoon peanut
butter.

Lunch: Cheese Salad

2oz (60g) hard cheese, grated and
served with 3oz (90g) beetroot,
1 tomato, sliced, shredded lettuce
and 3 spring onions, chopped.
1oz (30g) French bread spread with
1 teaspoon margarine.

1 medium tangerine

Dinner:

½ medium ogen melon

✳ Crispy-Topped Vegetables ✳

Small Green Salad – shredded endive,
sliced cucumber and spring onions.

2oz (60g) pineapple served with
5fl oz (150ml) low-fat natural yogurt.

Snacks:

½ pint (300ml) skimmed milk

Optional Calories 5

CRISPY-TOPPED VEGETABLES

Serves 2
345 Calories per serving

2 teaspoons vegetable oil

1 onion, chopped

1 stick celery, chopped

3oz (90g) fennel, sliced

1 courgette, sliced

1 small (8oz/227g) can chopped tomatoes

1 tablespoon tomato purée

½ teaspoon mixed herbs

6oz (180g) drained, canned or cooked kidney beans

9oz (270g) firm tofu, cubed

2oz (60g) bean sprouts

salt and pepper

2oz (60g) fresh wholemeal breadcrumbs

½oz (15g) Parmesan cheese, finely grated

1. Heat the oil in a deep flameproof casserole. Add the onion and stir-fry for 2–3 minutes.
2. Add the celery, fennel, courgette, tomatoes, tomato purée, herbs, kidney beans, tofu and bean sprouts, season with a little salt and pepper.
3. Bring to the boil, stirring occasionally, reduce the heat, cover and simmer for 25 minutes.
4. Mix the breadcrumbs and cheese together, sprinkle over the top of the tofu and bean mixture. Cook under a preheated grill until golden.

Exchanges per serving: Bread 1, Fat 1, Protein 2¾, Vegetable 4, Optional Calories 5

WEEK 5

Day 6

Breakfast: Breakfast Crunch (page 90)

Lunch: Cottage Cheese Salad

Mix 2oz (60g) cottage cheese with a large pinch of curry powder and 1 teaspoon mayonnaise.
Mixed Salad – shredded lettuce, fennel, sliced red and yellow peppers, chopped celery and spring onions.
1oz (30g) slice of bread spread with 1 teaspoon low-fat spread.
4fl oz (120ml) tomato juice

∗ Nut-Filled Peaches ∗

Dinner: Burger with Vegetables

1 vegetarian burger
Steamed or boiled cauliflower, mange-tout and carrots.
3oz (90g) boiled sweetcorn

2oz (60g) drained, canned apricots topped with 2½fl oz (75ml) low-fat natural yogurt.

Snacks:

½ pint (300ml) skimmed milk

Optional Calories 100

NUT-FILLED PEACHES

Serves 2
220 Calories per serving

2 medium peaches
lemon juice
4 teaspoons raspberry jam
2oz (60g) fromage frais
2oz (60g) curd cheese
1½ teaspoons set honey
2–3 drops almond essence
1oz (30g) flaked almonds

1. Halve and stone the peaches, brush the cut flesh with lemon juice.
2. Spoon a teaspoon of jam into each cavity left by the peach stone.
3. Mix together the fromage frais, curd cheese, honey and almond essence.
4. Toast the flaked almonds under a moderate grill until golden. Chop about three-quarters of the nuts, reserve the remainder for decoration.
5. Stir the chopped nuts into the fromage frais. Spoon the mixture onto each peach half, roughen the surface with a fork and top with the reserved toasted flaked almonds.

Exchanges per serving: Fat ½, Fruit 1, Protein 2, Optional Calories 50

Nut-Filled Peaches; cottage cheese salad; tomato juice

WEEK 5

Day 7

Breakfast:

½ medium banana, sliced
1oz (30g) cereal
¼ pint (150ml) skimmed milk

Lunch: Poached Egg and Beans on Toast

Toast 1 slice of reduced-calorie bread, spread with 1 teaspoon low-fat spread, top with 1 poached egg and 3oz (90g) baked beans.
3oz (90g) tomato, grilled
3oz (90g) mushrooms, stir-fried in 1 teaspoon margarine.

1 kiwi fruit

Dinner: ✴ Tofu Stir-Fry ✴

1oz (30g) cooked rice.

4oz (120g) fruit salad served with 5fl oz (150ml) low-fat natural yogurt.

Snacks:

¼ pint (150ml) skimmed milk

Optional Calories 50

TOFU STIR-FRY

Serves 1
340 Calories per serving

1 tablespoon soy sauce
2 tablespoons sherry
½ teaspoon honey
2 teaspoons lemon juice
1 clove garlic, crushed
6oz (180g) firm tofu
1½oz (45g) baby corn on the cob, halved or thickly sliced
2oz (60g) carrots, cut in matchstick lengths
1 teaspoon sesame oil
3 spring onions, cut in 1 inch (2.5cm) diagonal lengths
½ green pepper, seeded and sliced
2oz (60g) bean sprouts
1 teaspoon cornflour
2 teaspoons water
½oz (15g) cashew nuts, toasted

1. Mix together the soy sauce, sherry, honey, lemon juice and garlic.
2. Cut the tofu into cubes and stir into the marinade, leave for about 3 hours, stirring occasionally.
3. Plunge the baby corn into boiling water, boil for 4 minutes, then add the carrots and boil for a further 3 minutes, drain.
4. Heat the oil in a wok or small saucepan, add the spring onions and green pepper, stir-fry for 3–4 minutes. Add the corn and carrot and stir-fry for a further minute.
5. Drain the tofu and stir into the stir-fried vegetables with the bean sprouts, stir round until hot.
6. Blend the cornflour and water together, stir into the marinade and add to the wok. Bring to the boil stirring all the time. Add the cashew nuts and serve.

Exchanges per serving: Bread ½, Fat 1½, Protein 3, Vegetable 2½, Optional Calories 50

WEEKS AT A GLANCE
VEGETARIAN WEEK – 1

The first week's Menu Plan will ensure a good start to your weight-reducing diet. Tofu, beans, lentils and rice ensure a wide variety of recipes and tasty meals. It is important to weigh all food accurately and not to omit any. In addition to the food and drinks listed, ½ pint (300ml) skimmed milk must be included as a hot or chilled drink or used in cups of tea and coffee. Herbal and traditional teas, coffee and water may be drunk as desired.

Day 1

Breakfast:
4fl oz (120ml) orange juice
1 tablespoon peanut butter
2 rice cakes
Tea or coffee

Lunch:
Cottage Cheese Salad
4oz (120g) cottage cheese mixed with 1 tablespoon chopped chives.

Red Cabbage Salad (page 112)

Green Salad – shredded lettuce, sliced cucumber, green pepper, celery and sprigs of watercress.
Tea, coffee or mineral water

Dinner:
Stuffed Tomatoes (page 140)

3oz (90g) green beans
5oz (150g) cauliflower
4oz (120g) pineapple
Tea or coffee

Snacks:
5fl oz (150ml) low-fat natural yogurt
1 teaspoon honey

Optional Calories: 20

Day 2

Breakfast:
1 medium apple
1oz (30g) cereal
¼ pint (150ml) skimmed milk
Tea or coffee

Lunch:
Bean Salad (page 121) (½ of recipe)

1oz (30g) Cheddar cheese, grated

Tomato and Cucumber Salad – 1 tomato sliced, 1½ inch (4cm) wedge of cucumber, sliced and mixed with 2 teaspoons chopped spring onion.
1oz (30g) roll
1 teaspoon low-fat spread
Tea, coffee or mineral water

Dinner:
Peppered Frittata (page 177)

3oz (90g) carrots
3oz (90g) cabbage
Tea or coffee

Snacks:
5oz (150g) strawberries
2½fl oz (75ml) low-fat natural yogurt

Day 3

Breakfast:
½ medium grapefruit
1oz (30g) Cheddar cheese, grated
1oz (30g) bread, toasted
1 tomato, sliced
Tea or coffee

Lunch:
Cheese and Salad Sandwich
2 slices reduced-calorie bread
2 teaspoons low-fat spread
4oz (120g) cottage cheese mixed with 1 tablespoon chopped spring onion.
3 lettuce leaves
few slices of red pepper and cucumber
2 large sticks of celery
Tea, coffee or mineral water

Dinner:
Lentil-Coated Vegetables (page 184)

Spicy Fruit Salad (page 194)

5fl oz (150ml) low-fat natural yogurt
Tea or coffee

Snacks:
1 medium pear

Optional Calories: 30

Day 4

Breakfast:
2 inch (5cm) wedge of
honeydew melon
1oz (30g) cereal
¼ pint (150ml) skimmed milk
Tea or coffee

Lunch:
Baked Beans and Salad
¾oz (20g) French bread
1 teaspoon margarine
6oz (180g) baked beans
Green Salad – shredded
lettuce, sliced green pepper,
cucumber, celery and spring
onion.
Tea, coffee or mineral water

Dinner:
Blue Cheese Soufflé (page 145)

3oz (90g) green beans
3oz (90g) leeks
3oz (90g) carrots
4oz (120g) drained, canned
fruit salad with 2 tablespoons
natural juice.
2½ tablespoons low-fat natural
yogurt
Tea or coffee

Day 5

Breakfast:
4fl oz (120ml) grapefruit juice
1 egg, poached
1oz (30g) bread, toasted
1 teaspoon margarine
Tea or coffee

Lunch:
Tofu Salad
3oz (90g) smoked tofu, cubed
Tossed Mixed Salad –
shredded lettuce, slices of
tomato, cucumber, celery,
pepper and sprigs of
watercress.

2 teaspoons low-calorie French
dressing
1 rice cake
1 teaspoon low-fat spread
1 medium peach
Tea, coffee or mineral water

Dinner:
Nut Rissoles with Chilli Sauce
(page 181)

6oz (180g) broccoli
3oz (90g) carrots
Tea or coffee

Snacks:
5fl oz (150ml) low-fat natural
yogurt
1 teaspoon honey

Optional Calories: 40

Day 6

Breakfast:
4fl oz (120ml) orange juice
1 tablespoon peanut butter
Crispbread up to 40 Calories
Tea or coffee

Lunch:
Cheese Salad
1oz (30g) hard cheese, grated

Autumn Salad (page 122)

Green Salad – shredded
endive, sliced cucumber,
celery and green pepper.
2 teaspoons low-calorie
mayonnaise
Tea, coffee or mineral water

Dinner:
Savoury Rice and Beans
(page 185)

4oz (120g) courgettes
3oz (90g) red cabbage
1 medium pear, cored and
chopped and stirred into 5fl oz

(150ml) low-fat natural yogurt.
Tea or coffee

Day 7

Breakfast:
½ medium grapefruit
1oz (30g) cereal
¼ pint (150ml) skimmed milk
Tea or coffee

Lunch:
Baked Beans on Toast
1oz (30g) bread, toasted
1 teaspoon margarine
6oz (180g) baked beans
1 medium apple
1oz (30g) cottage cheese
Tea, coffee or mineral water

Dinner:
Burger and Salad
1 vegetarian burger
Mixed Salad – shredded
lettuce, sliced cucumber,
tomato, pepper, celery and
spring onion.
2 teaspoons mayonnaise

Honeycomb Mould (page 189)

Tea or coffee

Optional Calories: 40

Total Optional Calories for
Week 1: 130

WEEKS AT A GLANCE
VEGETARIAN WEEK – 2

The calorie intake increases this week and the introduction of ingredients such as tomato purée enables more adventurous recipes, such as Crispy-Topped Beans and Mixed Vegetable Stew, to be enjoyed. Bananas, gooseberries, raspberries and watermelon add variety as does the addition of asparagus and bean sprouts. Not all the recipes suitable for this week are included in this week's Menu Plans so make use of the recipe section for additional ideas. It is essential to add ½ pint (300ml) skimmed milk to every day's Menu Plan.

Day 1

Breakfast:
1 medium orange
1oz (30g) cereal
¼ pint (150ml) skimmed milk
Tea or coffee

Lunch:
Peach and Cottage Cheese Platter (page 129)

Tomato and Onion Salad
2½fl oz (75ml) low-fat natural yogurt mixed with ½ teaspoon honey.
Tea, coffee or mineral water

Dinner:
Lentil-Coated Vegetables (page 184)

3oz (90g) rice (cooked weight)
4oz (120g) fruit salad served with 2oz (60g) fromage frais.
Tea or coffee

Optional Calories: 10

Day 2

Breakfast:
4fl oz (120ml) orange juice
3oz (90g) baked beans
1oz (30g) bread, toasted
1 teaspoon low-fat spread
Tea or coffee

Lunch:
Peppered Frittata (page 177)

Green Salad – shredded lettuce, sliced celery, cucumber, sprigs of watercress.
1 medium apple
Tea, coffee or mineral water

Dinner:
Mixed Vegetable Stew (page 186)

4oz (120g) pineapple
5fl oz (150ml) low-fat natural yogurt
Tea or coffee

Optional Calories: 10

Day 3

Breakfast:
½ medium grapefruit
1oz (30g) hard cheese, grated
1oz (30g) bread, toasted
1 tomato, sliced
Tea or coffee

Lunch:
Cottage Cheese Salad
4oz (120g) cottage cheese
2 teaspoons chopped chives
Mixed Salad – shredded lettuce, grated carrot, sliced spring onion and cucumber

tossed in 1 tablespoon French dressing.
½ medium banana
2½fl oz (75ml) low-fat natural yogurt
Tea, coffee or mineral water

Dinner:
Crispy-Topped Beans (page 182)

Spicy Fruit Salad (page 194)

2½fl oz (75ml) low-fat natural yogurt
Tea or coffee

Optional Calories: 35

Day 4

Breakfast:
½ medium banana
1oz (30g) cereal
¼ pint (150ml) skimmed milk
Tea or coffee

Lunch:
Waldorf Salad (page 123)

3oz (90g) shredded white cabbage with
2oz (60g) grated carrot.
1 tablespoon low-calorie mayonnaise mixed with
2½ tablespoons low-fat natural yogurt.

Raspberry Bonanza (page 193)

Tea, coffee or mineral water

Dinner:
Poached Egg and Beans on Toast
6oz (180g) baked beans
1 egg, poached
1oz (30g) bread, toasted
1 teaspoon margarine
Tea or coffee

Optional Calories: 15

Day 5
Breakfast:
½ medium grapefruit
1oz (30g) cereal
¼ pint (150ml) skimmed milk
Tea or coffee

Lunch:
Smoked Tofu Salad
6oz (180g) smoked tofu, cubed
Mixed Salad – shredded lettuce, sliced red pepper, celery, tomato, sprigs of watercress.
Crispbread up to 80 Calories
2 teaspoons low-fat spread
1 medium pear
Tea, coffee or mineral water

Dinner:
Cheese and Spinach Soufflé (page 145)

6oz (180g) cauliflower
3oz (90g) carrots
5oz (150g) raspberries
2½ tablespoons low-fat natural yogurt
1 teaspoon honey
Tea or coffee

Optional Calories: 20

Day 6
Breakfast:
4oz (120g) drained, canned mandarins
2½fl oz (75ml) low-fat natural yogurt
2oz (60g) cottage cheese
1oz (30g) bread, toasted
1 teaspoon margarine
Tea or coffee

Lunch:
Peanut Butter Toast and Salad
1 tablespoon peanut butter
1oz (30g) bread, toasted

Autumn Salad (page 122)

3oz (90g) pineapple
2oz (60g) fromage frais
Tea, coffee or mineral water

Dinner:
Burger with Vegetables
1 vegetarian burger
3oz (90g) courgettes
6oz (180g) broccoli

Gooseberry Charlotte (page 192)

2½fl oz (75ml) low-fat natural yogurt
Tea or coffee

Snacks:
1 teaspoon carob or cocoa
¼ pint (150ml) skimmed milk

Optional Calories: 30

Day 7
Breakfast:
4fl oz (120ml) grapefruit juice
1 tablespoon peanut butter
Crispbread up to 80 Calories
Tea or coffee

Lunch:
Stuffed Egg Salad
1 hard-boiled egg halved and the yolk mashed with
1 teaspoon mayonnaise,
2oz (60g) curd cheese and
2 teaspoons chopped chives.
Mixed Salad – shredded lettuce, sliced red pepper, cucumber and celery.
5oz (150g) raspberries
2½fl oz (75ml) low-fat natural yogurt
Tea, coffee or mineral water

Dinner:
Filled Potato with Vegetables
6oz (180g) baked beans
6oz (180g) baked jacket potato
6oz (180g) tomatoes, grilled
3oz (90g) mushrooms, stir-fried in 1 teaspoon margarine.

Strawberry Dessert (page 191)

Tea or coffee

Snacks:
1 teaspoon carob or cocoa
¼ pint (150ml) skimmed milk

Optional Calories: 50

Total Optional Calories for Week 2: 170

WEEKS AT A GLANCE
VEGETARIAN WEEK – 3

The range of foods has increased yet again and the use of beetroot, aubergines and peas allows such recipes as Beetroot Salad, Aubergine Purée and Green Pea Soup to be enjoyed. Peas are one of the few vegetables to be limited to a total of 12oz (360g) per week. Grapes, nectarines and blackberries are added to meals and these, together with a snack of cream crackers on Day 7, will help you to continue losing weight. Remember to add ½ pint (300ml) skimmed milk to every day's menu.

Day 1

Breakfast:
4fl oz (120ml) orange juice
1oz (30g) bread, toasted
1 teaspoon margarine
6oz (180g) baked beans
Tea or coffee

Lunch:
Green Pea Soup (page 110)

1oz (30g) French bread
1 teaspoon margarine
4oz (120g) low-fat soft cheese mixed with
1 tablespoon chopped onion.
Mixed Salad – shredded lettuce, sliced tomato, cucumber and grated carrot.
2 inch (5cm) wedge of honeydew melon
Tea, coffee or mineral water

Dinner:
Stuffed Tomatoes (page 140)

6oz (180g) broccoli
3oz (90g) leeks
½ medium banana
2½fl oz (75ml) low-fat natural yogurt
Tea or coffee

Day 2

Breakfast:
½ medium banana
1oz (30g) cereal

¼ pint (150ml) skimmed milk
Tea or coffee

Lunch:
Toasted Cheese with Salad
2 slices reduced-calorie bread, toasted
2oz (60g) cheese
1 tomato and ½ onion, sliced and tossed in 2 teaspoons French dressing.
1 medium orange
Tea, coffee or mineral water

Dinner:
Nut Rissoles with Chilli Sauce (page 181)

3oz (90g) carrots
3oz (90g) courgettes
4oz (120g) fruit salad
2½fl oz (75ml) low-fat natural yogurt
Tea or coffee

Snacks:
Crispbread up to 40 Calories
2 teaspoons low-fat spread

Optional Calories: 20

Day 3

Breakfast:
4fl oz (120ml) grapefruit juice
2oz (60g) low-fat soft cheese
1oz (30g) bread, toasted
1 teaspoon low-fat spread
Tea or coffee

Lunch:
Hummus (page 126)

Waldorf Salad (page 123)

Tea, coffee or mineral water

Dinner:
Poached Egg and Beans with Vegetables
3oz (90g) baked beans
1 egg, poached
1oz (30g) bread, toasted
6oz (180g) tomatoes, grilled
3oz (90g) mushrooms, stir-fried in 1 teaspoon margarine.
4oz (120g) drained, canned pineapple pieces topped with 2½ tablespoons low-fat natural yogurt
Tea or coffee

Snacks:
1 teaspoon carob or cocoa
¼ pint (150ml) skimmed milk

Optional Calories: 10

Day 4

Breakfast:
4fl oz (120ml) orange juice
1 slice reduced-calorie bread, toasted
1 teaspoon margarine
1 tablespoon marmalade

Lunch:
Cheese Salad

4oz (120g) low-fat soft cheese

Savoury Fruit Salad (page 114)

1 slice reduced-calorie bread
1 teaspoon margarine
4oz (120g) drained, canned
pears
2½fl oz (75ml) low-fat natural
yogurt
Tea, coffee or mineral water

Dinner:
Burger with Vegetables
1 vegetarian burger

Aubergine Purée (page 125)
(⅓ of recipe)

6oz (180g) jacket potato
1 teaspoon low-fat spread
3oz (90g) green beans

Honeycomb Mould (page 189)
Tea or coffee

Optional Calories: 95

Day 5
Breakfast:
1 medium tangerine
1oz (30g) bread, toasted
1 tablespoon peanut butter
Tea or coffee

Lunch:
Smoked Tofu Salad
6oz (180g) smoked tofu, cubed

Beetroot Salad (page 116)

Mixed Salad – shredded
lettuce, sliced tomato,
cucumber and peppers.
1 teaspoon mayonnaise
5oz (150g) chunks of
watermelon
Tea, coffee or mineral water

Dinner:
Mixed Vegetable Stew
(page 186)

6oz (180g) jacket potato
topped with
1oz (30g) fromage frais.
5fl oz (150ml) low-fat natural
yogurt
1 teaspoon honey
Tea or coffee

Optional Calories: 50

Day 6
Breakfast:
½ medium grapefruit
1oz (30g) porridge oats
¼ pint (150ml) skimmed milk
Tea or coffee

Lunch:
Poached Egg and Beans on
Toast
1oz (30g) bread, toasted
1 teaspoon low-fat spread
3oz (90g) baked beans
1 poached egg
1 tomato, grilled
4oz (120g) drained, canned
sliced peaches
2½fl oz (75ml) low-fat natural
yogurt
Tea, coffee or mineral water

Dinner:
Crispy-Topped Beans
(page 182)

Green Salad – shredded
lettuce, endive, sliced
cucumber, celery and sprigs of
watercress tossed in
2 teaspoons French dressing.

Raspberry Bonanza (page 193)
Tea or coffee

Snacks:
½ pint (300ml) beer or cider

Optional Calories: 120

Day 7
Breakfast:
2 inch (5cm) wedge of
honeydew melon
1oz (30g) cereal
¼ pint (150ml) skimmed milk
Tea or coffee

Lunch:
4oz (120g) low-fat soft cheese
mixed with 1 tablespoon
chopped spring onion.

Sally's Special Salad (page 113)

1oz (30g) French bread
1 teaspoon low-fat spread
1 medium tangerine
Tea, coffee or mineral water

Dinner:
Peppered Frittata (page 177)

3oz (90g) courgettes
1 tomato, grilled
5oz (150g) gooseberries,
stewed
2½ tablespoons low-fat natural
yogurt
Tea or coffee

Snacks:
2 cream crackers
2 teaspoons low-fat spread
1oz (30g) cheese

Optional Calories: 5

Total Optional Calories for
Week 3: 300

WEEKS AT A GLANCE
VEGETARIAN WEEK – 4

The number of Optional Calories has now increased to 400! There is a wider range of fruit juices. Apricots, cherries, kiwi fruit, mangoes and ogen melons are just a few of the new Week 4 fruits and the introduction of even more vegetables results in a delicious Vegetable Curry. Oatcakes may be eaten in place of bread: allow one oatcake in place of 1oz (30g) bread. As usual, allow an additional ½ pint (300ml) skimmed milk every day.

Day 1

Breakfast:
½ medium banana
1oz (30g) bread, toasted
1 tablespoon peanut butter
Tea or coffee

Lunch:
Smoked Tofu Salad
3oz (90g) smoked tofu, cubed

Russian Salad (page 117)

1 tomato, sliced
4oz (120g) cherries
2½fl oz (75ml) low-fat natural yogurt
Tea, coffee or mineral water

Dinner:
Nut Rissoles with Chilli Sauce (page 181)

3oz (90g) baby corn on the cob
1 teaspoon margarine
3oz (90g) broad beans
3oz (90g) leeks

Mango Mix (page 197)

Tea or coffee

Optional Calories: 40

Day 2

Breakfast:
2 inch (5cm) wedge of honeydew melon

1oz (30g) cereal
¼ pint (150ml) skimmed milk
Tea or coffee

Lunch:
Poached Egg with Vegetables
6oz (180g) baked beans
1 egg, poached
6oz (180g) tomatoes, grilled
1 kiwi fruit
2½ tablespoons low-fat natural yogurt
Tea, coffee or mineral water

Dinner:
Blue Cheese Soufflé (page 145)

3oz (90g) fennel
3oz (90g) carrots

Pineapple Cheesecake (page 198)

Tea or coffee

Optional Calories: 35

Day 3

Breakfast:
1 medium apple
1oz (30g) porridge oats
¼ pint (150ml) skimmed milk
Tea or coffee

Lunch:
Cheese Salad
4oz (120g) low-fat soft cheese mixed with 1 tablespoon

chopped spring onion.
1oz (30g) French bread
1 teaspoon margarine
Mixed Salad – shredded lettuce, sliced tomato, cucumber, fennel, tossed in 2 teaspoons French dressing.
4fl oz (120ml) tomato juice
Tea, coffee or mineral water

Dinner:
Layered Vegetable Pâté (page 128)

Vegetable Curry (page 179)

3oz (90g) rice (cooked weight)
½ medium mango, cubed
2oz (60g) fromage frais
Tea or coffee

Snacks:
4fl oz (120ml) red or white wine
1 teaspoon carob or cocoa
¼ pint (150ml) skimmed milk

Optional Calories: 140

Day 4

Breakfast:
½ medium ogen melon
1oz (30g) cheese
1oz (30g) bread, toasted
1 tomato
Tea or coffee

Lunch:

Green Pea Soup (page 110)

Filled Potato with Salad
6oz (180g) jacket potato
6oz (180g) baked beans
Mixed Salad – shredded
lettuce, sliced tomato,
cucumber, radishes and celery.
1 teaspoon mayonnaise
3oz (90g) grapes
Tea, coffee or mineral water

Dinner:

Lentil-Coated Vegetables
(page 184)

2 medium apricots, served with
2½fl oz (75ml) low-fat natural
yogurt
Tea or coffee

Day 5

Breakfast:

1 medium orange
1oz (30g) cereal
¼ pint (150ml) skimmed milk
Tea or coffee

Lunch:

Peach and Cottage Cheese
Platter (page 129)

1oz (30g) French bread
1 teaspoon margarine
2½fl oz (75ml) low-fat natural
yogurt
½ teaspoon honey
Tea, coffee or mineral water

Dinner:

Burger with Vegetables
1 vegetarian burger

Aubergine Purée (page 125)
(⅓ of recipe)
3oz (90g) peas
3oz (90g) carrots

Sweet-Topped Fruit (page 200)

Tea or coffee

Snacks:

2 water biscuits
2 teaspoons low-fat spread
1oz (30g) curd cheese

Optional Calories: 35

Day 6

Breakfast:

½ medium ogen melon
1 egg, poached
1 slice reduced-calorie bread,
toasted
1 teaspoon low-fat spread
Tea or coffee

Lunch:

4fl oz (120ml) grape juice

Smoked Tofu Salad
6oz (180g) smoked tofu, cubed
1 tomato
Green Salad – shredded
lettuce, sliced cucumber,
celery and green pepper.
1 teaspoon low-calorie French
dressing
5fl oz (150ml) low-fat natural
yogurt
1 teaspoon honey
Tea, coffee or mineral water

Dinner:

Savoury Rice and Beans
(page 185)

3oz (90g) courgettes
3oz (90g) carrots

Flapjack Pudding (page 196)

1oz (30g) fromage frais
Tea or coffee

Optional Calories: 80

Day 7

Breakfast:

1 medium apple
1oz (30g) cereal
¼ pint (150ml) skimmed milk
Tea or coffee

Lunch:

Baked Beans and Salad
6oz (180g) baked beans
1oz (30g) slice of bread
6oz (180g) tomatoes, grilled
Green Salad – shredded
lettuce, sliced fennel,
cucumber, green peppers and
celery, topped with 1 teaspoon
low-calorie mayonnaise.
2 medium plums
2½fl oz (75ml) low-fat natural
yogurt
Tea, coffee or mineral water

Dinner:

Crispy-Topped Beans
(page 182)

3oz (90g) mushrooms stir-fried
in 1 teaspoon margarine.
3oz (90g) cabbage
5oz (150g) strawberries served
with 1 teaspoon caster sugar
and 2oz (60g) fromage frais
Tea or coffee

Optional Calories: 25

Total Optional Calories for
Week 4: 355

WEEKS AT A GLANCE
VEGETARIAN WEEK – 5

This is the last of the weekly Menu Plans which now allows up to 500 Optional Calories! It's impossible to show the whole range of foods now available in this food plan which results in weight loss and a healthy, well balanced outlook regarding food. It is important to continue accurately measuring all foods. By now you should have lost weight so make use of the recipes section of this book to continue with the diet until your goal weight has been achieved and then gradually introduce other foods until your goal weight is maintained. Always remember to add ½ pint (300ml) skimmed milk to every day's menu in this section.

Day 1

Breakfast:
½ medium mango
1oz (30g) cereal
¼ pint (150ml) skimmed milk
Tea or coffee

Lunch:
Baked Beans on Toast
1½oz (45g) slice bread
2 teaspoons margarine
6oz (180g) baked beans
Green Salad – shredded lettuce, sliced fennel, cucumber, green pepper and celery.
1 medium persimmon
Tea, coffee or mineral water

Dinner:
Smoked Tofu Salad
6oz (180g) smoked tofu, cubed

Nutty Fruit Rice (page 141)

1 tomato and ½ onion, sliced and tossed in 2 teaspoons low-calorie French dressing.

Scottish Cream (page 208)
Tea or coffee

Optional Calories: 90

Day 2

Breakfast:
½ medium grapefruit
1 tablespoon peanut butter
1oz (30g) bread, toasted
Tea or coffee

Lunch:
Filled Potato and Salad
6oz (180g) jacket potato
4oz (120g) fromage frais
Mixed Salad – shredded lettuce, sliced pepper, fennel, spring onion and tomato.
2 teaspoons French dressing

Honeycomb Mould (page 189)

Tea, coffee or mineral water

Dinner:
Peach and Cottage Cheese Platter (page 129)

Plum Mousse (page 216)

2½ tablespoons low-fat natural yogurt
Tea or coffee

Optional Calories: 90

Day 3

Breakfast:
2 inch (5cm) wedge of honeydew melon
1oz (30g) porridge
¼ pint (150ml) skimmed milk
Tea or coffee

Lunch:
Baked Beans and Salad
1oz (30g) French bread
1 teaspoon margarine
6oz (180g) baked beans
Mixed Salad – shredded lettuce, sliced pepper, fennel, spring onion and radish.
Tea, coffee or mineral water

Dinner:
Melon Appetiser with Raspberry Sauce (page 142)

Blue Cheese Soufflé (page 145)

2oz (60g) sweetcorn
6oz (180g) broccoli
4oz (120g) fruit salad
2oz (60g) fromage frais
Tea or coffee

Optional Calories: 25

Day 4

Breakfast:
½ medium grapefruit
1oz (30g) bread
1 teaspoon low-fat spread
2 teaspoons marmalade
Tea or coffee

Lunch:

Greek Feta Salad (page 120)

6oz (180g) jacket potato
1 teaspoon margarine
5fl oz (150ml) low-fat natural
yogurt
1 teaspoon honey
Tea, coffee or mineral water

Dinner:

Burger with Vegetables
1 vegetarian burger
6oz (180g) tomatoes, grilled
6oz (180g) broccoli

Frozen Banana Cream
(page 219)

Tea or coffee

Optional Calories: 105

Day 5

Breakfast:

1oz (30g) dried apricots,
chopped
1oz (30g) cereal
¼ pint (150ml) skimmed milk
Tea or coffee

Lunch:

Cottage Cheese Salad
4oz (120g) cottage cheese
mixed with 1 tablespoon
chopped spring onion.
3oz (90g) beetroot, sliced
Mixed Salad – shredded
lettuce, sliced cucumber,
tomato and celery.
1 medium orange
Tea, coffee or mineral water

Dinner:

Peppered Frittata (page 177)

3oz (90g) sweetcorn
3oz (90g) courgettes

Hazelnut Raspberry Crumble
(page 220)

Tea or coffee

Optional Calories: 30

Day 6

Breakfast:

4fl oz (120ml) orange juice
1oz (30g) cheese
1oz (30g) bread, toasted
1 tomato
Tea or coffee

Lunch:

4fl oz (120ml) tomato juice

Peanut Butter Toast
2 slices reduced-calorie bread,
toasted
2 tablespoons peanut butter
5fl oz (150ml) low-fat natural
yogurt
Tea, coffee or mineral water

Dinner:

Vegetable Curry (page 179)

3oz (90g) rice (cooked weight)

Caribbean Choice (page 212)

Tea or coffee

Optional Calories: 50

Day 7

Breakfast:

4fl oz (120ml) grapefruit juice
1 egg, poached
1oz (30g) bread, toasted
1 teaspoon margarine
Tea or coffee

Lunch:

Green Pea Soup (page 110)

Smoked Tofu Salad
3oz (90g) smoked tofu, cubed

Bean Salad (page 121) (½ of
recipe)

Green Salad – shredded
lettuce, sliced fennel,
cucumber, green pepper, bean
sprouts.
1 medium tangerine
2½fl oz (75ml) low-fat natural
yogurt
Tea, coffee or mineral water

Dinner:

Stuffed Tomatoes (page 140)

3oz (90g) baby corn on the cob
6oz (180g) cauliflower

Mixed Fruit Flambé (page 210)

Tea or coffee

Optional Calories: 80

Total Optional Calories for
Week 5: 470

The following recipes are divided into three categories: Snacks & Starters, Main Courses and Desserts. Each recipe is accompanied by a day's eating plan and indicates which week it may be introduced. As with the previous weekly recipes and daily food plans and the Weeks at a Glance sections, the recipe may be enjoyed from the week indicated and on subsequent weeks. The calorie count as well as the Weight Watchers Exchanges and Optional Calories are given for every recipe.

Presentation is important and the colour photographs throughout the book show how these little extras enhance even the simplest meal, and some suggestions have been made for garnishes, such as sprigs of fresh herbs for savoury dishes and twists of oranges and lemons for sweet recipes. By combining recipes from various categories it is possible to create a quick easy snack or an impressive dinner party. Unlike many slimming programmes, using these recipes means no one need know you are on a reducing diet or watching your weight.

The majority of recipes serve more than one person but, if you live alone, many dishes may be successfully frozen and reheated in single portions.

Recipes headed 'Vegetarian' may only be eaten by vegetarians and not by anyone who eats meat or fish.

SNACKS & STARTERS

WEEK 3

Breakfast:

½ medium grapefruit
1oz (30g) cereal
¼ pint (150ml) skimmed milk

Lunch: ✳ Green Pea Soup ✳

1oz (30g) French bread spread with
1 teaspoon margarine.

Apple and Cheese – 1 medium apple
and 1½oz (45g) hard cheese.

Dinner: Creole Swordfish (page 167)

3oz (90g) baked potato with
1 teaspoon margarine
Steamed or boiled Brussels sprouts
and leeks.

Spicy Fruit Salad (page 194)

Served with 2½fl oz (75ml) low-fat
natural yogurt.

Snacks:

¼ pint (150ml) skimmed milk

Optional Calories: 40

GREEN PEA SOUP

Serves 2
100 Calories per serving

12oz (360g) peas in the pod or 6oz (180g) shelled peas or frozen peas
¼ pint (150ml) vegetable stock
large sprig of mint
1 small onion, roughly chopped
¼ pint (150ml) skimmed milk
½–1 teaspoon lemon juice
salt and pepper
2½fl oz (75ml) low-fat natural yogurt
1 teaspoon mint, chopped

1. Shell the peas if bought fresh in their pods. Place the peas, stock, sprig of mint and onion in a saucepan. Bring to the boil, cover and reduce the heat, simmer frozen peas for 20 minutes, and fresh peas for 30 minutes.
2. Transfer the peas, stock etc. to a blender or food processor. Process until smooth.
3. Pour the pea purée back into a saucepan and stir in the milk, lemon juice and salt and pepper to taste.
4. Stir the soup over a moderate heat until boiling, pour into two warm soup bowls and swirl in the yogurt. Sprinkle with the chopped mint and serve.

Exchanges per serving: Milk ½, Vegetable 1½

WEEK 4

Breakfast:

4fl oz (120ml) orange juice
Toast a 1oz (30g) slice of bread,
spread with 1 teaspoon margarine
and top with 3oz (90g) baked beans.

Lunch: Open Sardine Sandwich

Spread a 1oz (30g) slice of bread with
1 teaspoon margarine, top with 2–3
lettuce leaves and alternate slices of
tomato and cucumber. Top with
2oz (60g) drained, canned sardines
and a wedge of lemon.
Green Salad – shredded lettuce,
sliced fennel, green pepper, celery
and spring onion.

3oz (90g) grapes

Dinner: ✳ Melon Soup ✳

Steak with Vegetables

4oz (120g) fillet steak. Brush with
½ teaspoon vegetable oil, grill for
4 minutes, turn, brush with
½ teaspoon vegetable oil and grill
until cooked.
3oz (90g) sweetcorn
Steamed or boiled broad beans and
cauliflower.

5oz (150g) loganberries, sprinkled
with 1 teaspoon caster sugar and
served with 2½fl oz (75ml) low-fat
natural yogurt.

Snacks:

¾ pint (450ml) skimmed milk

Optional Calories: 60

MELON SOUP

Serves 3
40 Calories per serving

1 medium galia melon

3 tablespoons chopped spring onion

1 teaspoon finely chopped fresh root ginger

juice of 1–2 lemons

½ pint (300ml) vegetable stock

sprig of mint

To serve:
3 slices lemon

3 sprigs of mint

1. Halve the melon, scoop out and discard the seeds, but catch and reserve any juices which drip from the fruit.
2. Using a spoon, scoop out the flesh of the melon into a saucepan, scrape the spoon against the skin then squeeze the skin to remove as many of the juices as possible.
3. Add the spring onion, ginger, juice of 1½ lemons, vegetable stock and mint to the saucepan. Cover and simmer for 15–20 minutes.
4. Transfer all the contents of the saucepan to a blender or food processor. Process until smooth.
5. If the soup is to be served hot, reheat adding more lemon juice as necessary. Pour into three warm soup bowls and garnish with the lemon slices and sprigs of mint. If the soup is to be served chilled, pour the liquidised mixture into a bowl and chill well. Before serving add more lemon juice if necessary. Pour into three cold soup bowls and decorate with the lemon slices and sprigs of mint.

Exchanges per serving: Optional Calories 40

WEEK 1

Breakfast:

4fl oz (120ml) orange juice
1oz (30g) cereal
¼ pint (150ml) skimmed milk

Lunch: Pork Salad

2oz (60g) lean roast pork, sliced.
Tomato and Courgette Salad – thinly
slice 1 tomato and 2 baby courgettes,
sprinkle with 2 teaspoons chopped
chives and 2 teaspoons French
dressing.

* Red Cabbage Salad *

1oz (30g) French bread spread with
1 teaspoon margarine.

Dinner: Poached Trout with Vegetables

4oz (120g) trout fillet poached in a
little water with a slice of lemon.
Steamed or boiled broccoli, celery
and leeks.

Honeycomb Mould (page 189)
Surrounded with 3oz (90g) drained,
canned pineapple pieces

Snacks:

½ pint (300ml) skimmed milk

Optional Calories: 40

RED CABBAGE SALAD

Serves 4
80 Calories per serving

10oz (300g) red cabbage, central core removed
1 red onion
1 medium red dessert apple, cored
4 tablespoons red wine vinegar
4 teaspoons olive oil
2 cloves garlic, crushed
good pinch of powdered mustard
¼ teaspoon mixed herbs
salt and pepper

1. Finely shred the red cabbage, grate the onion and apple. The
   simplest way of doing this preparation is by using a good
   processor fitted with a grating attachment.
2. Place the vinegar, oil, garlic, mustard, herbs and a sprinkling
   of salt and pepper in a screw-top jar, secure and shake well.
   Alternatively place all the ingredients in a small bowl and
   whisk well to mix.
3. Pour the dressing over the salad, stir well to thoroughly coat
   the cabbage, onion and apple. Transfer to a non-metallic
   bowl, cover and leave in a cool place for 3–4 hours.
4. Before serving stir once again and add extra seasoning if
   necessary.

Exchanges per serving: Fat 1, Fruit ¼, Vegetable 1

WEEK 3

Breakfast:

½ medium grapefruit
Toast a 1oz (30g) slice of bread,
spread with 1 tablespoon peanut
butter.

Lunch: Scrambled Egg and Baked Beans

Beat 1 egg with 2 tablespoons milk
taken from the snack allowance.
Season with salt and pepper. Heat
1 teaspoon margarine in a saucepan,
add the beaten egg and cook over a
low heat stirring all the time. Serve
with 3oz (90g) baked beans.
2 tomatoes, grilled

2½oz (75g) strawberries
5fl oz (150ml) low-fat natural yogurt

Dinner: ✳ Sally's Special Salad ✳

Ham Salad

2oz (60g) ham
Green Salad – shredded lettuce,
sliced green pepper and chopped
spring onion.
1oz (30g) French bread spread with
1 teaspoon margarine.

1 medium orange

Snacks:

1 digestive biscuit
7½fl oz (225ml) skimmed milk

Optional Calories: 5

SALLY'S SPECIAL SALAD

Serves 4
50 Calories per serving

1 medium pear
2 teaspoons lime juice
3oz (90g) seedless red grapes
2 sticks celery
4 inch (10cm) wedge of cucumber
2oz (60g) bean sprouts
5fl oz (150ml) low-fat natural yogurt
1 teaspoon honey
few sprigs of watercress

1. Peel and halve the pear, scoop out the core, dice and toss in ½–1 teaspoon lime juice.
2. Halve the red grapes, chop the celery and cucumber about the same size as the pear.
3. Mix the pear, grapes, celery, cucumber and bean sprouts together.
4. Stir the yogurt, remaining lime juice and honey together, pour over the salad and toss well. Decorate with the sprigs of watercress.

Exchanges per serving: Fruit ½, Milk ¼, Vegetable ¾, Optional Calories 5

WEEK 3

Breakfast:

½ medium banana
1oz (30g) cereal
¼ pint (150ml) skimmed milk

Lunch: Cottage Cheese Salad

4oz (120g) cottage cheese mixed with
1 tablespoon low-calorie mayonnaise
and 1 tablespoon chopped chives,
garnished with mustard and cress.

* Savoury Fruit Salad *

Green Salad – shredded endive,
lettuce, green pepper and celery.

Dinner: Trout with Vegetables

5oz (150g) trout poached in a little
water with a slice of lemon.
6oz (180g) baked potato with
1 teaspoon margarine.
Steamed or boiled cauliflower and
carrots.

Pineapple Buttermilk Froth – place
4oz (120g) drained, canned
pineapple pieces in a blender with
¼ pint (150ml) buttermilk and
1 teaspoon sugar, process until
smooth and frothy. Serve
immediately.

Snacks:

½ pint (300ml) skimmed milk

Optional Calories: 40

SAVOURY FRUIT SALAD

Serves 4
65 Calories per serving

| 1 medium grapefruit |
| 2 medium oranges |
| 3oz (90g) seedless grapes |
| 1oz (30g) watercress |
| 3 tablespoons chopped spring onion |
| 1 tablespoon lemon juice |
| 2 teaspoons olive oil |
| 1 teaspoon clear honey |
| 2 teaspoons chopped mint |
| salt and pepper |
| approximately 3 inch (7.5cm) wedge of cucumber |

1. Using a sharp knife peel the skin and white pith from the grapefruit and oranges. Cut in between each membrane to remove the segments, catching all the juices which drip from the fruit.
2. Halve the grapes, remove the sprigs from the watercress and chop the stalks. Mix the fruit, watercress and spring onion together.
3. Place the reserved juices, lemon juice, oil, honey, mint, salt and pepper in a small jar and shake well or whisk together in a small bowl.
4. Pour the dressing over the fruit etc. and toss to mix.
5. Thinly slice the cucumber and arrange round the edge of the serving dish or dishes. Pile the salad in the centre.

Exchanges per serving: Fat ½, Fruit 1, Optional Calories 20

Savoury Fruit Salad

WEEK 3

Breakfast:

Strawberry Buttermilk Froth – place 5oz (150g) strawberries, ¼ pint (150ml) buttermilk and 2 teaspoons sugar in a blender, process until frothy. Serve immediately.
Toast a 1oz (30g) slice of bread, spread with 1 teaspoon margarine and top with 2oz (60g) cottage cheese.

Lunch: Stuffed Egg Salad

Cut a hard-boiled egg in half horizontally, scoop out the yolk and mash with 1oz (30g) low-fat soft cheese, 1 teaspoon chopped chives and 1 teaspoon low-calorie mayonnaise. Pile into the egg whites.

✳ Beetroot Salad ✳

Green Salad – shredded lettuce, cucumber, green pepper and celery tossed in 2 teaspoons low-calorie French dressing.

Dinner: Ham with Vegetables

3oz (90g) boiled ham, sliced,
6oz (180g) baked potato
1 teaspoon margarine.
Steamed or boiled carrots and peas.

Blackberries and Apple – stew 1 medium cooking apple with 2½oz (75g) blackberries, sweeten with artificial sweetener.

Snacks:

¾ pint (450ml) skimmed milk

Optional Calories: 60

BEETROOT SALAD

Serves 4
65 Calories per serving

8oz (240g) cooked beetroot
1 medium pear
1 medium orange
4 sticks celery, sliced
2½fl oz (75ml) low-fat natural yogurt
1 teaspoon clear honey
approximately 2 teaspoons lemon juice
4 teaspoons chives, chopped
few lettuce, chicory or endive leaves

1. Remove and discard the skin from the beetroot and dice.
2. Peel, quarter, core and dice the pear. Using a sharp knife remove the peel and white pith from the orange. Thinly slice the orange, cut each slice into quarters.
3. Mix the beetroot, pear, orange and celery together in a bowl.
4. In a small bowl mix the yogurt, honey, lemon juice and chives together.
5. Mix the yogurt mixture into the fruit and vegetable salad, stir well adding a little more lemon juice if necessary.
6. Arrange the lettuce, chicory or endive leaves round the serving dish. Just before serving spoon the beetroot salad in the centre.

Exchanges per serving: Fruit ½, Vegetable 1, Optional Calories 20

WEEK 4

Breakfast:

4fl oz (120ml) apple juice
Toast a 1oz (30g) slice of bread,
spread with 1 tablespoon peanut
butter.

Lunch: Baked Beans Jacket Potato

4½oz (135g) baked potato
topped with 3oz (90g) baked beans.
Mixed Salad – shredded lettuce,
chopped red pepper, spring onion
and celery tossed in 2 teaspoons
French dressing.

✱ Russian Salad ✱

1 medium pear

Dinner: Grilled Liver with Vegetables

Brush 4oz (120g) slices of lamb's or
calf's liver with ½ teaspoon vegetable
oil, grill for 4 minutes, turn, brush
with ½ teaspoon vegetable oil and
grill until cooked.
Steamed or boiled cauliflower,
carrots and broccoli.

Gooseberries with Yogurt – stew
5oz (150g) gooseberries in a little
water, sweeten to taste with artificial
sweetener and serve with 2½fl oz
(75ml) low-fat natural yogurt.

Snacks:

12½fl oz (375ml) skimmed milk

RUSSIAN SALAD

Serves 4
90 Calories per serving

4oz (120g) carrot
3oz (90g) swede
3oz (90g) parsnip
6oz (180g) potato
3oz (90g) peas
salt
3oz (90g) dwarf beans, cut in 1 inch (2.5cm) lengths
3 tablespoons chopped spring onion
5fl oz (150ml) low-fat natural yogurt
½ teaspoon Dijon mustard

1. Cut the carrot, swede, parsnip and potato into ½ inch (1.25cm) dice.
2. If the peas are freshly shelled cook with the root vegetables, if frozen put to one side. Place the root vegetables in a saucepan of salted water and boil for 5 minutes.
3. Add the dwarf beans and boil for a further 5 minutes then add the peas and boil for a further 5 minutes or until all the vegetables are cooked but firm, drain well, leave to cool.
4. Mix the spring onion, yogurt and mustard together, stir into the cooked vegetables. Serve cold.

Exchanges per serving: Bread ½, Milk ¼, Vegetable 1¼

WEEK 5

Breakfast:

4 fl oz (120ml) orange juice
1 croissant spread with 1 teaspoon butter and 1 tablespoon strawberry jam.

Lunch: ✳ Salad Niçoise ✳

1½oz (45g) French bread spread with 1 teaspoon low-fat spread.
5fl oz (150ml) low-fat natural yogurt

Dinner: Fish Fingers with Vegetables

4 breadcrumbed fish fingers dotted with 1 teaspoon margarine and grilled
Steamed or boiled broad beans and cauliflower.
½ medium grapefruit

Apple and Cheese – 1 medium apple and 1½oz (45g) hard cheese.

Snacks:

½ pint (300ml) skimmed milk

Optional Calories: 250

SALAD NIÇOISE

Serves 2
205 Calories per serving

3oz (90g) dwarf beans

salt

8oz (240g) tomatoes

3 inch (7.5cm) wedge of cucumber

3oz (90g) drained and flaked, canned tuna

1 hard-boiled egg, chopped

½–1 teaspoon capers, rinsed and chopped

1 tablespoon olive oil

2 tablespoons white wine or cider vinegar

¼ teaspoon Dijon mustard

1 tablespoon finely chopped basil

1 teaspoon finely chopped parsley

½ clove garlic, crushed (optional)

4 anchovy fillets

6 black olives, pitted and halved

1. Cut the beans in half, plunge into boiling salted water, cover and boil for 6 minutes, drain.
2. While the beans are cooking finely slice the tomatoes and cucumber.
3. Arrange half the tomato slices in the base of the serving dish, spread half the slices of cucumber on top.
4. Lay half the beans on top of the cucumber and spoon over the tuna, egg and capers.
5. Place the olive oil, vinegar, mustard, basil, parsley and garlic in a small screw-top jar, secure and shake well. Alternatively whisk together in a small bowl. Spoon half the dressing over the tuna and egg.
6. Arrange the beans, the cucumber and lastly the tomato slices over the tuna, spoon over the remaining dressing.
7. Rinse the anchovy fillets and cut in half lengthways, arrange in a lattice pattern on top of the tomatoes. Place half an olive in each square of the lattice.

Exchanges per serving: Fat 1½, Protein 2, Vegetable 2½, Optional Calories 25

WEEK 5

Breakfast:

4fl oz (120ml) grapefruit juice
Spread a 1oz (30g) slice of bread with
1 teaspoon margarine and serve with
1 boiled egg.

Lunch: Baked Beans on Toast

Toast a 1oz (30g) slice of bread,
spread with 1 teaspoon margarine
and top with 6oz (180g) baked beans.
Serve with 1 grilled tomato.

1 medium persimmon

Dinner: Salmon with Mixed Salads

Poach a 4oz (120g) salmon fillet or
4½oz (135g) salmon cutlet in a little
water with a slice of lemon, bay leaf
and few sprigs of parsley. Leave until
cool.

* Mediterranean Salad *

Green Salad – shredded lettuce,
sliced green pepper, celery and
spring onion.
1oz (30g) French bread spread with
1 teaspoon butter.

5fl oz (150ml) low-fat fruit yogurt

Snacks:

½ medium ogen melon
½ pint (300ml) skimmed milk

Optional Calories: 85

MEDITERRANEAN SALAD

Serves 4
65 Calories per serving

6oz (180g) cherry tomatoes
6oz (180g) baby courgettes
1½oz (45g) very small button mushrooms
8 black olives, pitted
4 teaspoons olive oil
2 tablespoons red wine vinegar
1 small clove garlic, crushed
2–3 teaspoons chopped basil
¼ teaspoon Dijon mustard
salt and pepper
lamb's lettuce or watercress

1. Slice the tomatoes, courgettes, mushrooms and olives and place in a bowl.
2. Place the oil, vinegar, garlic, basil, mustard and a sprinkling of salt and pepper in a screw-top jar, secure and shake well to mix. Alternatively whisk together in a small bowl.
3. Pour the dressing over the salad, toss well to mix.
4. Spoon the salad into a serving dish and arrange the lamb's lettuce or watercress round the edge.

Exchanges per serving: Fat 1, Vegetable 1¼, Optional Calories 10

WEEK 5

Breakfast:

4fl oz (120ml) apple juice
1 egg, poached
1oz (30g) slice of bread
1 teaspoon low-fat spread

Lunch: ✳ Greek Feta Salad ✳

1oz (30g) French bread spread with
1 teaspoon margarine.

½ medium ogen melon, chopped,
served with 5fl oz (150ml) low-fat
natural yogurt.

Dinner: Poached Salmon with Vegetables

Poach a 4oz (120g) salmon fillet in a
little water with a slice of lemon and
bouquet garni.
Steamed or boiled asparagus and
cauliflower.
3oz (90g) baby corn, boiled and
dotted with 1 teaspoon margarine.

Strawberries and Cream – sprinkle
5oz (150g) strawberries with
1 teaspoon sugar, top with
1 tablespoon double cream.

Snacks:

½ pint (300ml) skimmed milk

Optional Calories: 85

GREEK FETA SALAD

Serves 4
150 Calories per serving

8oz (240g) tomatoes
8oz (240g) feta cheese
1 small yellow pepper
4 inch (10cm) wedge of cucumber
1 small onion
12 black olives, pitted
4 teaspoons olive oil
4 teaspoons white wine vinegar
1½ teaspoons chopped oregano
1½ teaspoons chopped parsley
1 small clove garlic, crushed
salt and pepper
lettuce

1. Cut the tomatoes into wedges, put in a large bowl.
2. Cut the feta cheese in ½ inch (1.25cm) cubes. Remove the core and seeds from the yellow pepper and cut the pepper and cucumber in the same size dice as the cheese.
3. Slice the onion and separate into rings, halve the olives, mix with the tomatoes, feta cheese, pepper and cucumber.
4. Whisk the oil, wine vinegar, herbs, garlic, salt and pepper together in a small bowl, pour over the salad, toss gently.
5. Arrange lettuce leaves, whole or shredded, round the edge of the serving dish and spoon the salad in the centre.

Exchanges per serving: Fat 1, Protein 2, Vegetable 1½, Optional Calories 15

VEGETARIAN WEEK 1/ MAIN MENU PLAN WEEK 3

Breakfast:

½ medium grapefruit
1oz (30g) cereal
¼ pint (150ml) skimmed milk

Lunch: Omelette

Beat together 2 eggs, 2 tablespoons water, 1 tablespoon chopped chives, salt and pepper. Heat 1 teaspoon margarine in a small omelette pan, add the egg mixture and cook over a gentle heat drawing the mixture from the edge towards the centre. When the underside is golden brown, fold over and serve.
2 tomatoes, grilled
1 slice of reduced-calorie bread spread with 1 teaspoon low-fat spread.

5oz (150g) strawberries sprinkled with 1 teaspoon caster sugar.

Dinner:

2oz (60g) cottage cheese

✳ Bean Salad ✳ (½ of recipe)

Green Salad – green pepper, celery, cucumber and lettuce.

Simple Milk Pudding (page 217) Served with 4oz (120g) drained, canned mandarins.

Snacks:

½ pint (300ml) skimmed milk

Optional Calories: 60

BEAN SALAD

Serves 2 as a main salad or 4 as a side salad
130/65 Calories per serving

2oz (60g) podded or frozen broad beans
salt
2oz (60g) dwarf beans, cut in 1 inch (2.5cm) lengths
3oz (90g) drained, canned or cooked cannellino or butter beans
3oz (90g) smoked tofu, diced
1–2 tablespoons chopped spring onions or chives
2 teaspoons olive oil
1 tablespoon red wine vinegar
¼ teaspoon Dijon mustard
1 clove garlic, crushed
1 teaspoon finely chopped basil
pepper

1. Boil the fresh broad beans in salted water for about 10 minutes or, if using frozen beans boil for 3 minutes. Drain, plunge into cold water and slip the beans out of their waxy skins.
2. Boil the dwarf beans in salted water for 5 minutes, drain.
3. Mix all the beans, tofu and spring onions or chives together.
4. Place the olive oil, vinegar, mustard, garlic, basil and a little salt and pepper in a small screw-top jar, secure and shake well. Alternatively whisk together in a small bowl.
5. Pour the dressing over the beans and toss well to coat.

Exchanges per serving for 2: Fat 1, Protein 1, Vegetable ½

Exchanges per serving for 4: Fat ½, Protein ½, Vegetable ¼

VEGETARIAN WEEK 1

Breakfast:

½ medium grapefruit
Toast 1 slice of reduced-calorie bread, spread with 1 tablespoon peanut butter.

Lunch:

4fl oz (120ml) orange juice
3oz (90g) low-fat soft cheese mixed with 1 tablespoon finely chopped red pepper and 1 teaspoon low-calorie mayonnaise.

✳ Autumn Salad ✳

1oz (30g) French bread spread with 1 teaspoon margarine.

5fl oz (150ml) low-fat natural yogurt

Dinner: Burger with Vegetables

1 vegetarian burger
Steamed or boiled Brussels sprouts, cauliflower and carrots.

Simple Milk Pudding (page 217)

Snacks:

¼ pint (150ml) skimmed milk

Optional Calories: 40

AUTUMN SALAD 🌰

Serves 4
75 Calories per serving

8oz (240g) carrots
6oz (180g) courgettes
1 leek
1 medium orange
1 teaspoon finely chopped fresh ginger
1oz (30g) cashew nuts, roughly chopped
lemon juice
head of chicory

1. Finely grate the carrots, courgettes and leek. This is most easily done with the grating attachment of a food processor. If you don't have a food processor finely grate the carrots and courgettes and finely chop the leek.
2. Squeeze the juice from the orange, mix with the ginger and pour over the prepared vegetables. Stir in the nuts and leave in a cool place for 1–2 hours.
3. Mix the salad once again and add lemon juice to taste.
4. Arrange the chicory leaves round the edge of the serving bowl or plate, spoon the salad in the centre.

Exchanges per serving: Fat ¼, Fruit ¼, Protein ½, Vegetable 2

VEGETARIAN WEEK 2

Breakfast:

4fl oz (120ml) orange juice
1oz (30g) cereal
¼ pint (150ml) skimmed milk

Lunch: ✳ Waldorf Salad ✳

Tomato and Cucumber Salad – slices
of tomato and 2 inch (5cm) wedge of
cucumber sliced, sprinkled with
2 teaspoons chopped chives.
2 rice cakes spread with
1½ teaspoons tahini.

Dinner: Mixed Vegetable
Stew (page 186)

Green Salad – shredded lettuce,
sliced green pepper, celery and
spring onion.

4oz (120g) drained, canned
mandarins served with 2 tablespoons
natural juice and topped with
2oz (60g) fromage frais.

Snacks:

12½fl oz (375ml) skimmed milk

Optional Calories: 10

WALDORF SALAD

Serves 2
220 Calories per serving

2oz (60g) Edam cheese
1 medium apple
4 teaspoons lemon juice
5oz (150g) small chunks watermelon, seeds removed
2 sticks celery, chopped
1oz (30g) walnuts or pecan nuts, roughly chopped
2½fl oz (75ml) low-fat natural yogurt
2 tablespoons chopped chives
a few lettuce or endive leaves

1. Dice the cheese.
2. Quarter, core and dice the apple. Toss in 2 teaspoons of the lemon juice.
3. Mix the cheese, apple, watermelon and celery together. Stir the walnuts or pecan nuts into the cheese etc.
4. Mix the yogurt, remaining lemon juice and chives together, spoon over the salad and toss well.
5. Line a serving bowl with the lettuce or endive leaves, pile the salad into the centre and serve.

Exchanges per serving: Fat ½, Fruit 1, Milk ¼, Protein 2, Vegetable ¾

VEGETARIAN WEEK 5

Breakfast:

2 inch (5cm) wedge of honeydew melon
2 rice cakes, spread with 1 teaspoon tahini and 2 teaspoons set honey.

Lunch: Cottage Cheese Salad

4oz (120g) cottage cheese mixed with 1 tablespoon chopped chives.

✳ Banana and Watercress Salad ✳

Mixed Salad – shredded lettuce, sliced tomato, cucumber, peppers and onion.
1oz (30g) French bread spread with 1 teaspoon low-fat spread.

Dinner: Vegetable Curry (page 179)

1oz (30g) long grain rice, boiled in a little water.

5fl oz (150ml) low-fat fruit yogurt

Snacks:

½ pint (300ml) skimmed milk

Optional Calories: 165

BANANA AND  WATERCRESS SALAD

Serves 3
185 Calories per serving

2 medium bananas
1 tablespoon lemon juice
2 tablespoons cream cheese
1 tablespoon low-fat natural yogurt
½ teaspoon honey
1oz (30g) watercress
1½oz (45g) pecan nuts, roughly chopped
cayenne pepper

1. Peel the bananas, cut in diagonal slices. Toss the banana in the lemon juice, remove from the lemon juice and place the banana in a bowl.
2. Blend the cream cheese with the yogurt and remaining lemon juice and stir in the honey.
3. Chop the stems of the watercress, reserve a few sprigs for decoration and chop the remaining leaves.
4. Stir the chopped watercress into the cream cheese mixture, spoon over the slices of banana, add the pecan nuts and stir to coat.
5. Transfer the banana and pecan nuts to a small serving bowl, garnish with the reserved sprigs of watercress and dust with a little cayenne pepper.

Exchanges per serving: Fat ½, Fruit 1, Protein 1, Optional Calories 85

WEEK 3

Breakfast:

1 medium orange
Toast a 1oz (30g) slice of bread, spread with 1 tablespoon peanut butter.

Lunch: ✳ Aubergine Dip ✳

(⅓ of recipe) with vegetable crudités
Turkey and Ham Salad

1oz (30g) turkey, sliced,
1oz (30g) lean ham, sliced
Mixed Salad – shredded lettuce, sliced red and green pepper, celery, spring onion and wedges of tomato.
1oz (30g) French bread spread with 1 teaspoon margarine.

Strawberries and Ice Cream –
5oz (150g) strawberries sprinkled with 1 teaspoon caster sugar.
2oz (60g) strawberry ice cream

Dinner: Omelette with Vegetables

Beat together 2 eggs, 2 tablespoons water, salt and pepper. Heat
1 teaspoon margarine in a small omelette pan, pour in the egg mixture and cook over a moderate heat drawing the edge towards the centre. When the underside is golden, fold over and serve.
Steamed or boiled green beans and cauliflower.
2 inch (5cm) wedge of honeydew melon
5fl oz (150ml) low-fat natural yogurt
1 teaspoon honey

Snacks:

1 digestive biscuit
½ pint (300ml) skimmed milk

Optional Calories: 140

AUBERGINE PURÉE OR DIP

Serves 3 or 9
95/30 Calories per serving

9–10oz (270–300g) aubergine

1 clove garlic, crushed

6oz (180g) curd cheese

1 teaspoon lemon juice

1 tablespoon chopped spring onion

salt and pepper

1. Place the whole aubergine under a moderately hot grill for 10–15 minutes, turning occasionally until evenly charred.
2. Allow the aubergine to cool then scoop out all the flesh and mash well, alternatively place in a blender or food processor and process until smooth.
3. Add all the remaining ingredients to the aubergine and blend well.
4. Serve cold or reheat over a gentle heat stirring all the time. Serve as a purée for three.
N.B. This purée makes an ideal dip for a buffet party surrounded by vegetable crudités. It will then serve nine people.

Exchanges per serving for 3: Protein 1, Vegetable 1

Exchanges per serving for 9: Protein ⅓, Vegetable ⅓

VEGETARIAN WEEK 1

Breakfast:
4fl oz (120ml) orange juice
1oz (30g) cereal
¼ pint (150ml) skimmed milk

Lunch: ✳ Hummus ✳
1 medium apple
1oz (30g) hard cheese

Dinner: Nut Rissoles with Chilli Sauce (page 181)
Mixed Salad – shredded lettuce, sliced peppers, cucumber, celery and radish tossed in 2 teaspoons French dressing.

Fruit and Fromage Frais – 4oz (120g) drained, canned fruit salad served with 2 tablespoons natural juice and topped with 1oz (30g) fromage frais mixed with ½ teaspoon clear honey.

Snacks:
¾ pint (450ml) skimmed milk

Optional Calories: 30

HUMMUS
Serves 4
170 Calories per serving

3oz (90g) chick peas

4 teaspoons tahini

juice of 1 lemon

1 large clove garlic, crushed

salt and pepper

paprika

sprigs of coriander

4 × 1oz (30g) pitta bread

few fresh vegetable crudités such as pepper and carrot sticks, cauliflower florets, etc.

1. Soak the chick peas in cold water overnight. The next day drain the chick peas, place in a saucepan and cover with cold water.
2. Bring the chick peas to a rapid boil, keep boiling rapidly for 10 minutes, then reduce the heat and simmer until cooked (about 1 hour).
3. Drain the chick peas, reserving the cooking liquid. Place the chick peas in a blender with the tahini, lemon juice and garlic. Blend until smooth adding a little of the reserved cooking liquid to form a stiff paste.
4. Season the mixture with salt and pepper and transfer to a small bowl, sprinkle with paprika and sprigs of coriander.
5. Serve the hummus with warm pitta bread and fresh vegetable crudités.

Exchanges per serving: Bread 1, Fat 1, Protein ¾, Vegetable ½

Hummus with crudités and pitta bread

WEEK 4

Breakfast:

½ medium banana, sliced
1oz (30g) cereal
¼ pint (150ml) skimmed milk

Lunch: Tuna Salad

2oz (60g) canned tuna, drained and flaked with 2 teaspoons chopped spring onion and lemon juice to taste, topped with 1 teaspoon mayonnaise. Mixed Salad – shredded lettuce, sliced red pepper, cucumber, tomato and celery with sprigs of watercress.

Mango and Honey Yogurt –
½ medium mango cubed and mixed into 5fl oz (150ml) low-fat natural yogurt with 1 teaspoon clear honey.

Dinner: ✳ Layered Vegetable Pâté ✳

Braised Beef (page 150)

6oz (180g) baked jacket potato with 1 teaspoon margarine.
Steamed or boiled green beans.
4fl oz (120ml) red wine

4oz (120g) fresh fruit salad

Snacks:

¼ pint (150ml) skimmed milk

Optional Calories: 160

LAYERED VEGETABLE PÂTÉ

Serves 6
120 Calories per serving

14oz (420g) spinach
salt
2 tablespoons chopped chives
6 tablespoons single cream
freshly grated nutmeg
1lb (480g) parsnips, diced
3oz (90g) fromage frais
8oz (240g) swede, diced
8oz (240g) carrots, diced
finely grated zest of ½ an orange
¼ pint (150ml) hot vegetable stock
2 tablespoons gelatine
few slices of carrot for garnish (optional)

1. Wash the spinach, shake well to remove excess water, place in a saucepan, sprinkle with a little salt, cover and simmer for 8–10 minutes. Drain well, pressing out all the excess water. Transfer to a blender or food processor, add the chives and 3 tablespoons single cream, process until smooth and season with freshly grated nutmeg.
2. While the spinach is cooking, place the parsnips in a saucepan of boiling salted water, boil until tender. Drain and mash with the fromage frais.
3. Boil the swede and carrots together in a saucepan of simmering water, drain and mash with the orange zest and remaining single cream. Alternatively blend in a food processor.
4. Pour the hot vegetable stock in a small basin, sprinkle in the gelatine and place in a saucepan of simmering water until dissolved.
5. If using the carrot for decoration, boil 6 slices until soft, drain, dip in the dissolved gelatine and arrange on the base of a 2lb (1kg) loaf tin. Divide the remaining stock between the three vegetable purées, stir well. Spoon the spinach purée into the tin, level, top with the parsnip purée and lastly the carrot and swede over the top, smooth and refrigerate for several hours.
6. To serve; dip in hot water and invert on a serving plate.

Exchanges per serving: Protein ¼, Vegetable 2½, Optional Calories 30

WEEK 2

Breakfast:

4fl oz (120ml) grapefruit juice
1oz (30g) cereal
¼ pint (150ml) skimmed milk

Lunch: ✳ Peach and Cottage Cheese Platter ✳

1oz (30g) French bread spread with 1 teaspoon margarine.

5fl oz (150ml) low-fat natural yogurt
1 teaspoon honey

Dinner: Grilled Lamb with Vegetables

Brush a 5oz (150g) lean, boneless lamb steak or chop with ½ teaspoon vegetable oil, grill for 4–5 minutes, turn, brush with another ½ teaspoon vegetable oil, sprinkle with a little mint and continue grilling until cooked.
Steamed or boiled asparagus, celery and carrots.

Raspberry Bonanza (page 193)

Snacks:

¼ pint (150ml) skimmed milk

Optional Calories: 35

PEACH AND COTTAGE CHEESE PLATTER

Serves 1
170 Calories per serving

3oz (90g) cottage cheese

2 teaspoons low-calorie mayonnaise

good pinch of curry powder

1 tablespoon finely chopped spring onion

1 tablespoon finely chopped red pepper

1 medium peach

lemon juice

2 sprigs of coriander

few lettuce leaves

4–5 slices cucumber

2 radishes, sliced

1 carrot, grated

1oz (30g) bean sprouts

1. Mix together the cottage cheese, low-calorie mayonnaise and curry powder. Stir in the spring onion and red pepper.
2. Cut halfway through the peach, twist the two halves in opposite directions and scoop out the stone. Brush the cut halves with lemon juice.
3. Pile the cottage cheese mixture on to each peach half and decorate with sprigs of coriander.
4. Arrange the lettuce, cucumber, radishes, carrot and bean sprouts decoratively on the serving plate with the cottage cheese-topped peaches.

Exchanges per serving: Fat 1, Fruit 1, Protein 1½, Vegetable 2

WEEK 4

Breakfast:

4fl oz (120ml) pineapple juice
Toast a 1oz (30g) slice of bread,
spread with 1 teaspoon low-fat spread
and top with 3oz (90g) baked beans.

Lunch: ✳ Special Scramble ✳

Green Salad – shredded lettuce,
sliced cucumber, green pepper and
spring onion.

1 kiwi fruit

Dinner: Plaice in Prawn Wine Sauce (page 170)

3oz (90g) boiled potatoes
Steamed or boiled mange-tout, fennel
and leeks.

5fl oz (150ml) low-fat natural yogurt

Snacks:

½ medium ogen melon
½ pint (300ml) skimmed milk

Optional Calories: 130

SPECIAL SCRAMBLE

Serves 2
290 Calories per serving

2 eggs

3 tablespoons single cream

pepper

1 tomato

1 teaspoon margarine

4 teaspoons chopped spring onion

1oz (30g) smoked salmon, chopped

To serve:

2 × 1oz (30g) slices bread

2 teaspoons margarine

1. Beat the eggs and single cream together and season with a little pepper.
2. Cover the tomato with boiling water, leave for 1 minute, drain and slip off the skin. Cut the tomato in half, scoop out and discard the seeds and chop the flesh.
3. Melt the margarine in a small saucepan, add the spring onion and stir-fry 1–2 minutes, add the tomato and stir-fry for a further 2 minutes.
4. Pour the beaten eggs and cream into the saucepan and stir over a moderate heat. When the mixture begins to thicken add the smoked salmon, do not overcook, the eggs should remain creamy.
5. While the eggs are cooking, toast the bread, spread with margarine and serve with the Special Scramble.

Exchanges per serving: Bread 1, Fat 1½, Protein 1½, Vegetable ½, Optional Calories 50

WEEK 3

Breakfast:

4fl oz (120ml) grapefruit juice
Toast a 1oz (30g) slice of bread,
spread with 1 teaspoon margarine
and 1 tablespoon marmalade.

Lunch: ✳ Ham and Cheese Salad ✳

1 oz (30g) slice of bread spread with
1 teaspoon margarine.

5fl oz (150ml) low-fat natural yogurt

Dinner: Roast Beef with Vegetables

3oz (90g) roast beef
3oz (90g) boiled potato
3oz (90g) peas, boiled or steamed
Steamed or boiled carrots.

Gooseberries and Custard –
5oz (150g) gooseberries stewed in a
little water and sweetened with
artificial sweetener, served with

Baked Egg Custard (page 190)

Snacks:

¼ pint (150ml) skimmed milk

Optional Calories: 85

HAM AND CHEESE SALAD

Serves 2
245 Calories per serving

2oz (60g) cooked ham

2 sticks celery, chopped

3oz (90g) grapes

1 medium orange

2 inch (5cm) wedge of cucumber, diced

½ red pepper, seeded and chopped

2 teaspoons olive oil

1 tablespoon lemon juice

¼ teaspoon Dijon mustard

salt and pepper

few chicory or lettuce leaves

2oz (60g) Danish Blue cheese

1. Cut the ham into small dice and place in a bowl with the celery.
2. Halve the grapes and discard any pips. Using a sharp knife cut the peel and white pith from the orange, cut in between each membrane to separate the segments. Reserve any juices which escape while preparing the fruit.
3. Mix the grapes, orange, cucumber and red pepper with the ham and celery.
4. Place the oil, lemon juice, mustard, salt and pepper together in a small screw-top jar, secure and shake well to mix. Alternatively whisk all the ingredients together in a small basin.
5. Pour the dressing over the ham etc. and toss well.
6. Arrange the chicory or lettuce leaves round the edge of the serving dish, spoon the salad in the centre and crumble over the Danish Blue cheese.

Exchanges per serving: Fat 1, Fruit 1, Protein 2, Vegetable 1½

Week 5

Breakfast:

4fl oz (120ml) vegetable juice
Toast 1 slice of reduced-calorie bread, sprinkle one side with 1oz (30g) Cheddar cheese, grated. Grill until bubbling and serve with 1 tomato, sliced.

Lunch: ✳ Creamy Prawn Pasta ✳

Green Salad – shredded lettuce, sliced cucumber, green pepper, celery and spring onion tossed in 2 teaspoons French dressing.
4 fl oz (120ml) tomato juice

Dinner: Grilled Liver with Vegetables

Brush 4oz (120g) sliced lamb's or calf's liver with ½ teaspoon vegetable oil, grill for 3–4 minutes, turn, brush with ½ teaspoon vegetable oil and grill until cooked.
1 corn-on-the-cob dotted with 1 teaspoon margarine.
Steamed or boiled green beans and carrots.

½ medium papaya
5fl oz (150ml) low-fat natural yogurt

Snacks:

½ medium ogen melon
½ pint (300ml) skimmed milk

Optional Calories: 120

CREAMY PRAWN PASTA

Serves 2
325 Calories per serving

3oz (90g) tagliatelle

salt

3oz (90g) broccoli florets

2 tablespoons cream cheese

2oz (60g) fromage frais

4 teaspoons grated Parmesan cheese

1 tablespoon chopped chervil

2 teaspoons chopped chives

3oz (90g) peeled prawns

pepper

1. Boil the tagliatelle in boiling salted water for 10–15 minutes according to the packaging instructions, drain.
2. Plunge the broccoli florets in boiling salted water for 4 minutes, drain.
3. While the tagliatelle is cooking, mix together the cream cheese, fromage frais, 2 teaspoons Parmesan cheese, chervil and chives, blend well, stir in the prawns.
4. Return the hot well-drained tagliatelle to the saucepan, add the broccoli and cream cheese mixture. Stir over a very low heat. Season with salt and pepper.
5. Divide the tagliatelle between two warm serving bowls, sprinkle each serving with a teaspoon of Parmesan cheese and serve.

Exchanges per serving: Bread 1½, Protein 2, Vegetable ½, Optional Calories 120

WEEK 5

Breakfast:

1 medium persimmon
1oz (30g) cereal
¼ pint (150ml) skimmed milk

Lunch: Stuffed Egg Salad

Cut a hard-boiled egg in half
lengthways, scoop out the yolk and
mash with 3oz (90g) low-fat soft
cheese, 2 teaspoons chopped chives,
salt and a dash of pepper sauce. Pile
the mixture back into the cavities left
by the removal of the yolk.
Mixed Salad – shredded endive,
sliced cucumber, fennel, celery and
tomato, chopped peppers and spring
onion tossed in 4 teaspoons low-
calorie French dressing.

5fl oz (150ml) low-fat natural yogurt

Dinner:

3fl oz (90ml) sherry

∗ Refreshing Prawn Cocktail ∗

Turkey with Vegetables

3oz (90g) roast turkey
2 teaspoons cranberry sauce
6oz (180g) baked jacket potato with
1 teaspoon margarine.
Steamed or boiled asparagus and
carrots.

½ medium papaya sprinkled with
lime juice.

Snacks:

¼ pint (150ml) skimmed milk

Optional Calories: 215

REFRESHING PRAWN COCKTAIL

Serves 3
155 Calories per serving

1½ medium grapefruit
½ medium avocado
1½oz (45g) peeled prawns
6 black olives, pitted and sliced
1 tablespoon olive oil
4 teaspoons lemon juice
pinch of powdered mustard
1–2 teaspoons chopped chives
salt and pepper
shredded lettuce

1. Using a sharp knife, remove the peel and white pith from the grapefruit, cut between each membrane to separate into segments. Reserve all the juice which runs from the fruit during preparation.
2. Remove the skin from the avocado and slice thinly.
3. Mix the grapefruit segments, avocado, prawns and olives together.
4. Place the reserved grapefruit juice, oil, lemon juice, mustard, chives and a little salt and pepper into a small jar and shake well to mix. Alternatively whisk the ingredients together in a small basin.
5. Pour the dressing over the salad and mix well.
6. Place a little shredded lettuce on each serving plate or in a small glass, top with the prawn cocktail and serve.

Exchanges per serving: Fat 1, Fruit 1, Protein ½, Optional Calories 80

WEEK 4

Breakfast:

1oz (30g) dried apricots, chopped
1oz (30g) cereal
¼ pint (150ml) skimmed milk

Lunch: * Spinach Roulade *

1 tomato cut into wedges
¾oz (20g) French bread
1 teaspoon margarine.

½ medium ogen melon

Dinner: Trout with Vegetables

4oz (120g) trout fillet, poached in a little water and served with a wedge of lemon.
3oz (90g) cooked potato tossed in 1 teaspoon margarine and 1 teaspoon chopped mint.
Steamed or boiled asparagus and carrots.

Rhubarb and Custard – 8oz (240g) rhubarb stewed in the juice of 1 medium orange and sweetened with artificial sweetener.

Baked Egg Custard (page 190)

Snacks:

½ pint (300ml) skimmed milk

Optional Calories: 85

SPINACH ROULADE

Serves 4
235 Calories per serving

4 teaspoons margarine

1 shallot, finely chopped

2½oz (75g) small button mushrooms, finely sliced

¼ pint (150ml) skimmed milk

4 teaspoons cornflour

4oz (120g) cooked chicken

3oz (90g) drained, canned sweetcorn

salt and pepper

2 tablespoons finely grated Parmesan cheese

1lb (480g) frozen leaf spinach

2 eggs, separated

freshly grated nutmeg

4 teaspoons single cream

1. Heat 1 teaspoon margarine in a small saucepan. Stir-fry the shallot for 2 minutes, add the mushrooms and stir-fry for 2–3 minutes.
2. Blend a little milk with the cornflour, put to one side. Finely chop the chicken.
3. Add the remaining milk, chicken and sweetcorn to the saucepan, heat until steaming. Add the cornflour paste and bring to the boil, stirring all the time. Boil for 1–2 minutes and season with salt and pepper.
4. Line an 8 × 12 inch (20 × 30cm) Swiss roll tin with non-stick baking parchment and sprinkle with 1 tablespoon Parmesan cheese.
5. Cook the leaf spinach according to the packaging instructions, drain very well. Chop the spinach and stir in the remaining margarine and egg yolks. Season with freshly grated nutmeg, salt and pepper.
6. Whisk the egg whites with a pinch of salt until peaking, carefully fold into the spinach and spoon into the prepared tin. Bake at 400°F/200°C/Gas Mark 6 for 12–15 minutes until firm to touch. Meanwhile sprinkle a sheet of non-stick paper with the remaining cheese and add the cream to the sauce and reheat.
7. Turn the roulade upside down on to the sheet of paper, peel off the baking parchment and spread the sauce to within ¾ inch (1cm) of the edge. Roll up Swiss roll style, cut into 8 slices and serve.

Exchanges per serving: Bread ¼, Fat 1, Protein 1½, Vegetable 1½, Optional Calories 50

WEEK 2

Breakfast:

½ medium grapefruit
Toast a 1oz (30g) slice of bread, sprinkle with 1oz (30g) grated cheese, grill until bubbling. Serve with 1 tomato, sliced.

Lunch: Peach and Cottage Cheese Platter (page 129)

Green Salad – shredded lettuce, celery and green pepper tossed in 2 teaspoons low-calorie French dressing.

2½fl oz (75ml) low-fat natural yogurt

Dinner:

3oz (90g) roast pork, sliced

✱ Braised Red Cabbage ✱

6oz (180g) baked potato with 1 teaspoon margarine.

4oz (120g) drained, canned fruit salad served with 2 tablespoons natural juice.
2½fl oz (75ml) low-fat natural yogurt

Snacks:

½ pint (300ml) skimmed milk

Optional Calories: 35

BRAISED RED CABBAGE

Serves 4
75 Calories per serving

2 teaspoons margarine
1 small onion, chopped
1lb (480g) red cabbage, shredded
4fl oz (120ml) red wine
2 tablespoons red wine vinegar
2 teaspoons clear honey
½ teaspoon salt
½–1 teaspoon caraway seeds

1. Melt the margarine in a saucepan, add the onion and stir-fry for 2–3 minutes.
2. Add the red cabbage to the saucepan and continue stirring for 2–3 minutes.
3. Mix the red wine, red wine vinegar, honey, salt and caraway seeds together, pour into the saucepan and stir well.
4. Bring to the boil over a moderate heat, reduce the heat as low as possible, cover the saucepan and simmer for about 1 hour, stirring occasionally until most of the liquid has been absorbed.
5. If desired this recipe may be cooked in the oven. The initial stir-frying should be carried out in a flameproof dish, then after bringing to the boil cover and transfer to a preheated oven, 325°F/160°C/Gas Mark 3, for about 1 hour, stirring occasionally during cooking.

Exchanges per serving: Fat ½, Vegetable 1½, Optional Calories 35

WEEK 5
Breakfast: Swiss Muesli
(page 52)

Lunch: Sardine and Tomato Roll

Cut a 1½oz (45g) roll in half and spread with 2 teaspoons low-fat spread. Cover one half with slices of tomato and carefully spread 2oz (60g) drained, canned and mashed sardine on top. Season with salt and pepper and sandwich together with the other half.
Green Salad – sliced cucumber, fennel, celery and sprigs of watercress tossed in 2 teaspoons low-calorie French dressing.
4fl oz (120ml) vegetable juice.

1 medium persimmon

Dinner:

5oz (150g) beef sausages, grilled

✲ Stir-Fried Vegetables ✲

5fl oz (150ml) low-fat fruit yogurt

Snacks:

¼ pint (150ml) skimmed milk

Optional Calories: 65

STIR-FRIED VEGETABLES
Serves 4
125 Calories per serving

2 tablespoons sesame oil

2 cloves garlic, chopped

2 teaspoons chopped fresh root ginger

1 leek, sliced

½ red pepper, seeded and cut in strips

2oz (60g) fennel, sliced

2oz (60g) green beans, cut in 1 inch (2.5cm) lengths

2oz (60g) carrots, cut in 1 inch (2.5cm) lengths

2oz (60g) mushrooms, sliced

4oz (120g) broccoli florets

3oz (90g) baby corn, halved or quartered if large

3oz (90g) water chestnuts, sliced

1 tablespoon tomato purée

5 tablespoons water

1 tablespoon soy sauce

2oz (60g) bean sprouts

1. Heat the oil in a large saucepan, add the garlic and ginger and stir-fry for 1–2 minutes.
2. Add the leek, red pepper and fennel and stir-fry for 2–3 minutes.
3. Remove the pan from the heat and add the beans, carrots, mushrooms, broccoli, corn and water chestnuts.
4. Mix the tomato purée, water and soy sauce together, pour into the saucepan and mix well.
5. Return the saucepan to the heat, stir until the liquid boils, reduce the heat, cover and simmer for 5 minutes. Stir in the bean sprouts and simmer for a further 2 minutes, serve.

Exchanges per serving: Bread ½, Fat 1½, Vegetable 1½, Optional Calories 5

WEEK 4

Breakfast:

½ medium banana, sliced
1oz (30g) cereal
¼ pint (150ml) skimmed milk

Lunch: Cottage Cheese Salad

Mix 4oz (120g) cottage cheese with
2 teaspoons low-calorie mayonnaise
and a good pinch of curry powder.

Russian Salad (page 117)

Tomato and Cucumber Salad –
1 tomato sliced and mixed with a
2 inch (5cm) wedge of cucumber,
sliced and sprinkled with 2 teaspoons
chopped chives and 2 teaspoons
French dressing.
Spread 1 slice of reduced-calorie
bread with 1 teaspoon low-fat spread

Dinner: * Scallops Gratinée *

4fl oz (120ml) white wine

Lamb with Vegetables

3oz (90g) roast lamb
Steamed or boiled mange-tout,
cauliflower and aubergine.

Kiwi and Raspberry Salad – 1 kiwi
fruit sliced and mixed with 5oz (150g)
raspberries and 1 teaspoon caster
sugar.

Snacks:

12½fl oz (375ml) skimmed milk

Optional Calories: 190

SCALLOPS GRATINÉE

Serves 3
205 Calories per serving

9oz (270g) potato
salt
1 tablespoon skimmed milk
4oz (120g) scallops
4 tablespoons white wine
1½ teaspoons margarine
1 tablespoon flour
3 tablespoons single cream
1 tablespoon chopped chives
pepper
2½ teaspoons finely grated Parmesan cheese
sprigs of parsley (optional)

1. Boil the potato in salted water until cooked, drain and mash with the milk. Place in a piping bag fitted with a ½ inch (1.25cm) fluted nozzle. Pipe round three rounded scallop shells, and put to one side.
2. Place the scallops and white wine in a saucepan, cover and simmer for about 8 minutes. Drain, reserving the liquid and roughly chop the scallops.
3. Melt the margarine in a small saucepan, add the flour and stir round. Gradually blend in the fish liquid, cream and chives. Bring to the boil, stirring all the time. Boil for 1 minute, stir in the scallops and season the sauce with salt and pepper.
4. Place the scallop shells with the piped potato under a hot grill until beginning to brown. Remove from the heat, spoon the scallop sauce into each shell, sprinkle with Parmesan cheese and grill until golden. Garnish with parsley and serve.

Exchanges per serving: Bread 1, Fat ½, Protein 1, Optional Calories 70

Scallops Gratinée, served with white wine

VEGETARIAN WEEK 1

Breakfast:

4fl oz (120ml) orange juice
Toast a 1oz (30g) slice of bread, spread with 1 tablespoon peanut butter.

Lunch: ✳ Stuffed Tomatoes ✳

Green Salad – shredded lettuce, sliced green pepper, celery, spring onion and sprigs of watercress tossed in 2 teaspoons French dressing.

1 medium pear

Dinner: Burger with Vegetables

1 vegetarian burger
Steamed or boiled carrots, cauliflower and leeks.

5fl oz (150ml) low-fat natural yogurt

Snacks:

½ pint (300ml) skimmed milk

STUFFED TOMATOES

Serves 2
305 Calories per serving

2 × 10oz (300g) tomatoes
salt
1 teaspoon vegetable oil
1 onion, chopped
2oz (60g) curd cheese
1oz (30g) pine nuts
2oz (60g) fresh breadcrumbs
1 egg, beaten
1 tablespoon finely chopped basil
pepper

1. Slice the top off each tomato and reserve. Scoop out the inside of the tomato and discard or put to one side for use in a tomato based recipe. Sprinkle the inside of the tomatoes with salt and leave upside down in a colander or on a rack to drain for about 15 minutes while preparing the stuffing.
2. Heat the oil in a saucepan, add the onion and stir-fry for 6–7 minutes until soft.
3. Mix the curd cheese and pine nuts into the onion. Add the breadcrumbs and mix well to evenly distribute the ingredients.
4. Add the egg and basil and mix once again, season to taste with salt and pepper.
5. Rinse the tomatoes well and pat dry with kitchen paper. Spoon the stuffing into the tomatoes, stand in a baking tin lined with a sheet of non-stick paper and bake at 350°F/180°C/Gas Mark 4 for 20–25 minutes, then replace the tomato tops and bake for a further 5–10 minutes.

Exchanges per serving: Bread 1, Fat 1, Protein 2, Vegetable 1½

VEGETARIAN WEEK 5

Breakfast:

½ medium papaya with a little lime juice squeezed over the fruit.
Toast a 1oz (30g) slice of bread and top with 3oz (90g) hot baked beans.

Lunch: ✳ Nutty Fruit Rice ✳

Green Salad – shredded lettuce, sliced cucumber, green pepper, celery and spring onion with sprigs of watercress.

5fl oz (150ml) low-fat natural yogurt

Dinner: Peppered Frittata (page 177)

3oz (90g) sweetcorn
Steamed or boiled green beans and cauliflower.

5oz (150g) raspberries sprinkled with 1 teaspoon caster sugar and topped with 1½ tablespoons double cream.

Snacks:

½ pint (300ml) skimmed milk

Optional Calories: 95

NUTTY FRUIT RICE

Serves 3
305 Calories per serving

3oz (90g) long-grain brown rice
6fl oz (180ml) orange juice
1½oz (45g) cashew nuts
½oz (15g) sultanas
2 medium apricots
4 teaspoons lemon juice
1 tablespoon walnut oil
pinch of powdered mustard
salt and pepper
1½oz (45g) blue cheese, crumbled
a few lettuce, radicchio or endive leaves

1. Place the rice in a saucepan, add the orange juice and cook according to the packaging instructions, adding more water if necessary. Boil until all the liquid has been absorbed.
2. Transfer the cooked rice to a bowl, stir in the cashew nuts and sultanas.
3. Cut the apricots in half, remove the stones and either cut the fruit into thin wedges or chop. Toss in 1 teaspoon of the lemon juice, and add to the rice.
4. Pour the remaining lemon juice, oil, mustard and a little salt and pepper into a small screw-top jar, secure and shake well. Alternatively whisk all the ingredients together in a small bowl.
5. Stir the dressing through the nutty rice, add the crumbled blue cheese and serve in a bowl surrounded by the lettuce, radicchio or endive leaves.

Exchanges per serving: Bread 1, Fat 1½, Fruit 1, Protein 1½, Vegetable ¼

WEEK 4

Breakfast:

4fl oz (120ml) orange juice
1oz (30g) cereal
¼ pint (150ml) skimmed milk

Lunch: Filled Baked Potato

Split a 6oz (180g) baked potato in half, and top with 6oz (180g) hot baked beans.
Green Salad – shredded lettuce, sliced cucumber, spring onion and celery tossed in 2 teaspoons French dressing.

Dinner: ✻ Melon Appetiser with Raspberry Sauce ✻

Poached Smoked Haddock with Vegetables

4oz (120g) poached smoked haddock
Grilled tomatoes
Steamed or boiled green beans.

5oz (150g) strawberries sprinkled with 1 teaspoon caster sugar, topped with 2½ tablespoons low-fat natural yogurt.

Snacks:

½ pint (300ml) skimmed milk

Optional Calories: 45

MELON APPETISER WITH RASPBERRY SAUCE

Serves 2
80 Calories per serving

5oz (150g) raspberries

1–1½ teaspoons chopped mint

2 teaspoons caster sugar

1 teaspoon arrowroot

2½fl oz (75ml) low-fat natural yogurt

½ medium cantaloupe melon, e.g. ogen or charentais

sprigs of fresh mint

1. Sieve the raspberries to remove all the seeds and press firmly against the sieve mesh to ensure all the juices are extracted.
2. Stir the chopped mint and sugar into the raspberry juice. Blend a little of the juice with the arrowroot and put to one side.
3. Heat the raspberry and mint juice until the sugar has dissolved, stir in the arrowroot mixture and bring to the boil, stirring all the time. Leave to cool then adjust the seasoning by adding a little extra chopped mint if necessary.
4. Add the yogurt and stir unevenly through the cold raspberry-mint sauce.
5. Scoop all the seeds out of the melon, peel off the skin and slice thinly. Arrange the slices of melon on to serving plates, pour over the raspberry-mint sauce and decorate with sprigs of fresh mint.

Exchanges per serving: Fruit 1, Milk ¼, Optional Calories 25

Melon Appetiser with Raspberry Sauce

MAIN COURSE RECIPES

WEEK 1

Breakfast:

1 medium pear
1oz (30g) cereal
¼ pint (150ml) skimmed milk

Lunch: Salmon Salad

2oz (60g) drained, canned salmon, flaked and mixed with 1 teaspoon chopped chives and squeeze of lemon juice.
Mixed Salad – shredded lettuce, sliced cucumber, tomato, spring onion and peppers.
Crispbread up to 60 Calories spread with 1 teaspoon margarine.

1 medium orange

Dinner: ✶ Blue Cheese Soufflé ✶

Steamed or boiled carrots and courgettes.

4oz (120g) drained, canned fruit salad with 2 tablespoons fruit juice and 2½fl oz (75ml) low-fat natural yogurt.

Snacks:

7½fl oz (235ml) skimmed milk

BLUE CHEESE SOUFFLÉ

Serves 2
415 Calories per serving

4 teaspoons margarine

½oz (15g) flour

¼ pint (150ml) skimmed milk

3oz (90g) blue cheese, e.g. Gorgonzola, grated

3 eggs, separated

1 tablespoon chopped chives

good pinch of powdered mustard

salt and pepper

1. Use a small amount of the margarine to grease a 6 inch (15cm) soufflé dish.
2. Heat the remaining margarine in a 2 pint (1.2 litre) saucepan, add the flour and cook over a low heat for 1–2 minutes, stirring continuously.
3. Remove from the heat and gradually blend in the milk. Bring to the boil, stirring all the time, boil for 1–2 minutes until very thick.
4. Allow to cool a little, stir in the cheese, egg yolks, chives and mustard and season to taste with salt and pepper.
5. Whisk the egg whites with a pinch of salt until peaking. Using a tablespoon fold the egg whites into the cheese sauce. Spoon into the prepared dish and bake at 350°F/180°C/Gas Mark 4 for 35–40 minutes until golden brown and well-risen. Serve immediately.

Exchanges per serving: Bread ¼, Fat 2, Milk ¼, Protein 3

Alternative – Cheese and Spinach Soufflé – replace the blue cheese with grated Cheddar or Gruyère cheese and add 3oz (90g) cooked, extremely well-drained chopped spinach to the sauce – add Vegetable Exchange ½

WEEK 2

Breakfast:

1 medium apple
1oz (30g) cereal
¼ pint (150ml) skimmed milk

Lunch: Peach and Cottage Cheese Platter (page 129)

Crispbread up to 40 Calories spread with 1 teaspoon low-fat spread.

5fl oz (150ml) low-fat natural yogurt

Dinner: ✱ Cottager's Pie ✱

Tomato and Cucumber Salad – slices of tomato and cucumber arranged in a bowl, sprinkled with 2 teaspoons chopped chives and 1 tablespoon low-calorie French dressing.

1 medium orange

Snacks:

¼ pint (150ml) skimmed milk

Optional Calories: 10

COTTAGER'S PIE

Serves 2
425 Calories per serving

8oz (240g) minced beef or lamb
1½ teaspoons vegetable oil
1 small leek, sliced
2oz (60g) mushrooms, chopped
1 teaspoon flour
1 tablespoon tomato purée
3oz (90g) carrot, diced
1 small (8oz/227g) can chopped tomatoes
1 teaspoon basil
¼ teaspoon celery seeds
salt and pepper
9oz (270g) peeled potatoes
1oz (30g) fromage frais
½oz (15g) mature Cheddar cheese, grated
¼ teaspoon mustard

1. Form the minced meat into patties, arrange on the rack of a grill pan and grill, turning once, under a moderate heat until the fat stops dripping.
2. Heat the oil in a saucepan, add the leek and stir-fry for 4 minutes. Add the mushrooms, stir round and mix in the flour. Remove from the heat.
3. Stir the tomato purée, carrot, chopped tomatoes, herbs, seasoning and crumbled mince into the saucepan. Bring to the boil and simmer gently for 4–5 minutes, stirring occasionally.
4. Boil the potatoes in salted water, drain and mash the potatoes with the fromage frais, cheese and mustard, season with salt and pepper.
5. Spoon the minced meat into an ovenproof dish, spread the potato over the top and roughen with a fork. Bake at 375°F/190°C/Gas Mark 5 for 30 minutes; if necessary brown under a moderate grill.

Exchanges per serving: Bread 1½, Fat ¾, Protein 3½, Vegetable 3, Optional Calories 10

WEEK 4

Breakfast:

½ medium banana
1oz (30g) cereal
¼ pint skimmed milk

Lunch: Smoked Salmon Roll

½oz (15g) slice of smoked salmon
spread with 3oz (90g) low-fat soft
cheese mixed with 2 teaspoons
chopped chives and a squeeze of
lemon juice then rolled up Swiss-roll
style.
Mixed Salad – shredded lettuce,
sliced fennel, peppers, radish, celery
and spring onion tossed in
1 tablespoon of low-calorie French
dressing.

2½fl oz (75ml) low-fat natural yogurt
½ medium mango

Dinner: ✳ Boeuf Bourguignon ✳

6oz (180g) potatoes, mashed with
1½ teaspoons margarine.
Steamed or boiled mange-tout and
carrots.

Strawberries and Ice Cream – 5oz
(150g) strawberries sprinkled with
1 teaspoon caster sugar and served
with 2oz (60g) vanilla ice cream.

Snacks:

½ pint (300ml) skimmed milk

Optional Calories: 195

BOEUF BOURGUIGNON

Serves 4
355 Calories per serving

1lb 2oz (540g) leg of beef, all visible fat removed

½ pint (300ml) Burgundy wine

bouquet garni

1 clove garlic, peeled but whole

a few rings of onion

1½oz (45g) lean back bacon

¼ pint (150ml) beef stock

1 tablespoon vegetable oil

12 baby onions

6oz (180g) mushrooms, sliced

4 teaspoons cornflour

2 teaspoons chopped parsley

1. This recipe is best prepared the day before it is to be eaten so do not pre-cook the meat as the fat can be skimmed off after the initial cooking. Cut the meat into large cubes, place in a non-metallic container, pour over the Burgundy and add the bouquet garni, garlic and onion. Leave in the cool to marinate for 3–4 hours.
2. Cut the bacon into thin strips, place the bacon, beef and marinade in a casserole with 4fl oz (120ml) stock. Cook at 325°F/160°C/Gas Mark 3 for 2½ hours. Leave overnight for the flavours to develop.
3. Heat the oil in a saucepan, stir-fry the onions until golden brown, add the mushrooms and remove from the heat.
4. Skim any fat from the surface of the casserole, remove the garlic and bouquet garni.
5. Blend the cornflour with the remaining beef stock. Stir the beef etc. and the stock into the saucepan, bring to the boil stirring all the time. Cover and simmer gently for 20–25 minutes. Transfer to a warm serving dish, sprinkle with parsley and serve.

Exchanges per serving: Fat ¾, Protein 4, Vegetable 1, Optional Calories 75

WEEK 3

Breakfast:

Pineapple Buttermilk Froth – place 4oz (120g) drained, canned pineapple pieces in a blender with ¼ pint (150ml) buttermilk and 1 teaspoon sugar. Process until frothy. Serve immediately.

Toast a 1oz (30g) slice of bread, sprinkle 1oz (30g) grated Cheddar cheese over one side and grill until bubbling. Serve with 1 tomato, sliced.

Lunch: Green Pea Soup (page 110)

1oz (30g) French bread spread with 1 teaspoon margarine.

Egg and Cottage Cheese Salad

1 hard-boiled egg, halved lengthways, the yolk scooped out and mashed with 2oz (60g) cottage cheese, 1 teaspoon low-calorie mayonnaise and 1 teaspoon chopped chives, then spooned back into the egg white halves.

Green Salad – shredded lettuce, sliced cucumber, spring onion and pepper.

Dinner: * Moussaka *

3oz (90g) boiled or baked potato

4oz (120g) canned mandarin segments topped with 3 tablespoons frozen whipped topping.

Snacks:

4fl oz (120ml) orange juice
7½fl oz (225ml) skimmed milk

Optional Calories: 95

MOUSSAKA

Serves 4
390 Calories per serving

12oz (360g) aubergines, sliced
salt
14oz (420g) minced lamb
2 teaspoons vegetable oil
1 clove garlic, chopped
3 onions, sliced
6 tomatoes, peeled and sliced
4 tablespoons water or vegetable stock
1 tablespoon tomato purée
¼ teaspoon mixed herbs
4 teaspoons margarine
3 tablespoons flour
½ pint (300ml) skimmed milk
2oz (60g) cheese, grated

1. Sprinkle the aubergines with salt, place in a sieve and leave to drain for 30 minutes. Then rinse well, plunge into boiling water and boil for 2–3 minutes, drain and put to one side.
2. Form the minced lamb into patties, place on the rack of a grill pan, grill until the fat stops dripping, turning from time to time.
3. Heat the oil, add the garlic and onion, stir-fry for 5 minutes or until the onion is soft and translucent.
4. Place half the onion on the base of an ovenproof dish, crumble over half the mince and top with half the tomatoes. Repeat these layers, cover with overlapping slices of aubergine.
5. Mix together the water or stock, tomato purée and herbs, pour over the aubergines.
6. Heat the margarine, add the flour and stir to mix. Remove from the heat and gradually blend in the milk. Bring to the boil, stirring all the time, boil for 1 minute, remove from the heat, add the cheese and stir until melted.
7. Pour the cheese sauce evenly over the aubergine and bake at 350°F/180°C/Gas Mark 4 for 30–40 minutes.

Exchanges per serving: Fat 1½, Milk ¼, Protein 3, Vegetable 3, Optional Calories 25

WEEK 4

Breakfast:

1oz (30g) dried apricots, chopped
1oz (30g) cereal
¼ pint (150ml) skimmed milk

Lunch: Cottage Cheese with Russian Salad

3oz (90g) cottage cheese mixed with
2 teaspoons chopped chives and
1 teaspoon mayonnaise.

Russian Salad (page 117)

1 slice of reduced-calorie bread
spread with 1 teaspoon margarine.

½ medium mango

Dinner: ✳ Somerset Casserole ✳

3oz (90g) potatoes, mashed
Steamed or boiled carrots and
courgettes.

Apple and Cheese – 1 medium apple
and 1oz (30g) hard cheese.

Snacks:

12½fl oz (375ml) skimmed milk

Optional Calories: 60

SOMERSET CASSEROLE

Serves 4
415 Calories per serving

4 × 4½oz (135g) boned lamb loin chops
4 teaspoons vegetable oil
2 leeks, sliced
1 green pepper, seeded and cut in strips
3 sticks celery, sliced
4 teaspoons flour
2 tablespoons cranberry sauce
½ pint (300ml) cider
2 tablespoons finely chopped mint
salt and pepper

1. Lay the chops on the rack of a grill pan, grill under a moderate heat, turning once until the fat stops dripping from the meat.
2. Heat the oil in a flameproof casserole, add the leeks and stir-fry for 3–4 minutes.
3. Stir the green pepper and celery into the casserole, sprinkle with the flour and remove from the heat.
4. Gradually blend in the cranberry sauce and cider. Mix in the mint, season with a little salt and pepper. Add the chops and bring to the boil, stirring all the time.
5. Cover the casserole and transfer to a moderate oven, 350°F/180°C/Gas Mark 4 for 45 minutes.

Exchanges per serving: Fat 1, Protein 3½, Vegetable 1¼, Optional Calories 60

WEEK 4

Breakfast:

1 medium apple
1oz (30g) cereal
¼ pint (150ml) skimmed milk

Lunch: Tuna and Cottage Cheese Salad

1½oz (45g) drained, canned tuna, flaked and mixed with 2oz (60g) cottage cheese, a large pinch of curry powder and 2 teaspoons low-calorie mayonnaise.
Tomato and Cucumber Salad –
1 tomato, sliced and mixed with a 2 inch (5cm) wedge of cucumber, sliced and sprinkled with 2 teaspoons chopped chives.
Green Salad – shredded lettuce, sliced celery, green pepper and spring onion with sprigs of watercress.

4oz (120g) cherries

Dinner: ✳ Braised Beef ✳

6oz (180g) baked jacket potato with 1 teaspoon margarine.
Steamed or boiled green beans.

4oz (120g) drained, canned mandarins with 2 tablespoons natural juice and 2½fl oz (75ml) natural yogurt.
4fl oz (120ml) red wine

Snacks:

½ pint (300ml) skimmed milk

Optional Calories: 110

BRAISED BEEF

Serves 6
395 Calories per serving

2½–3lb (1.2–1.4kg) topside – ask your butcher to prepare this without the usual covering of fat
2 tablespoons vegetable oil
8oz (240g) baby onions
4 large sticks celery, cut into 3 inch (8cm) lengths
1lb 12oz (840g) mixture of root vegetables, e.g. parsnip, swede, turnip, cut in large chunks
9oz (270g) carrots, leave whole if small or cut large carrots into big chunks
¾ pint (450ml) beef stock
bouquet garni
4 teaspoons cornflour
2 teaspoons chopped parsley

1. Place the topside on a grill rack and grill, turning from time to time until the fat stops dripping from the joint.
2. Heat the oil in a very large flameproof casserole and stir-fry the baby onions until beginning to brown.
3. Add all the remaining vegetables and stir well to mix, pour in the stock which should cover about half the vegetables. If necessary make a slight dip in the vegetables and lay the joint on the vegetable base, add the bouquet garni.
4. Bring to the boil over a low heat. Cover tightly, if necessary weigh down the casserole lid and place in a moderate oven, 325°F/160°C/Gas Mark 3 for 2½–3 hours until the topside is tender.
5. Remove the joint and strain the vegetables, discard the bouquet garni. Keep warm. Blend the cornflour to a paste with a little of the stock, bring to a rapid boil stirring all the time. Either serve the beef as a joint with vegetables sprinkled with parsley surrounding it or sliced. Allow 3½oz (105g) beef per person. Serve the gravy separately.

Exchanges per serving: Fat 1, Protein 3½, Vegetable 2½, Optional Calories 10

Braised Beef with a jacket potato and green beans, served with red wine

WEEK 1

Breakfast:

4fl oz (120ml) orange juice
1oz (30g) cereal
¼ pint (150ml) skimmed milk

Lunch: Tuna or Salmon Sandwich

Spread 2 slices of reduced-calorie bread with 2 teaspoons margarine. Arrange a few lettuce leaves over one slice and top with slices of cucumber. Flake 2oz (60g) drained, canned tuna or salmon, season with a little lemon juice, mix with 1 teaspoon mayonnaise and spread over the cucumber. Top with a few sprigs of watercress and sandwich together the slices of bread. Serve with 1 tomato.

Dinner: ✱ Barbecued Pork ✱

Steamed or boiled courgettes, carrots and cauliflower.

4oz (120g) drained, canned fruit salad served with 2 tablespoons natural juice and 2½fl oz (75ml) low-fat natural yogurt.

Snacks:

½ pint (300ml) skimmed milk

Optional Calories: 40

BARBECUED PORK

Serves 1
280 Calories per serving

2oz (60g) crushed pineapple

2 teaspoons set honey

2 teaspoons soy sauce

½ teaspoon chopped rosemary

good pinch of chilli powder

salt

4oz (120g) lean boned loin pork chop

1. Mix the crushed pineapple and its juices with the honey and soy sauce.
2. Stir in the rosemary, chilli powder and a little salt.
3. Lay the pork in a non-metallic dish, pour over the pineapple mixture and leave to marinate in the cool for about 3 hours, turn the pork or spoon the marinade over during this time.
4. Cook the pork chop over a barbecue or under a moderate grill, turning once, but continually spooning over the remaining marinade.

Exchanges per serving: Fruit ½, Protein 3, Optional Calories 40

WEEK 1

Breakfast:

4fl oz (120ml) grapefruit juice
1oz (30g) cereal
¼ pint (150ml) skimmed milk

Lunch: Cottage Cheese and Tuna Salad

Mix 2oz (60g) cottage cheese with
1oz (30g) drained and flaked, canned
tuna, 1 teaspoon chopped chives and
1½ teaspoons mayonnaise.
Mixed Salad – shredded lettuce,
sliced cucumber, red pepper,
radishes and sprigs of watercress.
1oz (30g) French bread spread with
1 teaspoon margarine.

Dinner: ✳ Orange Pork ✳

Steamed or boiled chicory.

4oz (120g) canned fruit salad
5fl oz (150ml) low-fat natural yogurt

Snacks:

¼ pint (150ml) skimmed milk

Optional Calories: 15

ORANGE PORK

Serves 4
275 Calories per serving

1lb (480g) fillet or loin of pork
2 teaspoons vegetable oil
3 leeks, thickly sliced
6oz (180g) carrots, sliced
2 sticks celery, sliced and leaves reserved
sprigs of rosemary
4fl oz (120ml) vegetable stock
8fl oz (240ml) orange juice
2 tablespoons cornflour
8oz (240g) calabrese broccoli
1 medium orange
salt and pepper

1. Place the pork on the rack of a grill pan and grill under a moderate heat until the fat stops dripping. Allow to cool then cut into cubes.
2. Heat the oil in a saucepan, add the leeks and stir-fry for 2 minutes. Add the carrots, sliced celery, rosemary, pork and vegetable stock.
3. Gradually blend the orange juice into the cornflour and stir into the saucepan. Bring to the boil, stirring all the time. Reduce the heat, cover and simmer very gently for 30 minutes, stirring occasionally.
4. Slice the stalk of the broccoli and separate the florets. Using a sharp knife remove the peel and white pith from the orange and separate into segments.
5. Stir the broccoli and orange into the pork mixture, season to taste and simmer for a further 5–10 minutes. Transfer to a warm serving dish.
6. Finely chop the reserved celery leaves and sprinkle over the pork and orange before serving.

Exchanges per serving: Fat ½, Fruit ¾, Protein 3, Vegetable 2, Optional Calories 15

WEEK 4

Breakfast:

4fl oz (120ml) orange juice
Toast a 1oz (30g) slice of bread,
spread with 1 teaspoon margarine
and top with a poached egg.

Lunch: Liver Sausage Salad

2oz (60g) liver sausage, sliced and
served with a mixed salad of
shredded lettuce, sliced fennel,
cucumber, tomato and peppers and
sprinkled with mustard and cress,
tossed in 2 teaspoons low-calorie
French dressing.

Pineapple Buttermilk Froth – place
4oz (120g) drained, canned
pineapple pieces in a blender with
¼ pint (150ml) buttermilk and
1 teaspoon sugar, process until
frothy, serve immediately.

Dinner: * Peppered Pork Stroganoff *

6oz (180g) long-grain rice or noodles
(cooked weight).

4oz (120g) cherries

Snacks:

¾ pint (450ml) skimmed milk

Optional Calories: 120

PEPPERED PORK STROGANOFF

Serves 2
350 Calories per serving

8oz (240g) tenderloin or fillet of pork
1 tablespoon sunflower oil
1 small onion, thinly sliced
½ green pepper, seeded and sliced
½ red pepper, seeded and sliced
½ yellow pepper, seeded and sliced
2oz (60g) mushrooms, thinly sliced
6 tablespoons soured cream
salt and pepper

1. Place the pork on a grill rack under a moderate heat, turning once, until the fat stops dripping. Allow to cool.
2. Heat the oil in a saucepan. Add the onion and stir-fry for 2 minutes. Add the peppers and continue cooking for 6–7 minutes until soft.
3. Thinly slice the pork and add to the saucepan with the mushrooms, stir-fry over a moderate heat for 4–5 minutes.
4. Remove from the heat and stir in the soured cream. Season to taste with salt and pepper.

Exchanges per serving: Fat 1½, Protein 3, Vegetable 1½, Optional Calories 100

Peppered Pork Stroganoff

WEEK 1

Breakfast:

½ medium grapefruit
1oz (30g) cereal
¼ pint (150ml) skimmed milk

Lunch: Toasted Cheese

Toast 2 slices of reduced-calorie
bread, sprinkle with 2oz (60g) grated
hard cheese and grill until bubbling.
Serve topped with slices of tomato.
Green Salad – lettuce, sliced
cucumber, celery and green pepper
with 1½ teaspoons mayonnaise.

Red Cabbage Salad (page 112)

Dinner: ✳ Veal Stew ✳

4oz (120g) fruit salad with 2½fl oz
(75ml) low-fat natural yogurt.

Snacks:

½ pint (300ml) skimmed milk

Optional Calories: 15

VEAL STEW

Serves 2
215 Calories per serving

1 onion
1 green pepper
3 sticks celery
1 clove garlic
8oz (240g) stewing veal
1 teaspoon safflower oil
1 tablespoon flour
1 small (8oz/227g) can chopped tomatoes
¼ pint (150ml) vegetable stock
½ teaspoon oregano
salt and pepper

1. Slice the onion. Remove the core and seeds from the pepper,
   cut into 1 inch (2.5cm) dice. Thickly slice the celery and
   finely chop the garlic.
2. Cut the veal into cubes and put to one side.
3. Heat the oil in a saucepan, add the garlic and stir-fry for
   1 minute, add the veal and stir round until it loses its
   pinkness.
4. Sprinkle the flour into the saucepan and mix well. Gradually
   stir in the tomatoes and stock, then the remaining
   ingredients.
5. Bring to the boil stirring continuously, reduce the heat, cover
   and simmer very gently for 50–60 minutes.

**Exchanges per serving: Fat ½, Protein 3, Vegetable 3,
Optional Calories 15**

WEEK 2

Breakfast:

½ medium banana, sliced
1oz (30g) cereal
¼ pint (150ml) skimmed milk

Lunch: Tuna and Cottage Cheese Salad

Mash 1oz (30g) drained, canned tuna
with 2oz (60g) cottage cheese,
1 teaspoon chopped chives,
2 teaspoons mayonnaise and a good
pinch of curry powder. Serve with a
tomato and cucumber salad sprinkled
with 1 tablespoon chopped spring
onion and 2 teaspoons low-calorie
French dressing, grated carrot and
sprigs of watercress.

Dinner: ✳ Spaghetti Bolognaise ✳

5oz (150g) chunks of watermelon
5fl oz (150ml) low-fat natural yogurt

Snacks:

4fl oz (120ml) grapefruit juice
¼ pint (150ml) skimmed milk

Optional Calories: 70

SPAGHETTI BOLOGNAISE

Serves 2
415 Calories per serving

1 teaspoon vegetable oil
1 clove garlic, chopped
1 onion, finely chopped
1 carrot, finely chopped
1 stick celery, finely chopped
8oz (240g) minced veal
4fl oz (120ml) white wine
1 small (8oz/227g) can chopped tomatoes
4fl oz (120ml) strong vegetable stock
good pinch of mixed herbs
salt and pepper
3oz (90g) spaghetti
4 teaspoons finely grated Parmesan cheese

1. Heat the oil in a saucepan, add the garlic and onion and stir-fry for 2–3 minutes.
2. Stir the carrot, celery, veal, wine, tomatoes and stock into the saucepan. Add the herbs and a little salt and pepper.
3. Bring to the boil, reduce the heat, partially cover and simmer for 30 minutes stirring occasionally. Remove the saucepan lid and cook for a further 5–10 minutes until reduced.
4. Cook the spaghetti according to the packaging instructions in boiling salted water, drain.
5. Divide the spaghetti between two serving plates, spoon over the sauce and sprinkle with the Parmesan cheese.

Exchanges per serving: Bread 1½, Fat ½, Protein 3, Vegetable 1½, Optional Calories 70

WEEK 5

Breakfast:

4fl oz (120ml) orange juice
1 croissant spread with 1 teaspoon butter and 1 tablespoon strawberry jam

Lunch: Scrambled Egg and Baked Beans

Beat 1 egg with 2 tablespoons skimmed milk from snack allowance, season with salt and pepper. Melt 1 teaspoon margarine in a saucepan, add the egg and stir over a low heat until thickened. Serve with 6oz (180g) baked beans and a 1oz (30g) slice of bread toasted and spread with 1 teaspoon margarine.

5fl oz (150ml) low-fat natural yogurt

Dinner: ∗ Curried Chicken Salad ∗

Green Salad – shredded lettuce, cucumber and celery tossed in 1 teaspoon low-calorie French dressing.

5oz (150g) blackberries sprinkled with 1 teaspoon caster sugar and served with 1 tablespoon double cream.

Snacks:

½ pint (300ml) skimmed milk

Optional Calories: 265

CURRIED CHICKEN SALAD

Serves 4
330 Calories per serving

1 tablespoon vegetable oil
1 onion, chopped
4oz (120g) long-grain rice
Approximately 1 tablespoon Madras curry powder
1 red pepper, seeded and chopped
3oz (90g) bean sprouts
6 radishes, sliced
8 black olives, pitted and halved
4oz (120g) drained, canned sliced peaches, or 1 medium fresh peach
lemon juice
1 medium orange
2 kiwi fruit
12oz (360g) cooked chicken or smoked chicken, diced
2 heads chicory

1. Heat the oil in a saucepan, add the onion and stir-fry for 4–5 minutes. Stir in the rice and curry powder. Pour in the recommended amount of water according to the packaging instructions and boil as directed until all the water has been absorbed.
2. Allow the rice to cool then stir in the red pepper, bean sprouts, radishes, olives and canned peaches. If using a fresh peach, cut in half, discard the stone, slice, toss in lemon juice and add to the rice.
3. Using a sharp knife cut the orange peel, including all the white pith from the orange. Cut between the membranes to remove the orange segments.
4. Peel and slice the kiwi fruit, leave the slices whole or cut in half. Stir the orange, kiwi fruit and chicken into the rice.
5. Separate the chicory leaves and arrange round the edge of the serving dish or individual dishes, chop the remaining leaves and add to the chicken and rice, pile into the lined dish.

Exchanges per serving: Bread 1, Fat ¾, Fruit 1, Protein 3, Vegetable 1½, Optional Calories 10

Curried Chicken Salad

WEEK 2

Breakfast:

Pineapple Buttermilk Froth – place 4oz (120g) drained, canned pineapple pieces in a blender with ¼ pint (150ml) buttermilk and 1 teaspoon sugar. Process until smooth and frothy. Serve immediately. Spread 2 rice cakes with 1 teaspoon margarine and 1 tablespoon marmalade.

Lunch: Sardine Salad

2oz (60g) drained, canned sardines served with a wedge of lemon Mixed Salad – shredded lettuce, sliced tomato, cucumber, peppers and onion tossed in 2 teaspoons French dressing.

1 medium orange

Dinner: * Chicken and Ham Bake *

3oz (90g) boiled potato
Steamed or boiled asparagus, carrots and Brussels sprouts.

4oz (120g) fruit salad served with 2½fl oz (75ml) low-fat natural yogurt.
½ pint (300ml) cider

Snacks:

½ pint (300ml) skimmed milk

Optional Calories: 170

CHICKEN AND HAM BAKE

Serves 1
265 Calories per serving

3½oz (105g) skinned, boned chicken breast
¼ teaspoon tarragon
½oz (15g) slice cooked ham
½oz (15g) Gruyère, grated
1 teaspoon margarine
½ small yellow or red pepper, seeded and cut in strips
1 tablespoon chopped spring onion
1 small courgette, cut in thin strips
2 teaspoons water or stock
salt and pepper

1. Cut horizontally almost through the chicken breast, sprinkle the inside with the tarragon. Lay the ham inside the chicken, sprinkle the cheese over the ham and fold back the top half of the chicken.
2. Melt the margarine in a saucepan, add the pepper strips and spring onion, stir-fry for 5 minutes. Add the courgette and stir-fry for a further 2 minutes.
3. Cut a piece of foil about 8 inches (20cm) square. Spoon the stir-fried vegetables in the centre and lay the chicken and ham on top. Add the stock, season with salt and pepper and fold the foil securely over the mixture.
4. Bake at 375°F/190°C/Gas Mark 5 for 25–30 minutes. Serve the chicken with the vegetables and their juices.

Exchanges per serving: Fat 1, Protein 4, Vegetable 2

WEEK 4

Breakfast:

4fl oz (120ml) apple juice
Toast 1 slice of reduced-calorie bread, spread with 1oz (30g) curd cheese and 1 tablespoon marmalade.

Lunch: Baked Potato with Baked Beans

Cut a hot 4½oz (135g) baked jacket potato in half, dot with 1 teaspoon margarine and top with 6oz (180g) hot baked beans.
Green Salad – shredded lettuce, sliced cucumber, celery and green pepper tossed in 2 teaspoons French dressing.

5fl oz (150ml) low-fat natural yogurt

Dinner: ✳ Liver in Pepper Sauce ✳

3oz (90g) sweetcorn
Steamed or boiled broccoli and cauliflower.

Cranberries and Custard –
5oz (150g) cranberries stewed in 4 tablespoons orange juice and sweetened to taste with artificial sweetener served with
Baked Egg Custard (page 190)

Snacks:

4fl oz (120ml) tomato juice
¼ pint (150ml) skimmed milk

Optional Calories: 110

LIVER IN PEPPER SAUCE

Serves 4
270 Calories per serving

2 red peppers
2 cloves unpeeled garlic
1 baby onion
3 tablespoons single cream
4 teaspoons vegetable oil
14oz (420g) lamb's liver, cut in thin strips
8oz (240g) courgettes, cut in thin strips
1 teaspoon cornflour
good pinch of chilli powder
salt

1. Remove the core and seeds from the red peppers, cut into large dice. Place the peppers, garlic and baby onion in boiling water. Boil for 10 minutes and drain.
2. Transfer the peppers and onion to a blender, slip the cloves of garlic out of their skins and add to the blender with the cream, process until smooth.
3. Heat the oil in a saucepan, add the liver and stir-fry for 3–4 minutes, add the courgettes and stir-fry for a further 2 minutes. Remove from the heat.
4. Blend the red pepper sauce into the cornflour. Season with the chilli powder and a little salt. Stir the sauce into the liver.
5. Stir the liver, courgettes and pepper sauce over a moderate heat, simmer for about 3 minutes. Do not overcook.

Exchanges per serving: Fat 1, Protein 2½, Vegetable 1¼, Optional Calories 25

WEEK 1

Breakfast:

4fl oz (120ml) orange juice
Toast a 1oz (30g) slice of bread,
sprinkle with 1oz (30g) grated hard
cheese, grill until bubbling.

Lunch: Cottage Cheese Salad

3oz (90g) cottage cheese mixed with
1 tablespoon low-calorie mayonnaise
and a good pinch of curry powder.
Mixed Salad – shredded chicory,
sliced tomato, grated carrot and
chopped celery and spring onion.
1oz (30g) French bread spread with
1 teaspoon margarine.

Dinner: ✳ Smoked Haddock Ring ✳

Mixed Salad – shredded endive,
chicory, radicchio and strips of
yellow pepper.

5oz (150g) strawberries, sprinkled
with 1 teaspoon caster sugar and
topped with 2½ tablespoons low-fat
natural yogurt.

Snacks:

¾ pint (450ml) skimmed milk

Optional Calories: 25

SMOKED HADDOCK RING

Serves 4
175 Calories per serving

10oz (300g) smoked haddock fillet

½ pint (300ml) skimmed milk

2 teaspoons margarine

2 teaspoons flour

3 tablespoons chopped parsley

2 eggs, separated

2 tablespoons hot water

1 sachet gelatine

pinch of cream of tartar

1 head chicory

slices of tomato and cucumber

1. Lay the haddock in a pan, cover with cold water and poach for 8–10 minutes until cooked. Remove the fish from the cooking water and discard the skin.
2. Place the haddock and milk in a blender or food processor and process for a few seconds.
3. Heat the margarine in a large saucepan, stir in the flour and stir over a low heat for 1 minute. Remove from the heat and gradually blend in the haddock, milk and parsley. Bring to the boil stirring all the time, boil for 1–2 minutes. Allow to cool a little then stir in the egg yolks. Leave to cool.
4. Pour the hot water into a cup or small basin, sprinkle in the gelatine and stand the cup in a saucepan of simmering water until the gelatine has dissolved. Stir the dissolved gelatine into the haddock sauce and leave until beginning to set.
5. Whisk the egg whites and cream of tartar until peaking. Using a metal tablespoon fold into the setting sauce. Spoon into a 1½ pint (900ml) ring mould. Chill well.
6. To serve; dip the ring mould in hot water, invert on to a serving dish. Arrange chicory leaves in the centre and fill with tomato and cucumber. Arrange a few half slices of tomato and cucumber round the edge.

Exchanges per serving: Fat ½, Milk ¼, Protein 2½, Vegetable ½, Optional Calories 5

Smoked Haddock Ring with salad

WEEK 1

Breakfast:

Pineapple Buttermilk Froth – place 4oz (120g) drained, canned pineapple pieces in a blender with ¼ pint (150ml) buttermilk and 1 teaspoon sugar, process until smooth and frothy. Serve immediately.

Toast 1 slice of reduced-calorie bread, spread with 1 teaspoon margarine and 2oz (60g) cottage cheese and 1 tomato cut in wedges.

Lunch: Chicken Open Sandwich

Spread 1 reduced-calorie slice of bread with 1 teaspoon margarine, arrange alternate slices of cucumber and tomato on top and sprinkle with 1 teaspoon chopped chives. Dice 1½oz (45g) chicken and arrange on top of the open sandwich.

Green Salad – shredded lettuce, celery, green pepper and watercress.

Dinner: ✳ Trout Pudding with Parsley Sauce ✳

Steamed or boiled cauliflower and carrots.

4oz (120g) drained, canned mandarins, and served with 2 tablespoons natural juice and 2½fl oz (75ml) low-fat natural yogurt.

Snacks:

7½fl oz (225ml) skimmed milk

Optional Calories: 40

TROUT PUDDING WITH PARSLEY SAUCE

Serves 4
330 Calories per serving

| 10oz (300g) trout fillets |
| 4oz (120g) white bread, weighed with crusts removed |
| ¼ pint (150ml) skimmed milk |
| 2 eggs |
| zest of ½ a lemon, finely grated |
| 3 tablespoons chopped spring onion |
| dash of pepper sauce |
| salt |
| 4½ teaspoons margarine |
| 3 tablespoons flour |
| ½ pint (300ml) skimmed milk |
| 2 tablespoons finely chopped parsley |
| pepper |

1. Remove and discard the skin from the trout fillets, cut into chunks. Break the bread into pieces.
2. Place the trout and bread in a food processor, process until smooth, add the ¼ pint (150ml) milk and process once again. Break the eggs into the mixture and process for a further few seconds until smooth and evenly mixed.
3. Transfer the trout purée to a bowl, add the lemon zest, spring onion, pepper sauce and a sprinkling of salt. Grease a 1 pint (600ml) pudding basin with ½ teaspoon margarine, spoon in the mixture and cover with a pleated piece of baking parchment to allow for the mixture to rise. Steam for 1 hour.
4. Melt the remaining margarine in a saucepan, mix in the flour and stir over a low heat for 1 minute. Gradually blend in ½ pint (300ml) milk, add the parsley and bring to the boil stirring all the time, boil for 1–2 minutes. Season with salt and pepper.
5. To serve; turn the Trout Pudding out on to a plate, cut into four wedges and serve with the parsley sauce.

Exchanges per serving: Bread 1, Fat 1, Milk ¼, Protein 2½, Optional Calories 40

WEEK 2

Breakfast:

Pineapple Buttermilk Froth – place 4oz (120g) drained, canned pineapple pieces in a blender with ¼ pint (150ml) buttermilk and 1 teaspoon sugar. Process until frothy and serve immediately.
Toast a 1oz (30g) slice of bread and spread with 1 teaspoon low-fat spread.

Lunch: Chicken Open Sandwich

Spread 1½oz (45g) of French bread with 1½ teaspoons low-fat spread, cover with two lettuce leaves and top with 2oz (60g) sliced chicken and garnish with a sprig of watercress.
Mixed Salad – toss some shredded lettuce, a few slices of cucumber, tomato and spring onion in 2 teaspoons low-calorie French dressing.

Dinner: ✳ Mexican Fish ✳

Steamed or boiled cauliflower and Brussels sprouts.

Simple Milk Pudding (page 217)

4oz (120g) drained, canned tangerines

Snacks:

½ pint (300ml) skimmed milk

Optional Calories: 65

MEXICAN FISH

Serves 3
170 Calories per serving

1 tablespoon vegetable oil

1 clove garlic, chopped

1 onion, chopped

½ green pepper, seeded and chopped

¼ teaspoon ground coriander

1 teaspoon mild chilli powder

1 teaspoon flour

1 small (8oz/227g) can chopped tomatoes

3 × 3½oz (105g) red snapper fillets

1. Heat the oil in a small flameproof casserole dish, add the garlic and stir-fry for 1 minute.
2. Add the onion and green pepper, stir round then cover the casserole and reduce the heat as low as possible. Leave to cook gently for 5 minutes.
3. Stir in the coriander, chilli powder (if you prefer use less chilli for a milder sauce) and flour. Gradually blend in the chopped tomatoes. Bring to the boil stirring all the time.
4. Remove from the heat, lay the fish fillets in the casserole, cover and transfer to a preheated oven, 350°F/180°C/Gas Mark 4 for 20 minutes.

Exchanges per serving: Fat 1, Protein 3, Vegetable 1¼, Optional Calories 5

WEEK 2

Breakfast:

1 medium pear
1oz (30g) cereal
¼ pint (150ml) skimmed milk

Lunch: Pork Salad

2oz (60g) sliced pork
Green salad – shredded lettuce,
spring onions, sliced green pepper
and cucumber, tossed in 2 teaspoons
low-calorie French dressing.
1 slice of reduced-calorie bread
spread with 1 teaspoon margarine.

1 medium tangerine
5fl oz (150ml) low-fat natural yogurt

Dinner: ✳ Tuna and Pasta Mix ✳

Mixed Salad – shredded lettuce,
sliced peppers, tomatoes, spring
onion and radish with 1½ teaspoons
mayonnaise.

4oz (120g) canned fruit salad

Snacks:

¼ pint (150ml) skimmed milk

Optional Calories: 25

TUNA AND PASTA MIX

Serves 2
300 Calories per serving

3oz (90g) pasta spirals
salt
1 medium orange
2 inch (5cm) wedge cucumber
1 stick celery, sliced
½ red pepper, seeded and diced
6oz (180g) drained and flaked, canned tuna
2½fl oz (75ml) low-fat natural yogurt
2 teaspoons lemon juice
½ teaspoon Dijon mustard
1 tablespoon chopped parsley

1. Boil the pasta according to the packaging instructions in salted water, drain.
2. Using a sharp knife, cut the peel and white pith from the orange, cut between each membrane to separate the segments and reserve any juices which drip during preparation.
3. Dice the cucumber and mix with the orange, celery, red pepper, tuna and pasta spirals.
4. Mix the yogurt, reserved orange juice, lemon juice, mustard and parsley well together, pour over the salad and gently toss through all the ingredients.

Exchanges per serving: Bread 1½, Fruit ½, Protein 3, Vegetable 1, Optional Calories 25

WEEK 2

Breakfast:

½ medium grapefruit
1oz (30g) cereal
¼ pint (150ml) skimmed milk

Lunch: Ham Open Sandwich

Spread a 1oz (30g) slice of bread with
1 teaspoon margarine, cover with
slices of tomato and cucumber.
Spread 1½oz (45g) thin slices of
cooked ham with mustard, roll up
and lay on the tomato and cucumber,
add 1 teaspoon mayonnaise.

Buttermilk and Peach Froth – place
1 medium stoned peach in a blender,
add ¼ pint (150ml) buttermilk and
1 teaspoon sugar. Process until
smooth and frothy. Serve
immediately.

Dinner: ✳ Creole Swordfish ✳

Steamed or boiled courgettes and
carrots.

5oz (150g) drained, canned
raspberries with 2 tablespoons of the
canned fruit juice and
2½fl oz (75ml) low-fat natural yogurt.

Snacks:

¼ pint (150ml) skimmed milk

Optional Calories: 30

CREOLE SWORDFISH

Serves 2
230 Calories per serving

8oz (240g) tomatoes
2 teaspoons vegetable oil
1 clove garlic, chopped
1 small onion, sliced
½ green pepper, seeded and chopped
1 tablespoon tomato purée
1 teaspoon cornflour
¼ pint (150ml) vegetable stock
1½ teaspoons chopped basil
2 × 5oz (150g) swordfish steaks
salt and pepper

1. Plunge the tomatoes in boiling water, leave for 1 minute, rinse in cold water and slip off the skins. Cut the tomatoes in half, scoop out and discard the seeds, and chop the flesh.
2. Heat the oil in a medium-sized saucepan, stir-fry the garlic for 1 minute, add the onion and green pepper, stir-fry for a further 3–4 minutes.
3. Stir the chopped tomatoes and tomato purée into the saucepan. Blend the cornflour into the vegetable stock and add to the saucepan with the chopped basil.
4. Bring to the boil, stirring all the time, reduce the heat to a gentle simmer, place the swordfish steaks on top of the vegetables, season with salt and pepper, cover and simmer for 10–12 minutes until cooked.
5. Remove the fish and keep warm. Boil the sauce rapidly for 1–2 minutes, pour on to a warm serving plate and arrange the swordfish on top.

Exchanges per serving: Fat 1, Protein 3½, Vegetable 2, Optional Calories 10

WEEK 4

Breakfast:

1 medium apple
1oz (30g) cereal
¼ pint (150ml) skimmed milk

Lunch: Pork Salad

2oz (60g) sliced pork
Mixed salad – shredded lettuce, bean sprouts, grated carrot.

Red Cabbage Salad (page 112)

1oz (30g) slice of bread spread with 1 teaspoon margarine.

3oz (90g) cherries

Dinner: ✱ Cod Bonne Femme ✱

3oz (90g) boiled baby corn on the cob
Steamed or boiled mange-tout and carrots.
4fl oz (120ml) white wine

Strawberries and Cream – 5oz (150g) strawberries sprinkled with 1 teaspoon caster sugar and served with 2 tablespoons single cream.

Snacks:

¾ pint (450ml) skimmed milk

Optional Calories: 275

COD BONNE FEMME

Serves 3
220 Calories per serving

12oz (360g) cod fillet
6fl oz (180ml) white wine
slice of onion
4oz (120g) small button mushrooms, sliced
1 tablespoon margarine
7 teaspoons flour
2 tablespoons single cream
squeeze of lemon juice
salt and pepper

1. Remove the skin from the cod fillet. Lay the fish in a saucepan, pour over the wine and add the onion and mushrooms.
2. Simmer over a low heat for 10–12 minutes or until the cod is cooked.
3. While the cod is cooking melt the margarine in a small saucepan, add the flour, stir round and remove from the heat.
4. Carefully transfer the cod to a warm serving dish and keep warm in a low oven. Discard the onion slice.
5. Strain the wine and reserve the mushrooms. Gradually blend the wine into the margarine and flour. Bring to the boil stirring all the time.
6. Add the mushrooms, cream, lemon juice and salt and pepper to taste. Simmer gently, stirring all the time for 1 minute. Pour over the cod and serve.

Exchanges per serving: Fat 1, Protein 3, Vegetable ¼, Optional Calories 95

WEEK 4

Breakfast:

4fl oz (120ml) pineapple juice
Toast a 1oz (30g) slice of bread,
spread with 1 teaspoon low-fat spread
and top with a poached egg.

Lunch: Beans on Toast

Toast 1 slice of reduced-calorie
bread, spread with 1 teaspoon low-fat
spread and top with 6oz (180g) hot
baked beans.
4fl oz (120ml) tomato juice

5fl oz (150ml) low-fat fruit yogurt

Dinner: ✳ Plaice
Florentine ✳

4½oz (135g) baked potato with
1 teaspoon low-fat spread.
Steamed or boiled carrots and
mange-tout.

3 medium plums
4fl oz (120ml) white wine

Snacks:

7½fl oz (225ml) skimmed milk

Optional Calories: 190

PLAICE FLORENTINE

Serves 2
325 Calories per serving

9oz (270g) spinach

salt

6oz (180g) plaice fillet, black skin removed

¼ pint (150ml) skimmed milk

slice of onion

1 tablespoon margarine

4½ teaspoons flour

1 tablespoon single cream

freshly grated nutmeg

1oz (30g) mature Cheddar cheese, grated

pepper

2 teaspoons grated Parmesan cheese

1 tomato, sliced

1. Wash the spinach well, roughly chop and place in a saucepan with a sprinkling of salt. Cover and place over a low heat for 8–10 minutes while cooking the plaice.
2. Cut the plaice into six pieces, lay in a saucepan, add the milk and onion, cover and simmer for about 8 minutes or until the fish is cooked.
3. Grease a small au gratin dish with as little of the margarine as possible. Melt the remaining margarine in a small saucepan, add the flour, stir well and remove from the heat.
4. Drain the spinach well, add the cream and nutmeg and spread round the edge of the au gratin dish. Keep warm in a low oven.
5. Remove the plaice from the milk, strain and gradually blend the milk into the margarine and flour. Bring to the boil stirring all the time. Boil for 1 minute, lower the heat and add the plaice and Cheddar cheese. Season with salt and pepper.
6. When the cheese has melted pour the sauce into the au gratin dish, sprinkle with the Parmesan cheese and grill until golden. Arrange the tomato slices on top and return to the grill for 1–2 minutes.

Exchanges per serving: Fat 1½, Milk ¼, Protein 3, Vegetable 1½, Optional Calories 50

WEEK 4

Breakfast:

1 kiwi fruit
1oz (30g) cereal
¼ pint (150ml) skimmed milk

Lunch: Ham and Cheese Salad (page 131)

1oz (30g) French bread spread with
1 teaspoon margarine.

Dinner: ✳ Plaice in Prawn Wine Sauce ✳

3oz (90g) baked or boiled potato
Steamed or boiled mange-tout and
leeks.

Apricot Yogurt Fool (page 204)

Snacks:

12½fl oz (375ml) skimmed milk

Optional Calories: 170

PLAICE IN PRAWN WINE SAUCE

Serves 4
240 Calories per serving

| 4 × 4oz (120g) plaice fillets |
| 4fl oz (120ml) white wine |
| 2–3 tablespoons finely chopped chives or spring onion |
| salt and pepper |
| 4 teaspoons margarine |
| 2 tablespoons flour |
| ¼ pint (150ml) skimmed milk |
| 2oz (60g) peeled prawns |
| 3 tablespoons single cream |

1. Remove the black skin from the plaice fillets. Roll each fillet up, with the side which had the skin attached inside. Transfer the plaice rolls to a saucepan, add the wine and chives and season with a little salt and pepper.
2. Cover the saucepan, place over a low heat and poach for about 8 minutes until the plaice is cooked.
3. While the plaice is cooking, melt the margarine in a small saucepan, mix in the flour and stir over a low heat for 1 minute. Gradually blend in the milk and put to one side.
4. Remove the plaice from the wine and keep warm. Boil the wine for 2 minutes to reduce a little and stir into the milk.
5. Bring the sauce to the boil, stirring continuously, add the prawns and cream and boil for 1–2 minutes, stirring all the time. Adjust the seasoning to taste.
6. Pour the Prawn Wine Sauce over the plaice rolls, sprinkle with a few extra chopped chives and serve.

Exchanges per serving: Fat 1, Protein 3½, Optional Calories 80

Plaice in Prawn Wine Sauce with
mange-tout and leeks

WEEK 5

Breakfast: Swiss Muesli (page 52)

Lunch: Cheese Omelette with Tomatoes and Mange-tout

Beat together 2 eggs, 2 tablespoons water, salt and pepper. Heat 1 teaspoon margarine in a small omelette pan, pour in the egg mixture and cook over a gentle heat drawing the mixture from the edge towards the centre. When the underside is golden brown, sprinkle with 1oz (30g) grated cheese. Cook for a further minute, fold over and serve. Halve two tomatoes, sprinkle with basil and grill until cooked. Steamed or boiled mange-tout.

Dinner: ✳ Smoked Mackerel Salad ✳

3oz (90g) beetroot, diced
1oz (30g) bread, spread with 1 teaspoon margarine.

5oz (150g) drained, canned gooseberries served with 2 tablespoons of the canned juice and 2½fl oz (75ml) low-fat natural yogurt.

Snacks:

1 digestive biscuit
½ pint (300ml) skimmed milk

Optional Calories: 120

SMOKED MACKEREL SALAD

Serves 2
380 Calories per serving

2 medium apricots	
½ medium avocado	
2 tablespoons lemon juice	
6½ oz (195g) smoked mackerel fillets	
2oz (60g) courgettes, diced	
6 radishes, sliced	
1 teaspoon capers, well rinsed	
2 teaspoons olive oil	
good pinch of powdered mustard	
salt and pepper	
few lettuce, endive or chicory leaves	
1–2 teaspoons chopped chives	

1. Halve and stone the apricots, cut into thin wedges. Remove the skin from the avocado and slice the flesh. Toss the fruit in 1 tablespoon of the lemon juice, this will help to prevent discolouration.
2. Remove the skin from the mackerel fillets and flake into large pieces.
3. Mix the apricots, avocado, mackerel, courgettes and radishes together in a bowl.
4. Finely chop the capers, place in a small screw-top jar with the remaining lemon juice, oil, mustard and a little salt and pepper, shake well to mix. Alternatively place all the ingredients in a small basin and whisk together. Pour the dressing over the salad and toss gently.
5. Arrange lettuce leaves round the edge of the serving dish, pile the salad in the centre and sprinkle with the chopped chives.

Exchanges per serving: Fat 1, Fruit ½, Protein 3, Vegetable ½, Optional Calories 100

WEEK 5

Breakfast:

4fl oz (120ml) tomato juice
Toast a 1oz (30g) slice of bread and spread with 1 tablespoon peanut butter.

Lunch: Chicken Pitta Bread

Spread a 1oz (30g) pitta bread with 1 teaspoon low-fat spread, fill with 1½oz (45g) diced chicken, a few whole lettuce leaves, sliced tomatoes and celery.
Pepper and Fennel Salad – seeded and sliced red and yellow peppers mixed with sliced fennel and tossed in 1 tablespoon low-calorie French dressing and 2 teaspoons chopped chives.

5fl oz (150ml) low-fat natural yogurt

Dinner: ✳ Curried Fish ✳

3oz (90g) rice (cooked weight)
Green Salad – lettuce, sliced cucumber, sprigs of watercress, chopped celery and spring onions.

Caribbean Choice (page 212)
4fl oz (120ml) orange juice

Snacks:

½ pint (300ml) skimmed milk

Optional Calories: 50

CURRIED FISH

Serves 4
170 Calories per serving

1 tablespoon margarine
1 clove garlic, chopped
1 chilli, seeded and finely chopped
1 teaspoon finely chopped fresh root ginger
½ teaspoon ground cumin
½ teaspoon ground coriander
½ teaspoon turmeric
2 onions, chopped
1 small (8oz/227g) can chopped tomatoes
6fl oz (180ml) vegetable stock
1 medium cooking apple
1oz (30g) sultanas
10oz (300g) haddock, cod or coley fillet
4oz (120g) peeled prawns

1. Melt the margarine in a saucepan, add the garlic and stir-fry for 1 minute. Add the chilli (use less if you prefer a mild curry), ginger and spices, stir well to mix.
2. Mix the onion into the saucepan, stir in the tomatoes and stock.
3. Peel, quarter, core and chop the apple, add to the mixture with the sultanas, partially cover and simmer for 25 minutes.
4. Remove the skin from the fish fillet, cut across the fillet in 1½ inch (4cm) strips. Add to the curry sauce, cover and simmer gently for 6–7 minutes.
5. Add the prawns, stir and simmer for a further 5 minutes.

Exchanges per serving: Fat ¾, Fruit ½, Protein 3, Vegetable 1½

WEEK 5

Breakfast:

4fl oz (120ml) vegetable juice
Toast a 1oz (30g) slice of bread,
spread with 1 tablespoon peanut
butter.

Lunch: Toasted Cheese and Ham

Toast 2 slices of reduced-calorie
bread and spread with 2 teaspoons
low-fat spread. Cover each with ½oz
(15g) cooked lean sliced ham and
sprinkle each with ½oz (15g) grated
hard cheese, grill until bubbling.
Mixed Salad – shredded lettuce,
tomato, peppers and celery.

½ medium mango, sliced and stirred
into 5fl oz (150ml) low-fat natural
yogurt with 1 teaspoon honey.

Dinner: ✳ Kipper Salad ✳

1oz (30g) French bread spread with
1 teaspoon low-fat spread.
Pepper and Fennel Salad – ½ green
and ½ red pepper, seeded and sliced,
mixed with 2oz (60g) sliced fennel
and tossed in 2 teaspoons low-calorie
French dressing.

3oz (90g) grapes

Snacks:

7½fl oz (225ml) skimmed milk

Optional Calories: 40

KIPPER SALAD

Serves 2
150 Calories per serving

6oz (180g) kipper with skin and bones removed (poached weight)
1 medium apple
1–2 tablespoons lemon juice
1½ inch (4cm) wedge of cucumber, sliced
4 radishes, sliced
4 black olives, pitted and sliced
2½fl oz (75ml) low-fat natural yogurt
1 teaspoon horseradish sauce
1 tablespoon chives, chopped
few lettuce leaves

1. Roughly flake the kipper and place in a bowl.
2. Quarter and remove the core from the apple, slice and toss in 1 tablespoon lemon juice.
3. Mix the kipper, apple, cucumber, radishes and olives together.
4. Just before serving, mix the yogurt, horseradish sauce and chives together, add lemon juice to taste. Stir into the kipper salad.
5. Line two serving plates with lettuce leaves, pile the salad on top and serve immediately.

Exchanges per serving: Fruit ½, Milk ¼, Protein 3, Vegetable ½, Optional Calories 20

WEEK 5

Breakfast:

1 large fresh fig
1 croissant spread with 1 teaspoon butter and 1 tablespoon black cherry jam.

Lunch: Tuna and Cottage Cheese Salad

3oz (90g) cottage cheese mixed with 1½oz (45g) drained and flaked, canned tuna, 2 teaspoons low-calorie mayonnaise, a good pinch of curry powder and 2 teaspoons chopped chives.
Mixed Salad – shredded lettuce, sliced cucumber, tomatoes and pepper with 1 tablespoon French dressing
3oz (90g) beetroot, diced.

1 kiwi fruit

Dinner: ✳ Squid and Prawn Gumbo ✳

1oz (30g) long grain rice, boiled.

Gooseberries and Egg Custard – 5oz (150g) gooseberries, stewed in a little water and sweetened with artificial sweetener, served with

Baked Egg Custard (page 190)

Snacks:

1 digestive biscuit
¾ pint (450ml) skimmed milk

Optional Calories: 240

SQUID AND PRAWN GUMBO

Serves 4
140 Calories per serving

2 teaspoons vegetable oil

1 clove garlic, chopped

1 onion, chopped

½ red pepper, seeded and chopped

1 small (8oz/227g) can chopped tomatoes

½ pint (300ml) vegetable stock

6oz (180g) okra

8oz (240g) squid, head removed and cleaned

1oz (30g) long grain rice

4oz (120g) peeled prawns

salt and pepper

1. Heat the oil in a saucepan, add the garlic and stir-fry for 1 minute. Add the onion and red pepper and stir-fry for a further 3–4 minutes.
2. Stir the tomatoes and stock into the saucepan, partially cover and simmer for 10 minutes.
3. Cut the stalk end off the okra and slice. Prepare the squid, ensure all the purple mottled skin has been removed and discard the hard piece joining all the tentacles, rinse well and cut in thin rings.
4. Stir the okra, squid and rice into the saucepan, cover and simmer for 25 minutes.
5. Stir in the prawns and simmer for a further 5 minutes. Season to taste with salt and pepper.

Exchanges per serving: Fat ½, Protein 2½, Vegetable 1¾, Optional Calories 20

WEEK 1

Breakfast:

1 kiwi fruit
1oz (30g) cereal
¼ pint (150ml) skimmed milk

Lunch: Tuna Salad

2oz (60g) drained and flaked, canned tuna mixed with ½ teaspoon chopped capers and a little lemon juice.
Mixed Salad – shredded lettuce, sliced tomatoes, peppers, celery, cucumber and spring onion tossed in 2 teaspoons low-calorie French dressing.

5fl oz (150ml) low-fat natural yogurt

Dinner: ✳ Peppered Frittata ✳

Tomato and Cucumber Salad – slices of tomato and cucumber served in a bowl lined with a few lettuce leaves and sprinkled with 1–2 teaspoons chopped chives.
1oz (30g) French bread spread with 1 teaspoon margarine.

Spicy Fruit Salad (page 194)

Snacks:

¼ pint (150ml) skimmed milk

Optional Calories: 30

PEPPERED FRITTATA

Serves 1
370 Calories per serving

1½ teaspoons vegetable oil

1 small clove garlic, finely chopped

1 tablespoon chopped spring onion

¼ green pepper, seeded and chopped

¼ red pepper, seeded and chopped

2 eggs

2 tablespoons water

½oz (15g) Double Gloucester or Cheddar cheese, finely grated

½oz (15g) Parmesan cheese, finely grated

salt and pepper

1. Heat ½ teaspoon oil in a 7 inch (18 cm) omelette pan. Add the garlic, onion and peppers and stir-fry for 4–5 minutes until soft.
2. Beat the eggs and water together in a bowl, add the stir-fried vegetables, about half the cheeses and a little salt and pepper.
3. Add the remaining oil to the omelette pan, place over a low heat and swirl round the pan.
4. Pour the egg mixture into the pan, turn the heat down to low and cook very slowly without stirring for 10–12 minutes until the underside is golden. Remove from the heat, sprinkle with the remaining cheese.
5. Transfer to a preheated grill and cook until the cheese has melted and is bubbling. Slide on to a warm serving plate.

Exchanges per serving: Fat 1½, Protein 3, Vegetable 1

WEEK 3

Breakfast:

½ medium grapefruit
Toast a 1oz (30g) slice of bread
spread with 1 teaspoon margarine
and top with 3oz (90g) baked beans.

Lunch: Fish Fingers with Vegetables

4 fish fingers dotted with 1 teaspoon
margarine and grilled.
1 grilled tomato and 3oz (90g) boiled
peas

3oz (90g) grapes

Dinner: ✳ Stuffed Marrow ✳

Mixed Salad – shredded lettuce,
sliced cucumber, peppers, radish and
spring onion tossed in 2 teaspoons
low-calorie French dressing.

Gooseberries with Custard –
5oz (150g) gooseberries stewed in a
little water and sweetened to taste
with artificial sweetener.
Custard: mix 1 tablespoon custard
powder with a little skimmed milk
taken from ¼ pint (150ml). Heat the
remaining milk with 1 teaspoon sugar
until steaming, add the custard
powder paste and bring to the boil,
stirring all the time, boil for 1 minute.

Snacks:

5fl oz (150ml) low-fat natural yogurt
¼ pint (150ml) skimmed milk

Optional Calories: 95

STUFFED MARROW

Serves 4
280 Calories per serving

1 medium marrow, approximately 2¼lb (1kg)
salt
2 teaspoons margarine
1 onion, chopped
1 small green pepper, seeded and chopped
1 tablespoon tomato purée
¼ teaspoon mixed herbs
8oz (240g) corned beef
2oz (60g) fresh breadcrumbs
1 egg, beaten
dash of pepper sauce
1oz (30g) mature Cheddar cheese, grated

1. Lightly peel the marrow, cut in half horizontally and scoop out all the seeds. Plunge the marrow in boiling salted water for 4–5 minutes, if the marrow is too long for a large saucepan use a deep baking tin. Drain the marrow well on a cooling rack.
2. Melt the margarine in a saucepan, add the onion and green pepper and stir-fry for 6–7 minutes. Remove from the heat.
3. Stir the tomato purée and herbs into the saucepan. Mash the corned beef and mix into the onion etc. Add the breadcrumbs and egg. Season with a little salt and the pepper sauce.
4. Spoon the stuffing into the marrow halves. Line a baking sheet with a large piece of foil, lay the marrow halves on the foil and fold the foil over to enclose them. Bake at 350°F/180°C/Gas Mark 4 for about 40 minutes or until the marrow is tender. Sprinkle the cheese over the marrow and return to the oven for a few minutes until melted.
N.B. The marrow may be cut into 4 rings instead of halves, but only pre-boil for 2 minutes before stuffing.

Exchanges per serving: Bread ½, Fat ½, Protein 2½, Vegetable 2, Optional Calories 5

WEEK 4

Breakfast:

½ medium banana, sliced
1oz (30g) cereal
¼ pint (150ml) skimmed milk

Lunch: Cottage Cheese Salad

4oz (120g) cottage cheese
1oz (30g) Cheddar cheese, grated and
mixed with 2 teaspoons low-calorie
mayonnaise, pinch of curry powder
and 1 tablespoon chopped chives.
Mixed Salad – shredded lettuce,
sliced cucumber, tomatoes, onion
and pepper.
1oz (30g) slice of bread spread with
1 teaspoon margarine.

Dinner: ✽ Vegetable Curry ✽

1oz (30g) long-grain rice, boiled

5fl oz (150ml) low-fat fruit yogurt

Snacks:

1 medium orange
¼ pint (150ml) skimmed milk

Optional Calories: 40

VEGETABLE CURRY

Serves 2
325 Calories per serving

2 teaspoons vegetable oil
1 teaspoon finely chopped fresh root ginger
1 clove garlic, finely chopped
1 chilli, seeded and finely chopped
½ teaspoon turmeric
1 teaspoon ground coriander
½ teaspoon ground cumin
½ teaspoon cayenne
2 leeks, thickly sliced
12oz (360g) root vegetables, e.g. parsnip, swede, carrot, cut into 1 inch (2.5cm) cubes
3oz (90g) peas
9oz (270g) firm tofu, cut in 1 inch (2.5cm) cubes
6oz (180g) drained, canned chick peas
8fl oz (240ml) mixed vegetable juice
salt
lemon juice

1. Heat the oil in a saucepan, add the ginger, garlic and chilli, stir-fry for 1–2 minutes. Remove from the heat.
2. Stir the turmeric, coriander, cumin and cayenne into the saucepan.
3. Add the prepared vegetables, tofu and chick peas. Stir in the vegetable juice. Bring to the boil over a moderate heat, cover and reduce the heat, simmer for 30 minutes.
4. Remove from the heat, season to taste with salt and lemon juice.

Exchanges per serving: Fat 1, Fruit ½, Protein 2½, Vegetable 3½

WEEK 5
Breakfast: Swiss Muesli (page 52)

Lunch: Ploughman's Lunch

2oz (60g) French bread spread with 2 teaspoons margarine and served with 2oz (60g) mature Cheddar cheese, 1 tablespoon chutney and a small salad of shredded lettuce, sliced tomato, celery and cucumber. 4fl oz (120ml) tomato juice

Dinner: * Savoury Squash *

Steamed or boiled mange-tout.

Strawberry Milk Shake – sieve 5oz (150g) strawberries, place in a blender with ¼ pint (150ml) skimmed milk, 2oz (60g) fromage frais and 1 teaspoon sugar, process until smooth. Serve immediately.

Snacks:

½ pint (300ml) skimmed milk

Optional Calories: 120

SAVOURY SQUASH

Serves 2
275 Calories per serving

Approximately 1lb 8oz (720g) spaghetti squash
2 teaspoons vegetable oil
4 spring onions, sliced
½ red pepper, seeded and chopped
1 clove garlic, crushed
2 teaspoons chopped dill
4oz (120g) quark or curd cheese
4oz (120g) peeled prawns
2 tablespoons grated Parmesan cheese
salt
dash of pepper sauce

1. Cut the squash in half horizontally, scoop out the seeds. Place the squash in boiling water, cover and boil for 20 minutes.
2. While the squash is cooking, heat the oil in a separate saucepan, add the spring onions and red pepper, stir round then reduce the heat as low as possible, cover and leave for 6–7 minutes.
3. Mix the garlic, dill and quark or curd cheese together.
4. Remove the spring onions and red pepper from the heat. Stir in the cheese mixture.
5. Drain the squash well and, holding the skin firmly with a thick cloth, scoop out the flesh in spaghetti-like strands, stir into the cheese and red pepper.
6. Add all the remaining ingredients and place over a low heat, stirring all the time until piping hot.

Exchanges per serving: Fat 1, Protein 3, Vegetable 3, Optional Calories 30

VEGETARIAN WEEK 1

Breakfast:

Pineapple Buttermilk Froth – place 4oz (120g) drained canned pineapple pieces in a blender with ¼ pint (150ml) buttermilk and 1 teaspoon sugar or honey. Process until smooth and frothy, serve immediately.
Toast a 1oz (30g) slice of bread spread with 1 tablespoon peanut butter.

Lunch: Cottage Cheese Salad

2oz (60g) cottage cheese mixed with 1 teaspoon chopped chives and a pinch of curry powder.
Mixed Salad – shredded lettuce, sliced cucumber, peppers and celery.
1 rice cake spread with 1 teaspoon margarine.

1 medium orange

Dinner: ✳ Nut Rissoles with Chilli Sauce ✳

Steamed or boiled carrots, cauliflower and cabbage.

5fl oz (150ml) low-fat natural yogurt

Snacks:

¼ pint (150ml) skimmed milk

Optional Calories: 40

NUT RISSOLES WITH ◗ CHILLI SAUCE

Serves 3
260 Calories per serving

2oz (60g) bread

6oz (180g) firm or smoked tofu

1 onion

1½oz (45g) roasted hazelnuts, finely chopped

1½oz (45g) walnuts, finely chopped

¼ teaspoon yeast extract

1 egg, beaten

1 small (8oz/227g) can chopped tomatoes

1 teaspoon cornflour

¼ teaspoon oregano

Approximately 1 teaspoon chilli sauce

sprigs of oregano or coriander

1. Place the bread in a blender, process to form breadcrumbs, add the tofu and process once again until smooth. Transfer to a bowl.
2. Grate half the onion into the tofu mixture. Stir in the nuts and yeast extract, blend well. Bind together with the egg.
3. Shape the tofu mixture into six rissoles, place on a baking tray and grill for 10–12 minutes until golden, turning once.
4. Sieve the tomatoes, blend a little of the juice with the cornflour and put to one side.
5. Grate the remaining onion into the tomato juice, add the oregano and ½ teaspoon chilli sauce, heat gently. Add the cornflour and bring to the boil. Boil for 1–2 minutes. Add more chilli sauce to taste.
6. Serve the hot nut rissoles with the chilli sauce garnished with sprigs of oregano or coriander.

Exchanges per serving: Bread ½, Fat 1, Protein 3, Vegetables 1¼, Optional Calories 20

WEEK 3/VEGETARIAN WEEK 2

Breakfast:

½ medium grapefruit
1oz (30g) cereal
¼ pint (150ml) skimmed milk

Lunch: Mushroom Omelette

Beat together 2 eggs, 2 tablespoons water, salt and pepper. Heat ½ teaspoon margarine in a small omelette pan and stir-fry 3oz (90g) sliced mushrooms for 3–4 minutes, remove. Heat another teaspoon margarine in the omelette pan, add the egg mixture and cook over a gentle heat, drawing the mixture from the edge towards the centre. When the underside is golden, spoon the mushrooms over half the omelette, cook for a further minute, fold over and serve.

5oz (150g) chunks of watermelon

Dinner: * Crispy-Topped Beans *

Mixed Salad – lettuce, sliced peppers, cucumber, wedges of tomato.

4oz (120g) drained, canned mandarins with 2 tablespoons natural juice and 2½fl oz (75ml) low-fat natural yogurt.
½ pint (300ml) beer

Snacks:

½ pint (300ml) skimmed milk

Optional Calories: 105

CRISPY-TOPPED BEANS

Serves 4
395 Calories per serving

12oz (360g) mixture of dried beans, e.g. kidney, haricot, cannellino
2 teaspoons vegetable oil
1 large onion, chopped
2 tablespoons tomato purée
1 medium (15oz/497g) can chopped tomatoes
1 teaspoon basil
1 bay leaf, torn into three or four pieces
large pinch of chilli powder
1 tablespoon soy sauce
salt
4oz (120g) French bread
4 teaspoons margarine
2 cloves garlic, crushed

1. Cover the beans with plenty of cold water and leave overnight. Drain, transfer to a saucepan, cover with fresh cold water and boil rapidly for 10–15 minutes, skimming off the scum which rises to the surface. Then cover, reduce the heat and simmer for 30–40 minutes until tender.
2. Heat the oil in a flameproof casserole, add the onion and stir-fry for 6–7 minutes. Stir in the tomato purée, chopped tomatoes, basil, bay leaf, chilli powder, soy sauce and a sprinkling of salt.
3. Drain the beans, reserve ¼ pint (150ml) of the cooking liquid. Stir the beans and reserved liquid into the casserole, bring to the boil, cover and simmer gently for 30–35 minutes.
4. Cut the French bread into about eight thin slices, sufficient to cover the top of the casserole.
5. Mash the margarine and garlic together, spread over the bread and arrange the bread on top of the beans, pushing down slightly to soak up some of the juices. Simmer uncovered for a further 4–5 minutes, then transfer to a low to medium grill and cook until golden.

Exchanges per serving: Bread 1, Fat 1½, Protein 3, Vegetable 1¾, Optional Calories 5

Crispy-Topped Beans, served with beer

VEGETARIAN WEEK 1

Breakfast:

4fl oz (120ml) grapefruit juice
Toast a 1oz (30g) slice of bread,
spread with 1 teaspoon margarine
and top with 3oz (90g) baked beans.

Lunch: Egg Salad

1 hard-boiled egg, sliced and served
with shredded lettuce, wedges of
tomato, sliced cucumber and peppers
and garnished with mustard and
cress.

1 medium orange
5fl oz (150ml) low-fat natural yogurt

Dinner: * Lentil-Coated Vegetables *

1oz (30g) long grain rice, boiled

Spicy Fruit Salad (page 194)

Snacks:

½ pint (300ml) skimmed milk

Optional Calories: 30

LENTIL-COATED VEGETABLES

Serves 1
370 Calories per serving

2oz (60g) split red lentils
1 small onion, chopped
1 clove garlic, crushed
Approximately 8fl oz (240ml) water
¼ teaspoon mild chilli powder
1½ teaspoons vegetable oil
½ teaspoon cumin seeds
¼ teaspoon coriander seeds, crushed
6–8oz (180–240g) mixture of broccoli and cauliflower
1 carrot, cut in 2 inch (5cm) lengths
4 tablespoons vegetable stock or water
salt
½ teaspoon garam masala
½oz (15g) pine nuts or flaked almonds, toasted

1. Place the lentils, onion, garlic and 8fl oz (240ml) water in a saucepan, add the chilli powder, cover and boil for 10 minutes. Reduce the heat and simmer for about 15–20 minutes until soft. If necessary add a little more water. Stir occasionally to prevent sticking.
2. Pour the oil into a saucepan over a low heat, add the cumin and coriander and stir until the cumin seeds start popping.
3. Add the broccoli, cauliflower and carrot, stir round and pour in the vegetable stock. Cover and simmer for 12 minutes.
4. Remove the lid from the saucepan and boil for 1 minute to reduce the liquid.
5. Transfer the lentil mixture to a blender, process until smooth, pour over the vegetables and boil for 3–4 minutes, season to taste with salt and garam masala. Remove from the heat and stir in the nuts. Serve in a bowl.

Exchanges per serving: Fat 2, Protein 3, Vegetable 4

VEGETARIAN WEEK 1

Breakfast:

4fl oz (120ml) grapefruit juice
Toast 1 slice of reduced-calorie bread, spread with 1 teaspoon margarine and top with a poached egg.

Lunch: Cheese Salad

1½oz (45g) hard cheese, grated
Mixed salad – shredded lettuce, sliced tomato, cucumber and spring onion topped with 1 teaspoon low-calorie mayonnaise.

Dinner: ✳ Savoury Rice and Beans ✳

Tossed Green Salad – shredded endive and chicory, sliced cucumber and green pepper tossed in 1 tablespoon low-calorie French dressing.

4oz (120g) canned fruit salad served with 2½fl oz (75ml) low-fat natural yogurt.

Snacks:

2½fl oz (75ml) low-fat natural yogurt
½ pint (300ml) skimmed milk

SAVOURY RICE AND BEANS

Serves 2
375 Calories per serving

1 teaspoon vegetable oil
1 onion, chopped
3oz (90g) basmati or long-grain rice
1 large clove garlic, finely chopped
1 teaspoon chopped fresh root ginger
2 whole cloves
1 teaspoon cumin seeds
1 inch (2.5cm) stick of cinnamon, crumbled
¼ teaspoon mild chilli powder
6oz (180g) firm tofu, diced
salt
1 small yellow or red pepper
6oz (180g) drained, canned or cooked kidney beans
½–1 teaspoon garam masala
½oz (15g) split or flaked almonds, toasted

1. Heat the vegetable oil in a saucepan, add the onion and stir-fry for 5–6 minutes. Stir in the rice and remove from the heat.
2. Add the garlic, ginger, cloves, cumin, cinnamon, chilli and firm tofu, the recommended amount of water on the packaging instructions and a sprinkling of salt.
3. While the rice and tofu are cooking, place the pepper under a hot grill and cook until black and blistered all over, plunge into cold water and peel off the skin. Remove the core and seeds and chop the flesh.
4. Five minutes before the end of the rice cooking time add the chopped pepper and kidney beans to the saucepan, stir well, cover and continue cooking.
5. Remove from the heat, stir in the garam masala and divide between two warm serving bowls, sprinkle with the toasted almonds and serve.

Exchanges per serving: Bread 1½, Fat ¾, Protein 2½, Vegetable 1

VEGETARIAN WEEK 2/ MAIN MENU PLAN WEEK 3

Breakfast:

1 medium apple
1oz (30g) cereal
¼ pint (150ml) skimmed milk

Lunch: Red Pepper Omelette

Beat together 2 eggs, 2 tablespoons water, salt and pepper. Heat ½ teaspoon margarine in a small omelette pan, stir-fry ½ seeded and chopped red pepper, for 3–4 minutes, remove. Heat 1 teaspoon margarine in the same pan, add the egg mixture and cook over a gentle heat, drawing the mixture from the edge towards the centre. When the underside is golden, spoon the red pepper over half the omelette, cook for a further minute, fold over and serve.
1oz (30g) slice of bread spread with 1 teaspoon low-fat spread.

5oz (150g) chunks of watermelon

Dinner: ✳ Mixed Vegetable Stew ✳

3oz (90g) pasta (cooked weight)

5fl oz (150ml) low-fat natural yogurt

Snacks:

¼ pint (150ml) skimmed milk

Optional Calories: 10

MIXED VEGETABLE STEW

Serves 2
280 Calories per serving

2 teaspoons vegetable oil

2 leeks, sliced

2 tablespoons tomato purée

1 clove garlic, crushed

1 tablespoon chopped basil

1 small (8oz/227g) can chopped tomatoes

2oz (60g) split red lentils

9oz (270g) firm tofu, diced

2oz (60g) mushrooms, diced or thinly sliced

¼ pint (150ml) water or vegetable stock

2 tablespoons soy sauce

salt and pepper

1. Heat the oil in a saucepan, add the leeks and stir-fry for 3–4 minutes.
2. Stir in all the remaining ingredients and season with a little salt and pepper.
3. Bring to the boil, stirring all the time, reduce the heat, cover and simmer for 30 minutes stirring occasionally and if necessary adding a little extra water.

Exchanges per serving: Fat 1, Protein 2½, Vegetable 3, Optional Calories 10

DESSERTS

WEEK 1

Breakfast:

1 medium apple
1oz (30g) cereal
¼ pint (150ml) skimmed milk

Lunch: Cottage Cheese Open Sandwich

Spread a 1oz (30g) slice of bread with 1 teaspoon low-fat spread. Top with a few endive leaves and alternate slices of tomato and cucumber. Pile 4oz (120g) cottage cheese in the centre.

5oz (150g) strawberries
5fl oz (150ml) low-fat natural yogurt

Dinner: Grilled Cod with Vegetables

Dot a 4oz (120g) fillet of cod with ½ teaspoon margarine, grill for 3–4 minutes, turn, dot with ½ teaspoon margarine and continue grilling until cooked.
Steamed or boiled Brussels sprouts, cauliflower and carrots.

✳ Baked Lemon Soufflé ✳

Snacks

¼ pint (150ml) skimmed milk

Optional Calories: 80

BAKED LEMON SOUFFLÉ

Serves 3
245 Calories per serving

4½ teaspoons margarine
7 teaspoons flour
1 lemon, finely grated zest and juice
¼ pint (150ml) skimmed milk
2 tablespoons caster sugar
3 eggs, separated
pinch of cream of tartar

1. Use as little margarine as possible to grease a 6½ inch (16.5cm) soufflé dish.
2. Melt the rest of the margarine in a large saucepan, stir in the flour and cook over a low heat for 30 seconds.
3. Remove the saucepan from the heat, gradually blend in the lemon juice and zest, then the skimmed milk.
4. Bring to the boil, stirring all the time, boil for 1 minute. Remove from the heat, add the sugar and stir round until dissolved. Add the egg yolks and put to one side.
5. Whisk the egg whites and cream of tartar until peaking. Using a metal tablespoon, fold the egg whites into the lemon sauce. Spoon into the greased soufflé dish. Bake at 350°F/180°C/Gas Mark 4 for 30–35 minutes until well-risen. Serve immediately.

Exchanges per serving: Fat 1½, Protein 1, Optional Calories 80

WEEK 1

Breakfast:

½ medium grapefruit
1oz (30g) cereal
¼ pint (150ml) skimmed milk

Lunch: Tuna Salad

2oz (60g) drained and flaked, canned
tuna, mixed with 2 teaspoons
low-calorie mayonnaise and
1 teaspoon chopped chives.
Tomato and Cucumber Salad – slices
of tomato and cucumber sprinkled
with ½ teaspoon chopped basil.
Green Salad – shredded lettuce,
sliced celery, green pepper and sprigs
of watercress.
Crispbread, up to 80 Calories
2 teaspoons margarine

✳ Honeycomb Mould ✳

Served with 4oz (120g) drained,
canned mandarin segments and
arranged around each individual
serving.

Dinner: Roast Chicken with Vegetables

2½oz (75g) roast chicken
Steamed or boiled Brussel sprouts,
cauliflower and carrots.

4oz (120g) fruit salad served with
2½fl oz (75ml) low-fat natural yogurt.

Snacks:

¼ pint (150ml) skimmed milk

Optional Calories: 40

HONEYCOMB MOULD

Serves 2
145 Calories per serving

½ pint (300ml) skimmed milk

1 egg, separated

4 teaspoons caster sugar

few drops of vanilla essence

1 tablespoon hot water

2 teaspoons gelatine

pinch of cream of tartar

1. Beat a few tablespoons of the milk with the egg yolk and put to one side.
2. Heat the remaining milk until steaming, pour on to the egg yolk mixture. Return to the saucepan and place over a very low heat, stirring all the time for 1 minute. Do not boil.
3. Remove from the heat, stir in the sugar and vanilla essence and leave until cool.
4. Pour the hot water into a cup, sprinkle in the gelatine and place in a saucepan of simmering water until the gelatine has dissolved.
5. Stir the dissolved gelatine into the egg and milk, leave until the mixture thickens, not until it is beginning to set.
6. Whisk the egg white and cream of tartar until peaking, fold into the mixture. Transfer to a 1 pint (600ml) mould or two individual moulds and leave to set.
7. To serve; dip in hot water, then invert the mould on to a serving plate. The mixture will have separated into layers. Serve alone or with fruit.

Exchanges per serving: Milk ½, Protein ½, Optional Calories 40

WEEK 1

Breakfast:

2 inch (5cm) wedge of honeydew melon
1oz (30g) cereal
¼ pint (150ml) skimmed milk

Lunch: Tuna Salad

2oz (60g) drained and flaked, canned tuna with 1 teaspoon mayonnaise and a little lemon juice.
Mixed Salad – shredded lettuce, sliced tomatoes, peppers, celery and onion tossed in 2 teaspoons French dressing.
1oz (30g) French bread spread with 1 teaspoon margarine.

Dinner: Lamb with Vegetables

2½oz (75g) roast lamb
Steamed or boiled green beans, leeks and onions.

Spicy Fruit Salad (page 194)

✳ Baked Egg Custard ✳

Snacks:

½ pint (300ml) skimmed milk

Optional Calories: 65

BAKED EGG CUSTARD

Serves 2
130 Calories per serving

¼ teaspoon margarine

1 egg

1 tablespoon caster sugar

½ pint (300ml) skimmed milk

freshly grated nutmeg

1. Grease a ¾ pint (450ml) pie dish or ovenproof dish with the margarine.
2. Beat the egg, sugar and a tablespoon of the milk together. Heat the remaining milk until steaming and stir into the egg mixture.
3. Strain the custard into the greased dish and sprinkle with the freshly grated nutmeg.
4. Stand the dish in a baking tin containing warm to hot water to a depth of ½ inch (1.25cm). Bake at 325°F/160°C/Gas Mark 3 for about 40 minutes. To check the custard is set, make a slit in the top with a knife and gently press each side of the slit. If no milk oozes out, the custard is cooked.

Exchanges per serving: Milk ½, Protein ½, Optional Calories 35

WEEK 2

Breakfast:

1 medium apple
1oz (30g) cereal
¼ pint (150ml) skimmed milk

Lunch: Curried Prawn Salad (page 16)

1oz (30g) slice of bread spread with 1 teaspoon margarine.

Dinner: Roast Lamb with Vegetables

3oz (90g) roast lamb
3oz (90g) boiled or baked potatoes
Steamed or boiled courgettes and carrots.

✳ Strawberry Dessert ✳

Snacks:

12½fl oz (375ml) skimmed milk

Optional Calories: 40

STRAWBERRY DESSERT

Serves 2
130 Calories per serving

5oz (150g) strawberries

1 tablespoon clear honey

4fl oz (120ml) orange juice

2½ teaspoons gelatine

4oz (120g) fromage frais

1 egg white

pinch of cream of tartar

1. Reserve two strawberries for decoration. Place the remaining strawberries, honey and 3fl oz (90ml) orange juice in a blender. Process until smooth, pour into a bowl.
2. Pour the remaining orange juice in a cup, sprinkle in the gelatine and stand the cup in a saucepan of simmering water until dissolved.
3. Stir the dissolved gelatine into the strawberry and orange purée and leave until beginning to set.
4. Stir the fromage frais into the setting mixture.
5. Whisk the egg white with the cream of tartar until peaking. Using a metal spoon, carefully fold the egg white into the purée. Spoon into two serving glasses and chill until set.
6. To serve; slice the strawberries and arrange on top of each serving of Strawberry Dessert.

Exchanges per serving: Fruit 1, Protein 1, Optional Calories 40

WEEK 2

Breakfast:

2 inch (5cm) wedge of honeydew melon
Toast a 1oz (30g) slice of bread, spread with 1 tablespoon peanut butter.

Lunch: Salmon Salad

2oz (60g) drained and flaked, canned salmon, mixed with 1 teaspoon low-calorie French dressing and lemon juice to taste.
Mixed Salad – shredded lettuce, sliced peppers, celery and bean sprouts.

Peach Buttermilk Froth – place 1 stoned medium peach in blender, add ¼ pint (150ml) buttermilk and 1 teaspoon sugar. Blend until smooth and frothy. Serve immediately.

Dinner: Roast Lamb with Vegetables

3oz (90g) roast lamb, sliced
3oz (90g) boiled potato tossed in 1 teaspoon margarine and sprinkled with mint.
Steamed or boiled Brussels sprouts and cauliflower.

✻ Gooseberry Charlotte ✻

Served with 2½fl oz (75ml) low-fat natural yogurt

Snacks:

½ pint (300ml) skimmed milk

Optional Calories: 40

GOOSEBERRY CHARLOTTE

Serves 2
140 Calories per serving

10oz (300g) gooseberries, topped and tailed

sprig of fresh elderflowers or ¼–½ teaspoon dried elderflowers

1–2 tablespoons water

artificial sweetener

2oz (60g) fresh breadcrumbs

1½ teaspoons margarine

2 teaspoons demerara sugar

1. Place the gooseberries, elderflowers and water in a saucepan. Heat gently and simmer until just cooked but the gooseberries remain whole.
2. Remove the gooseberries from the heat and sweeten to taste with artificial sweetener. Spoon about a quarter of the gooseberries into each of two 4 inch (10cm) ramekins.
3. Sprinkle ½oz (15g) breadcrumbs over each of the gooseberries in the ramekins, spoon over the remaining gooseberries.
4. Mix together the remaining 1oz (30g) breadcrumbs with the margarine and demerara sugar, sprinkle evenly over each ramekin.
5. Bake at 375°F/190°C/Gas Mark 5 for about 20 minutes until golden.

Exchanges per serving: Bread 1, Fat ¾, Fruit 1, Optional Calories 20

WEEK 2

Breakfast:

1 medium pear
1oz (30g) cereal
¼ pint (150ml) skimmed milk

Lunch: Peach and Cottage Cheese Platter (page 129)

1oz (30g) slice of bread spread with 1 teaspoon margarine.

5fl oz (150ml) low-fat natural yogurt
1 teaspoon honey

Dinner: Trout with Vegetables

4½oz (135g) fillet of trout, poached in a little water.
3oz (90g) potato with 1 teaspoon margarine.
Steamed or boiled asparagus and carrots.

✳ Raspberry Bonanza ✳

Snacks:

¼ pint (150ml) skimmed milk

Optional Calories: 35

RASPBERRY BONANZA

Serves 3
100 Calories per serving

1 medium banana

5oz (150g) drained, canned raspberries, juice reserved

2 teaspoons honey

1 large egg, separated

1 teaspoon gelatine

pinch of cream of tartar

1oz (30g) fromage frais

1. Place the banana and raspberries in a blender, process until smooth.
2. Sieve the banana and raspberry purée into a saucepan, pressing the purée against the sieve with a wooden spoon and scraping the purée off the sieve with a metal spoon.
3. Gently heat the purée, add the honey and stir until steaming. Remove from the heat, allow to cool a little, then stir in the egg yolk. Leave to cool.
4. Pour 2 tablespoons of the reserved fruit juice into a cup and sprinkle in the gelatine. Stand the cup in a saucepan of simmering water and leave until the gelatine has dissolved.
5. Stir the dissolved gelatine into the fruit purée. Leave until beginning to set.
6. Whisk the egg white with the cream of tartar until peaking, gently fold into the setting mixture. Spoon the raspberry mixture into three small glasses and swirl the fromage frais into each serving. Chill until completely set.

Exchanges per serving: Fruit 1, Protein ½, Optional Calories 15

WEEK 1

Breakfast:

½ medium grapefruit
Toast a 1oz (30g) slice of bread,
spread with 1 teaspoon margarine
and 1 tablespoon marmalade.

Lunch: Smoked Haddock Ring (page 162)

1oz (30g) French bread spread with
1 teaspoon margarine.
Green Salad – lettuce, sliced
cucumber, green pepper, celery and
chopped spring onion tossed in
2 teaspoons low-calorie French
dressing.

5fl oz (150ml) low-fat natural yogurt

Dinner: Roast Turkey with Vegetables

3oz (90g) roast turkey
Steamed or boiled carrots,
cauliflower and green beans.

✳ Spicy Fruit Salad ✳

Snacks:

7½fl oz (225ml) skimmed milk

Optional Calories: 85

SPICY FRUIT SALAD

Serves 2
75 Calories per serving

4 tablespoons water

juice of ½ a lemon

1 tablespoon honey

½ teaspoon finely chopped fresh root ginger

1½ inch (4cm) stick cinnamon

1 medium orange

1 medium pear

1. Place the water, lemon juice, honey and ginger in a small saucepan. Crumble the cinnamon into the saucepan and add the finely grated zest of half the orange.
2. Using a sharp knife remove the orange skin and white pith, cut between the membranes and separate the segments. Pour any juice which escapes while preparing the orange into the saucepan.
3. Peel the pear, cut in half lengthways, scoop out the core and cut each half into three or four wedges.
4. Place the saucepan over a low heat until the honey has dissolved. Add the pear, cover and simmer gently for 6 minutes. Add the orange segments and simmer uncovered for 3 minutes until heated through.
5. Remove the fruit with a slotted spoon, boil the remaining liquid rapidly for 1 minute and pour over the fruit. Serve hot, warm or chilled.

Exchanges per serving: Fruit 1, Optional Calories 30

WEEK 2

Breakfast:

½ medium banana
1oz (30g) cereal
¼ pint (150ml) skimmed milk

Lunch:

2fl oz (60ml) orange juice
2 rice cakes spread with
2 tablespoons peanut butter.
1 tomato, cut in wedges

4oz (120g) pineapple
5fl oz (150ml) low-fat natural yogurt

Dinner: Trout with Vegetables

4oz (120g) poached trout fillets
3oz (90g) baked potato with
1 teaspoon margarine.
Steamed or boiled courgettes, carrots,
and cauliflower.

✳ Strawberry Sherbet ✳

Snacks:

¼ pint (150ml) skimmed milk

Optional Calories: 80

STRAWBERRY SHERBET

Serves 6
90 Calories per serving

10oz (300g) strawberries

1 medium orange, zest and juice

4fl oz (120ml) water

7 tablespoons caster sugar

2 large egg whites (size 1)

pinch of cream of tartar

1. Place the strawberries in a blender. Remove the orange zest with a potato peeler, put to one side, squeeze the juice from the orange and add to the strawberries.
2. Process the strawberries and orange juice until completely smooth.
3. Pour the water into a saucepan, add the sugar and reserved orange zest. Heat gently until the sugar has dissolved then increase the heat and boil fiercely for 2 minutes. Allow to cool.
4. Pour the strawberry purée into a bowl. Remove the zest from the syrup and stir the syrup into the purée, mix well. Transfer to a shallow container and freeze for 2–3 hours until half frozen and a slushy consistency.
5. Whisk the egg whites and cream of tartar until peaking, carefully fold into the slushy strawberry purée. Return to the freezer for several hours.
6. Place in the refrigerator for about 20 minutes before serving. Scoop into glasses or dishes and serve immediately.

Exchanges per serving: Fruit ½, Optional Calories 80

WEEK 3

Breakfast:

4fl oz (120ml) orange juice
Toast a 1oz (30g) slice of bread,
spread with 1 teaspoon low-fat spread
and top with a poached egg.

Lunch: Turkey Salad

2oz (60g) cooked turkey
Mixed Salad – shredded lettuce,
sliced peppers, radish, cucumber,
chopped celery and spring onion
tossed in 2 teaspoons French
dressing.

1 medium orange

Dinner: Roast Beef with Vegetables

3oz (90g) roast beef
3oz (90g) boiled peas
3oz (90g) baked or boiled potato
Steamed or boiled cauliflower and
carrots.

* Flapjack Pudding *

Served with 2½fl oz (75ml) low-fat
natural yogurt.

Snacks:

¾ pint (450ml) skimmed milk

Optional Calories: 60

FLAPJACK PUDDING

Serves 2
275 Calories per serving

4oz (120g) peeled, cored, quartered and sliced apples
5oz (150g) blackberries
¼ teaspoon ground allspice
2 tablespoons honey
1 tablespoon margarine
2oz (60g) porridge oats
finely grated zest of ½ a lemon

1. Place the apples and blackberries in a 5 inch (13cm) soufflé dish or small pie dish. Sprinkle the allspice over the fruit and drizzle 1 tablespoon honey evenly over the top.
2. Heat the remaining honey and margarine over a low heat until the margarine has melted.
3. Mix the porridge oats and lemon zest together in a bowl, stir in the margarine and honey and mix well.
4. Sprinkle the honeyed oats over the fruit and bake at 350°F/180°C/Gas Mark 4 for 25 minutes.
N.B. The sweetness of the fruit influences the amount of honey required. This recipe was tested with ripe Bramley apples. I suggest you follow the recipe using either Bramleys or a dessert apple, alternatively increase the amount of honey to sweeten the fruit but increase the amount of Optional Calories accordingly; for example ½ teaspoon honey would increase each serving by 10 Calories.

Exchanges per serving: Bread 1, Fat 1½, Fruit 1, Optional Calories 60

WEEK 4

Breakfast:

4fl oz (120ml) orange juice
Toast a 1oz (30g) slice of bread,
spread with 1 teaspoon margarine
and top with 3oz (90g) baked beans.

Lunch: Stuffed Egg Salad

1 hard-boiled egg, cut in half
horizontally. Scoop out the yolk and
mash with 2oz (60g) low-fat soft
cheese, 2 teaspoons low-calorie
mayonnaise and 1 teaspoon chopped
chives. Replace mixture in hollow
centres of each half of egg.
Mixed Salad – shredded lettuce,
sliced radish, tomato, cucumber and
spring onion.

1 medium tangerine

Dinner: Vegetable Curry (page 179)

2oz (60g) long grain rice, boiled

∗ Mango Mix ∗

Snacks:

5fl oz (150ml) low-fat natural yogurt
7½fl oz (225ml) skimmed milk

Optional Calories: 90

MANGO MIX

Serves 2
130 Calories per serving

1 medium mango
3oz (90g) firm tofu
2 teaspoons set honey
1 lime
½ teaspoon orange flower water
2½fl oz (75ml) low-fat natural yogurt
slices of lime to decorate (optional)

1. Cut the mango lengthways down the broadside of the fruit about ½ inch (1.25cm) away from the centre. Cut through the other side about the same distance from the centre. Scrape the flesh from each half and from round the stone into a blender. Add the tofu and honey. Process until smooth.
2. Squeeze the juice from the lime and add to the blender with the orange flower water and process again until smooth.
3. Spoon the mango and tofu purée into a bowl, swirl in the yogurt and transfer to two glasses, chill well.
4. Just before serving, garnish each glass with a twist of lime.

Exchanges per serving: Fruit 1, Milk ¼, Protein ½, Optional Calories 20

WEEK 4

Breakfast:

Mango Froth – blend ½ medium mango with 2½fl oz (75ml) low-fat natural yogurt, ¼ pint (150ml) buttermilk and 1 teaspoon sugar. Serve immediately.

1 oatcake spread with 1 teaspoon margarine and 1 tablespoon marmalade.

Lunch: Salmon Salad

2oz (60g) drained, canned salmon served with a lemon wedge.
Mixed Salad – shredded lettuce, sliced cucumber, tomato and peppers with sprigs of watercress.
2 slices of reduced-calorie bread spread with 1 teaspoon margarine.

1 medium apple

Dinner: Ham with Vegetables

3oz (90g) cooked ham, sliced, served with mustard.
Steamed or boiled mange-tout and carrots.

✳ Pineapple Cheesecake ✳

Snacks:

½ pint (300ml) skimmed milk

Optional Calories: 105

PINEAPPLE CHEESECAKE

Serves 4
210 Calories per serving

3 large digestive biscuits

4 teaspoons margarine

4oz (120g) low-fat soft cheese

2 tablespoons caster sugar

8oz (240g) crushed pineapple

4oz (120g) fromage frais

finely grated zest of ½ a lemon

¼ teaspoon ground ginger

2 teaspoons gelatine

1 large egg white (size 1)

pinch of cream of tartar

1 kiwi fruit, sliced

1. Place the biscuits in a plastic bag and crush with a rolling pin to make fine crumbs.
2. Melt the margarine, stir in the biscuit crumbs and mix well. Press firmly into a 6 inch (15cm) loose-bottomed cake tin.
3. Mix the soft cheese and caster sugar together. Drain the crushed pineapple into a sieve standing over a small basin. Reserve the pineapple juice. Stir the pineapple, fromage frais, lemon zest and ginger into the soft cheese mixture.
4. Sprinkle the gelatine into the pineapple juice in the basin and stand in a saucepan of simmering water until the gelatine has dissolved.
5. Stir the dissolved gelatine mixture into the cheese and fromage frais and leave until beginning to set.
6. Whisk the egg white and cream of tartar until peaking. Using a metal tablespoon carefully fold the egg white into the cheese mixture, spoon over the biscuit base, and chill until completely set.
7. To serve; remove the base from the cake tin, slide a spatula under the biscuit base and transfer the cheesecake on to a serving plate. Decorate with the slices of kiwi fruit.

Exchanges per serving: Bread ¾, Fat 1, Fruit ¾, Protein 1, Optional Calories 35

WEEK 4

Breakfast:

4fl oz (120ml) apple juice
1oz (30g) bap spread with 1 teaspoon margarine and 1 tablespoon marmalade.

Lunch: Prawn Salad

2oz (60g) peeled prawns mixed with 2 teaspoons low-calorie mayonnaise, seasoned with a large pinch of curry powder and a squeeze of lemon juice. Served with a wedge of lemon and mixed salad of shredded lettuce, chopped red pepper, celery, spring onions and mustard and cress.

4oz (120g) fresh or drained, canned cherries with 2½fl oz (75ml) low-fat natural yogurt

Dinner: Grilled Pork with Vegetables

Brush a 4oz (120g) lean boned pork chop with ½ teaspoon vegetable oil, grill for 4–5 minutes, turn and brush with ½ teaspoon vegetable oil. Return to the grill until cooked through.
6oz (180g) baked jacket potato
Steamed or boiled cauliflower and cabbage.

✳ Sweet-Topped Fruit ✳

Snacks:

¾ pint (450ml) skimmed milk

Optional Calories: 75

SWEET-TOPPED FRUIT

Serves 4
100 Calories per serving

| juice of 1 lemon |
| 5 tablespoons water |
| 1 tablespoon sugar or honey |
| 2 thin slices of fresh root ginger |
| 5oz (150g) strawberries, halved or sliced |
| 5oz (150g) blueberries |
| ½ medium galia melon, cut in chunks or balls |
| 1 kiwi fruit, sliced |
| For the topping:
8oz (240g) fromage frais |
| 2 teaspoons honey |
| 4 sprigs of mint |

1. Place the lemon juice, water, sugar or honey and ginger in a saucepan. Bring to the boil over a moderate heat. Boil for 2 minutes, remove from the heat and leave until cool.
2. Mix all the prepared fruits together in a bowl, pour over the strained syrup and leave for 2–3 hours.
3. Divide the fruit salad evenly between four serving dishes.
4. Mix together the fromage frais and honey. Spoon a quarter of the mixture on top of each fruit salad and decorate with a sprig of mint.

Exchanges per serving: Fruit 1, Protein 1, Optional Calories 25

WEEK 4

Breakfast:

1½oz (45g) chopped dried apricots
1oz (30g) cereal
¼ pint (150ml) skimmed milk

Lunch: Green Pea Soup (page 110)

Cottage Cheese and Tuna Sandwich

Spread 2 × 1oz (30g) slices of bread with 2 teaspoons margarine. Mix 2oz (60g) cottage cheese with 1oz (30g) drained and flaked, canned tuna, 1 tablespoon chopped chives and a little lemon juice. Season with salt and pepper. Spread the filling on one slice of bread, sandwich together with the remaining slice.

5oz (150g) wedge of honeydew melon
2½fl oz (75ml) low-fat natural yogurt

Dinner: Grilled Steak with Vegetables

Brush a 4oz (120g) lean fillet steak with ½ teaspoon vegetable oil, grill for 4 minutes, turn, brush with ½ teaspoon vegetable oil and continue grilling until cooked. Serve with 1½ teaspoons horseradish sauce, 1 grilled tomato and steamed or boiled broccoli and swede.

✳ Blueberry Mousse ✳

Snacks:

¼ pint (150ml) skimmed milk

Optional Calories: 100

BLUEBERRY MOUSSE

Serves 6
130 Calories per serving

15oz (450g) blueberries
4fl oz (120ml) white wine
5 tablespoons sugar
1 tablespoon cornflour
2 tablespoons water
3 eggs, separated
pinch of cream of tartar

1. Place the blueberries, wine and sugar in a saucepan, cover and simmer for 10 minutes.
2. Transfer the blueberries and wine to a blender, process until smooth.
3. Pour the purée back into the saucepan. Blend the cornflour to a smooth paste with the water, stir into the blueberry purée and bring to the boil stirring all the time. Boil for 1–2 minutes.
4. Remove the saucepan from the heat, stir in the egg yolks, mix well and leave until cool.
5. When the purée is cold whisk the egg whites with the cream of tartar until peaking. Using a metal tablespoon, fold a little of the egg whites into the purée to lighten the mixture, then fold in the remaining egg whites.
6. Spoon the mixture into six serving glasses, chill for about an hour before serving.

Exchanges per serving: Fruit ½, Protein ½, Optional Calories 75

WEEK 5

Breakfast:

1oz (30g) dried apricots, chopped
1oz (30g) cereal
¼ pint (150ml) skimmed milk

Lunch: Ploughman's Lunch

1¾oz (50g) wedge French bread,
2 teaspoons margarine, 2oz (60g)
Cheddar cheese, 1 tablespoon
chutney garnished with 1 tomato and
few sticks of celery.
4fl oz (120ml) tomato juice

Dinner: Roast Turkey with Vegetables

3oz (90g) roast turkey
Steamed or boiled mange-tout,
carrots and cauliflower.

✳ Creamy Strawberry Sundae ✳

Snacks:

½ pint (300ml) skimmed milk

Optional Calories: 170

CREAMY STRAWBERRY SUNDAE

Serves 4
255 Calories per serving

For the base:
10oz (300g) strawberries, sliced

4 teaspoons caster sugar

3 tablespoons medium sherry

For the custard:
1oz (30g) cornflour

1 pint (600ml) skimmed milk

2 eggs

few drops of vanilla essence

2 tablespoons caster sugar

For the topping:
4 small violets or primroses

1½ teaspoons caster sugar

3 tablespoons double cream

1. Mix the strawberries, caster sugar and sherry together. Leave to marinate for 1 hour.
2. Meanwhile make the custard: mix the cornflour to a smooth paste with a little milk and put to one side.
3. Separate one of the eggs, lightly beat the white and measure 2 teaspoons into a cup, this will be used to frost the flowers. Whisk the remaining egg white with the egg yolk and the other egg.
4. Heat the remaining milk until steaming, pour in the cornflour paste and bring to the boil, stirring all the time, boil for 1 minute. Remove from the heat, stir in the vanilla essence and sugar. Allow to cool a little then stir in the beaten eggs (do not add the eggs to the boiling sauce).
5. Divide the strawberries between four serving glasses, spoon over the cool custard and chill until set.
6. Dust a small piece of greaseproof paper with ¼ teaspoon caster sugar. Using a fine paint brush paint the back and front of the flowers with the reserved egg white, sprinkle both sides evenly with the caster sugar. Lay on the greaseproof paper in a warm dry place to dry.
7. Whip the cream, either pipe or swirl on top of the custard and decorate with the frosted flowers just before serving.

Exchanges per serving: Bread ¼, Fruit ½, Milk ½, Protein ½, Optional Calories 120

Creamy Strawberry Sundae

WEEK 4

Breakfast:

4fl oz (120ml) grapefruit juice
Toast a 1oz (30g) slice of bread,
spread with 1 teaspoon margarine
and top with a poached egg.

Lunch: Cottage Cheese Salad

Mix together 3oz (90g) cottage
cheese, 2 teaspoons chopped chives
or spring onions, salt and pepper.
Mixed Salad – shredded lettuce,
chicory, sliced tomato, radish and
cucumber.

½ medium mango with
2½fl oz (75ml) low-fat natural yogurt.

Dinner: Plaice in Prawn Wine Sauce (page 170)

6oz (180g) baked jacket potato with
1 teaspoon margarine.
Steamed or boiled mange-tout, leeks
and mushrooms.

✳ Apricot Yogurt Fool ✳

Snacks:

12½fl oz (375ml) skimmed milk

Optional Calories: 170

APRICOT YOGURT FOOL

Serves 4
130 Calories per serving

8 medium apricots
finely grated zest of 1 orange
juice of ½ an orange
4 tablespoons sugar
2 tablespoons custard powder
¼ pint (150ml) skimmed milk
5fl oz (150ml) low-fat natural yogurt

1. Halve the apricots, remove the stones and place in a saucepan with the orange zest and juice.
2. Cover the saucepan, place over a moderate heat and simmer for about 10 minutes until the apricots are cooked.
3. Transfer the apricots and the juices into a blender and process until smooth. Stir in the sugar.
4. Blend the custard powder with a little milk until smooth, heat the remaining milk, pour on to the custard powder mixture and return to the saucepan. Stir in the apricot purée and bring to the boil, stirring continuously. Boil for 1–2 minutes. Leave to cool.
5. Reserve 4 teaspoons of yogurt, stir the remainder into the cold purée. Spoon the Apricot Yogurt Fool into four serving glasses and swirl the remaining teaspoons of yogurt into each fool. Chill well.

Exchanges per serving: Fruit 1, Milk ¼, Optional Calories 90

WEEK 4

Breakfast:

4fl oz (120ml) apple juice
Toast a 1oz (30g) slice of bread,
spread with 1 tablespoon peanut
butter.

Lunch: Luncheon Meat Open Sandwich

Spread 1 reduced-calorie slice of
bread with 1 teaspoon margarine.
Top with 2–3 lettuce leaves and
alternate slices of tomato and
cucumber. Arrange 1½oz (45g) slices
of luncheon meat on top.
4fl oz (120ml) tomato juice

5fl oz (150ml) low-fat natural yogurt
½ medium ogen melon

Dinner: Grilled Liver with Vegetables

Brush 4oz (120g) lamb's or calf's liver
with ½ teaspoon vegetable oil, grill
for about 4 minutes then turn, brush
with ½ teaspoon vegetable oil and
continue grilling until cooked. Serve
with 1 tomato, halved, sprinkled with
chopped basil and grilled.
3oz (90g) sweetcorn
Boiled or steamed broccoli.

✳ Clafouti ✳

Snacks:

½ pint (300ml) skimmed milk

Optional Calories: 100

CLAFOUTI

Serves 4
195 Calories per serving

12oz (360g) sweet black cherries
1 teaspoon margarine
2oz (60g) plain flour
pinch of salt
4 tablespoons icing sugar
2 eggs
¼ pint (150ml) skimmed milk
½–1 teaspoon vanilla essence
For the topping: ½ teaspoon icing sugar

1. Stone all the cherries. Grease a shallow ovenproof dish with the margarine and spread all the cherries over the dish to just cover the base.
2. Sieve the flour, salt and icing sugar into a bowl. Make a well in the centre and beat an egg into it. Mix in the egg and gradually add the other one in the same way to make a smooth mixture.
3. Gradually add the milk and vanilla essence.
4. Pour the thin batter over the cherries and bake at 350°F/180°C/Gas Mark 4 for about 1 hour until the edges have risen well and a knife can be inserted into the centre and remains clean when removed.
5. Sprinkle the remaining icing sugar through a fine sieve all over the pudding and serve immediately.

Exchanges per serving: Bread ½, Fruit ½, Protein ½, Optional Calories 100

WEEK 5
Breakfast: Swiss Muesli (page 52)

Lunch: Prawn Omelette with Tomatoes

Beat together 2 eggs, 2 tablespoons water, salt and pepper. Heat 1 teaspoon margarine in a small omelette pan, pour in the mixture and cook over a gentle heat drawing the mixture from the edge towards the centre. When the underside is golden sprinkle 2 teaspoons chopped chives and 1oz (30g) peeled prawns over one half of the omelette, cook for a further minute, fold over and serve with 2 grilled tomatoes.
1oz (30g) French bread spread with 1 teaspoon margarine.

1 small tangerine

Dinner: Roast Chicken with Vegetables

3oz (90g) roast chicken
3oz (90g) boiled or baked potato with 1 teaspoon margarine.
Steamed or boiled Brussels sprouts and parsnips.

✳ Ice-Cream with Cherry Sauce ✳

Snacks:

2½fl oz (75ml) low-fat natural yogurt
½ pint (300ml) skimmed milk

Optional Calories: 180

ICE-CREAM WITH CHERRY SAUCE
Serves 4
200 Calories per serving

1lb 2oz (540g) sweet dark cherries
4fl oz (120ml) red wine
2 inch (5cm) stick of cinnamon
1 long strip of orange zest, removed with a potato peeler
2 tablespoons sugar
1½ teaspoons arrowroot
3 tablespoons water
4 × 2oz (60g) scoops vanilla ice-cream

1. Remove the stalks and stones from the cherries using a cherry stoner. Place the cherries in a saucepan with the wine, cinnamon and orange zest, cover and simmer for 10 minutes.
2. Stir the sugar into the cherries and remove from the heat.
3. Blend the arrowroot to a paste with the water, stir into the cherries and wine and return to the heat, bring to the boil, stirring all the time. Boil for 1 minute and remove from the heat.
4. Chill the cherry sauce until cold. Remove the cinnamon and orange zest.
5. Place the ice-cream in four serving dishes, pour over the cherry sauce.

Exchanges per serving: Fruit 1, Optional Calories 160

Ice-Cream with Cherry Sauce

WEEK 5

Breakfast:

4fl oz (120ml) orange juice
Toast a 1½oz (45g) slice of bread,
spread with 1 teaspoon margarine
and top with 3oz (90g) baked beans.

Lunch: Ham Salad

1½oz (45g) cooked, sliced ham
served with a mixed salad of
shredded lettuce, sliced tomato,
cucumber, spring onions and celery
tossed in 2 teaspoons French
dressing.

4oz (120g) drained, canned sliced
peaches, served with 2½fl oz (75ml)
low-fat natural yogurt.

Dinner: Poached Salmon with Vegetables

3oz (90g) poached salmon
Steamed or boiled mange-tout,
courgettes and carrots
3oz (90g) sweetcorn topped with
1 teaspoon margarine.

✳ Scottish Cream ✳

Snacks:

2 inch (5cm) wedge of honeydew
melon
½ pint (300ml) skimmed milk

Optional Calories: 70

SCOTTISH CREAM

Serves 4
195 Calories per serving

1 pint (600ml) skimmed milk
good pinch of ground allspice
2oz (60g) porridge oats
3 tablespoons honey
3 tablespoons whisky
4oz (120g) fromage frais

1. Heat the milk and allspice until steaming, stir in the porridge oats and bring to the boil, stirring all the time.
2. Reduce the heat and simmer for about 10 minutes, stirring continuously until very thick. Continue stirring to prevent the mixture burning.
3. Remove the thick sauce from the heat and allow to cool.
4. Reserve a teaspoon of honey, stir the remaining honey and whisky into the sauce. When completely cold, stir in the fromage frais and spoon into four serving glasses, chill.
5. Just before serving, drizzle the reserved honey over the top of each Scottish Cream.

Exchanges per serving: Bread ½, Milk ½, Protein ½, Optional Calories 70

WEEK 5

Breakfast:

4fl oz (120ml) orange juice
1 croissant spread with 1 teaspoon margarine and 1 tablespoon strawberry jam.

Lunch: Mushroom Omelette

Beat together 2 eggs, 2 tablespoons water, salt and pepper. Heat ½ teaspoon margarine in a small omelette pan, stir-fry 3oz (90g) sliced mushrooms for 3–4 minutes, remove. Heat 1 teaspoon margarine in the omelette pan, pour in the egg mixture and cook over a gentle heat drawing the mixture from the edge towards the centre. When the underside is golden, spoon the mushrooms over half the omelette, cook for a further minute, fold over and serve.

5fl oz (150ml) low-fat natural yogurt

Dinner: Poached Smoked Haddock with Vegetables

Poach 4½oz (135g) fillet smoked haddock in a little cold water.
6oz (180g) baked jacket potato with ½ teaspoon margarine.
Steamed or boiled peas and carrots.

✳ Apples with Blackberry Sauce ✳

Snacks:

½ pint (300ml) skimmed milk

Optional Calories: 230

APPLES WITH BLACKBERRY SAUCE

Serves 2
165 Calories per serving

12oz (360g) cooking apples, weighed when peeled, quartered and cored
4 tablespoons water
2½ tablespoons caster sugar
strip of lemon zest
good pinch of ground cinnamon
5oz (150g) blackberries
1 teaspoon arrowroot

1. Slice the apple quarters, place in a saucepan with the water, 2 tablespoons sugar, a strip of lemon zest and the cinnamon. Cover the saucepan and place over a low heat until the apple is just cooked, but not mushy, about 10–15 minutes.
2. Push the blackberries through a sieve or purée in a blender, then sieve. Press hard to remove all the seeds but extract as much juice as possible.
3. Blend a little of the blackberry juice with the arrowroot and put to one side.
4. Remove the cooked apple slices from the saucepan with a slotted spoon and keep warm. Remove the lemon zest.
5. Pour the blackberry purée and remaining sugar into the saucepan and stir over a gentle heat until the sugar has dissolved.
6. Stir in the arrowroot and bring to the boil stirring all the time, boil for 1 minute, pour over the apples and serve.

Exchanges per serving: Fruit 2, Optional Calories 80

WEEK 5

Breakfast:

4fl oz (120ml) tomato juice
Toast a 1oz (30g) slice of bread, sprinkle 1oz (30g) grated cheese on one side and return to the grill until bubbling.

Lunch: Sausage and Beans

Grill a 2oz (60g) pork sausage and serve with 3oz (90g) baked beans. Mixed Salad – shredded lettuce, sliced tomato, cucumber, spring onion and celery, tossed in 4 teaspoons French dressing.

5fl oz (150ml) low-fat natural yogurt

Dinner: Roast Turkey with Vegetables

3oz (90g) roast turkey
1½ teaspoons cranberry sauce
3oz (90g) sweetcorn dotted with 1 teaspoon margarine.
Steamed or boiled asparagus and carrots.

✳ Mixed Fruit Flambé ✳

Snacks:

½ pint (300ml) skimmed milk

Optional Calories: 105

MIXED FRUIT FLAMBÉ

Serves 4
135 Calories per serving

2 medium nectarines
4oz (120g) cherries
1 medium banana
½ medium firm papaya
4fl oz (120ml) water
grated zest of ½ a lemon
5 teaspoons sugar
1 teaspoon arrowroot
1 teaspoon water
6 tablespoons kirsch or rum

1. Halve the nectarines, remove the stones and cut each nectarine half into four wedges.
2. Stone the cherries, slice the banana diagonally into thick slices. Scoop the seeds out of the papaya, peel and dice.
3. Place all the fruit, water and lemon zest in a saucepan, cover and simmer for about 10 minutes until the fruit is just cooked.
4. Stir in the sugar and remove from the heat. Remove the fruit. Blend the arrowroot with the water, stir into the syrup, bring to the boil, simmer for 1 minute, stirring all the time.
5. Replace the fruit, stir gently over a low heat, add the kirsch or rum, set alight and serve immediately.

Exchanges per serving: Fruit 1½, Optional Calories 80

WEEK 5

Breakfast:

4fl oz (120ml) orange juice
1 croissant spread with 1 teaspoon margarine and 1 tablespoon raspberry jam.

Lunch: Corned Beef and Tomato Sandwich

Spread 2 × 1oz (30g) slices of bread with 2 teaspoons margarine, lay 2oz (60g) of corned beef over one slice, cover with slices of tomato and sandwich together with the other slice of bread.
Green Salad – shredded lettuce, sliced cucumber, green pepper, celery and sprigs of watercress.

1 medium persimmon

Dinner: Kipper with Vegetables

4½oz (135g) kippers, poached or grilled
Steamed or boiled courgettes, peas and carrots.

✳ Caribbean Choice ✳

Snacks:

5fl oz (150ml) low-fat natural yogurt
½ pint (300ml) skimmed milk

Optional Calories: 200

CARIBBEAN CHOICE

Serves 4
130 Calories per serving

½ medium papaya
½ medium mango
1 medium banana, sliced
4 tablespoons orange juice
4oz (120g) curd cheese
2 tablespoons set honey
juice of 1 lime
2 egg whites
pinch of cream of tartar
4 slices of lime

1. Scoop out and discard the black seeds from the papaya. Spoon the papaya into a blender scraping all the flesh from the skin.
2. Using a spoon remove the mango flesh from the skin and round the stone, add to the papaya in the blender.
3. Add the banana and orange juice to the blender, and process until smooth. Add the curd cheese, honey and lime juice and process again until smooth. Transfer the purée to a bowl.
4. Whisk the egg whites with the cream of tartar until peaking. Using a metal tablespoon, fold the egg whites into the fruit purée.
5. Spoon the mixture into four serving dishes and chill well. Just before serving decorate each dish with a slice of lime.

Exchanges per serving: Fruit 1, Protein ½, Optional Calories 50

WEEK 5

Breakfast:

½oz (15g) raisins
1oz (30g) cereal
¼ pint (150ml) skimmed milk

Lunch: Chicken Salad

2oz (60g) chicken, sliced
Tomato and Cucumber Salad –
1 tomato, sliced and 1½ inch (4cm)
wedge of cucumber sliced, tossed in
2 teaspoons low-calorie French
dressing and 2 teaspoons chopped
chives.
Mixed Salad – shredded lettuce,
sliced cucumber, peppers and radish.
4fl oz (120ml) tomato juice

Cheese, apple and crackers –
2 cream crackers spread with
1 teaspoon low-fat spread, 1oz (30g)
hard cheese and 1 medium apple.

Dinner: Pineapple and Ham with Vegetables

3oz (90g) boiled ham, sliced, served
with 1 drained, canned slice of
pineapple.
Steamed or boiled carrots and
cauliflower.

✳ Fruit Shortbread ✳

Snacks:

5fl oz (150ml) low-fat natural yogurt
¼ pint (150ml) skimmed milk

Optional Calories: 45

FRUIT SHORTBREAD

Serves 6
205 Calories per serving

For the shortbread:
4 tablespoons margarine

2 tablespoons caster sugar

few drops of vanilla essence

3½oz (105g) plain flour

For the filling:
6oz (180g) fromage frais

4 teaspoons caster sugar

1 fresh medium peach or 4oz (120g) drained, canned peaches

5oz (150g) strawberries, halved or sliced

1 passion fruit

To finish:
½ teaspoon icing sugar

1. Line two baking sheets with non-stick baking parchment.
2. Make the shortbread; cream the margarine and caster sugar together, add the vanilla essence. Reserve 1 tablespoon flour and stir the remaining flour into the creamed mixture.
3. Sprinkle the reserved flour over the rolling pin and work surface, divide the mixture into two. Roll half the mixture into a 5¾ inch (14.5cm) circle, then roll the second half into a slightly smaller circle and mark into six. Bake at 350°F/180°C/Gas Mark 4 for about 20 minutes until lightly browned. Cool on a wire rack.
4. Place the larger circle of shortbread on the serving plate.
5. Mix the fromage frais and caster sugar together. Chop the peaches and mix into the fromage frais with the strawberries. Cut the passion fruit in half, scoop out the seeds and flesh and stir into the mixture.
6. Just prior to serving, sieve the icing sugar over the smaller individual shortbread. Pile the fruit mixture evenly over the shortbread base, divide the marked shortbread into six and arrange on top of the fruit.

Exchanges per serving: Bread ½, Fat 2, Fruit ½, Protein ½, Optional Calories 45

WEEK 5

Breakfast:

4fl oz (120ml) tomato juice
Toast 1 reduced-calorie slice of bread, spread with 1 teaspoon margarine and top with a poached egg.

Lunch: Ploughman's Lunch

1oz (30g) French bread spread with 1 teaspoon margarine, 1oz (30g) hard cheese, tomato, cucumber and 1 tablespoon chutney.

1 medium apple

Dinner: Salmon with Vegetables

4oz (120g) fillet of salmon poached in a little water and served with a wedge of lemon.
4½oz (135g) baked potato with 1 teaspoon margarine.
Steamed or boiled mange-tout and carrots.

∗ Luxury Orange Mousse ∗

Snacks:

½ medium ogen melon
5fl oz (150ml) low-fat natural yogurt
½ pint (300ml) skimmed milk

Optional Calories: 170

LUXURY ORANGE MOUSSE

Serves 6
210 Calories per serving

| 3 medium oranges |
| 1 tablespoon lemon juice |
| 6 tablespoons caster sugar |
| 3 large eggs (size 1 or 2) separated plus 1 extra egg white |
| 2 tablespoons hot water |
| 4 teaspoons gelatine |
| 3 tablespoons Grand Marnier |
| 6oz (180g) fromage frais |
| pinch of cream of tartar |
| ½oz (15g) plain chocolate |
| 6 rose leaves |
| 3 tablespoons double cream |

1. Finely grate the zest from the oranges, cut one orange in half horizontally and reserve. Squeeze the juice from 2½ oranges and place in a large bowl with the lemon juice, sugar and egg yolks. Place over a bowl of simmering water and whisk for about 15 minutes until beginning to thicken. Remove from the heat and whisk until cool.
2. Pour the hot water into a cup or small basin and sprinkle in the gelatine. Place the cup in a saucepan of simmering water, leave until the gelatine has dissolved.
3. Stir the Grand Marnier then the dissolved gelatine into the whisked mixture, leave until almost set – don't worry if the mixture separates into a sauce with a foamy top.
4. Meanwhile, tie a band of greaseproof paper around a 6 inch (15cm) soufflé dish.
5. Whisk the almost set mixture, then add the fromage frais. Whisk all the egg whites together with the cream of tartar, fold into the orange mixture, transfer to the prepared soufflé dish and chill until set.
6. Melt the chocolate and using a small paint brush, brush the chocolate on the back of the rose leaves. Allow to set then peel off the rose leaves.
7. Whisk the cream until thick. Using a ½ inch (1.25cm) fluted nozzle pipe rosettes on top of the mousse. Using a sharp knife remove the skin and pith from the reserved half an orange, divide into segments. Remove the paper from the mousse, decorate with chocolate leaves and orange segments.

Exchanges per serving: Fruit ½, Protein 1, Optional Calories 120

WEEK 5

Breakfast:

Pineapple Buttermilk Froth – place 4oz (120g) drained, canned pineapple pieces in a blender with ¼ pint (150ml) buttermilk and 1 teaspoon sugar. Process until smooth, serve immediately.
Toast a 1oz (30g) slice of bread, spread with 1 tablespoon peanut butter.

Lunch: Poached Egg and Baked Beans

Toast a 1½oz (45g) slice of bread, spread with 1 teaspoon margarine, top with 1 poached egg and 3oz (90g) baked beans.

5oz (150g) strawberries served with 2 tablespoons low-fat natural yogurt.

Dinner: Fishcakes with Vegetables

2 × 2oz (60g) breadcrumbed fish cakes, dotted with 1 teaspoon margarine and grilled.
Steamed or boiled mange-tout and carrots.

✳ Plum Mousse ✳

Snacks:

½ pint (300ml) skimmed milk

Optional Calories: 110

PLUM MOUSSE

Serves 4
195 Calories per serving

1lb (480g) plums
2 tablespoons water
artificial sweetener
2 eggs, separated
3 tablespoons port
2 tablespoons hot water
4 teaspoons gelatine
4oz (120g) fromage frais
5fl oz (150ml) low-fat natural yogurt
pinch of cream of tartar
3 tablespoons double cream

1. Tie a band of greaseproof paper round a 5 inch (13cm) soufflé dish, the paper should stand about 2 inches (5cm) above the rim of the dish.
2. Cut the plums in half and place in a saucepan with the cold water, cover and simmer gently until the plums are cooked.
3. Remove the plum stones then transfer the plums and their juices to a blender, process until smooth.
4. Pour the plum purée back into the saucepan, sweeten to taste with artificial sweetener and bring to the boil stirring all the time. Remove from the heat, allow to cool a little, beat in the egg yolks and port. Leave to cool.
5. Pour the hot water into a small basin or cup, sprinkle in the gelatine and stand in a saucepan of simmering water until dissolved.
6. Stir the dissolved gelatine into the plum purée and leave until beginning to set. Fold in the fromage frais and yogurt.
7. Whisk the egg whites and cream of tartar until peaking, carefully fold into the plum mixture. Transfer to the prepared dish and leave until completely set.
8. To serve; remove the greaseproof band. Whisk the double cream and, using a ½ inch (1.25cm) fluted nozzle pipe rosettes on the top.

Exchanges per serving: Fruit 1, Milk ¼, Protein 1, Optional Calories 50

WEEK 2

Breakfast:

4fl oz (120ml) orange juice
1oz (30g) cereal
¼ pint (150ml) skimmed milk

Lunch: Chicken Salad

2oz (60g) cooked chicken, sliced
Mixed Salad – shredded lettuce,
sliced cucumber, tomato, celery and
peppers tossed in 1 tablespoon
low-calorie French dressing.
1oz (30g) slice of bread spread with
1 teaspoon margarine.

1 medium pear

Dinner: Cheese Omelette with Vegetables

Beat together 2 eggs, 2 tablespoons
water, salt and pepper. Heat
1 teaspoon margarine in a small
omelette pan, pour in the egg mixture
and cook over a gentle heat, drawing
the mixture from the edge towards
the centre. When the underside is
golden brown, sprinkle 1oz (30g)
grated hard cheese over the omelette,
cook for a further minute, fold over
and serve.
Steamed or boiled carrots and
Brussels sprouts.

✱ Simple Milk Pudding ✱

Served with 1 medium cooking apple,
peeled, quartered, cored and sliced,
stewed in a little water and
sweetened with artificial sweetener.

Snacks:

½ pint (300ml) skimmed milk

Optional Calories: 40

SIMPLE MILK PUDDING

Serves 2
150 Calories per serving

½ teaspoon margarine

1oz (30g) short grain pudding rice or tapioca

finely grated zest of ½ a lemon

1 tablespoon caster sugar

12fl oz (360ml) skimmed milk

¼ teaspoon ground cinnamon

1. Grease a small ovenproof dish with the margarine.
2. Stir the rice or tapioca, lemon zest, sugar, milk and ground cinnamon into the greased dish and transfer to an oven 300°F/150°C/Gas Mark 2 for 30 minutes.
3. Remove the pudding from the oven, stir well, return to the oven at the same temperature and bake for a further 1½–2 hours.
4. Serve hot or allow to cool and serve cold.

Exchanges per serving: Bread ½, Fat ¼, Milk ½, Optional Calories 40

VEGETARIAN WEEK 2

Breakfast:

1 medium apple
1oz (30g) cereal
¼ pint (150ml) skimmed milk

Lunch: Filled Potato and Salad

6oz (180g) baked potato
6oz (180g) baked beans
1oz (30g) Cheddar cheese
Green Salad – shredded lettuce, sliced cucumber, celery and spring onions tossed in 3 teaspoons low-calorie French dressing.

1 medium orange

Dinner: Tomato Omelette

Beat together 2 eggs, 2 tablespoons water, salt and pepper. Heat 2 teaspoons margarine in a small omelette pan, add the egg mixture and cook over a gentle heat drawing the mixture from the edge towards the centre. When the underside is golden brown lay slices of tomato over half the omelette and cook for a further 1–2 minutes. Fold the omelette in half and serve.
Steamed or boiled green beans and cauliflower.

✳ Raspberry Hazelnut Meringues ✳

Snacks:

5fl oz (150ml) low-fat natural yogurt
¼ pint (150ml) skimmed milk

Optional Calories: 90

RASPBERRY HAZELNUT MERINGUES

Serves 3
125 Calories per serving

1 egg white

pinch of cream of tartar

4 tablespoons caster sugar

¾oz (20g) hazelnuts, very finely chopped

5oz (150g) raspberries

1. Line a baking sheet with non-stick baking parchment.
2. Whisk the egg white and cream of tartar until peaking, add a tablespoon of caster sugar and whisk again until peaks form. Repeat this process until all the sugar has been added.
3. Using a metal spoon, fold in the chopped hazelnuts.
4. Transfer the meringue mixture to a piping bag fitted with a ½ inch (1.25cm) fluted nozzle. Pipe a circle about 3 inches (7.5cm) in diameter on the baking parchment. Pipe one or two rings on top of the base circle to form a basket. Alternatively, pipe a single circle about 4½ inches (11.5cm) in diameter.
5. Bake at 250°F/120°C/Gas Mark ½ for about 3 hours until the meringue is firm and crisp.
6. Cool on a wire rack and fill with the raspberries no more than half an hour before serving. If the meringues are to be stored, place them in an airtight tin.

Exchanges per serving: Fat ¼, Fruit ¼, Protein ½, Optional Calories 90

VEGETARIAN WEEK 5

Breakfast:

4fl oz (120ml) tomato juice
1 croissant spread with 2 teaspoons low-fat spread and 1 tablespoon black cherry jam.

Lunch: Cottage Cheese Salad

3oz (90g) cottage cheese mixed with 2 teaspoons chopped chives and dash of pepper sauce.
Mixed Salad – shredded lettuce, sliced cucumber, tomato, peppers and radish.
2oz (60g) French bread spread with 1 teaspoon low-fat spread.

5fl oz (150ml) low-fat natural yogurt

Dinner: Vegetable Curry (page 179)

✱ Frozen Banana Cream ✱

Snacks:

½ pint (300ml) skimmed milk

Optional Calories: 190

FROZEN BANANA CREAM
Serves 2
240 Calories per serving

2 medium bananas

4oz (120g) fromage frais

2 teaspoons set honey

4 teaspoons rum

1oz (30g) flaked almonds

cinnamon

1. Peel the bananas and wrap each one in foil, freeze for 6–8 hours.
2. Mix together the fromage frais, honey and rum.
3. Toast the flaked almonds until golden.
4. About 10–15 minutes before serving remove the bananas from the freezer. Stir about threequarters of the almonds into the fromage mixture.
5. Unwrap the bananas and slice. Fold the bananas into the fromage frais. Spoon into two serving glasses. Dust with a little cinnamon and sprinkle with the reserved toasted almonds. Serve immediately.

Exchanges per serving: Fat ½, Fruit 2, Protein 2, Optional Calories 40

VEGETARIAN WEEK 5

Breakfast:

4fl oz (120ml) orange juice
Toast a 1oz (30g) slice of bread
spread with 1 tablespoon peanut
butter.

Lunch: Smoked Tofu Salad

3oz (90g) smoked tofu, cubed
Mixed Salad – sliced peppers,
mushrooms, cucumber, tomato and
celery, with sprigs of watercress.

Apple and Cheese – 1 medium apple
and 1oz (30g) hard cheese.

Dinner: Burger with Vegetables

1 vegetarian burger, grilled
Steamed or boiled celeriac, leeks and
carrots.
1 medium corn on the cob, boiled
and dotted with 1 teaspoon low-fat
spread.

✳ Hazelnut Raspberry Crumble ✳

4fl oz (120ml) white or red wine

Snacks:

¼ pint (150ml) buttermilk
½ pint (300ml) skimmed milk

Optional Calories: 130

HAZELNUT RASPBERRY CRUMBLE

Serves 1
290 Calories per serving

| 5oz (150g) raspberries |
| 1½ teaspoons honey |
| For the crumble:
1oz (30g) wholemeal flour |
| ½oz (15g) hazelnuts |
| 1 teaspoon margarine |
| To serve:
2½fl oz (75ml) low-fat natural yogurt |

1. Place the raspberries in a deep 4½ inch (11.5cm) ovenproof dish or ramekin, drizzle the honey over the fruit.
2. Place the wholemeal flour in a bowl. Grind the hazelnuts in a mouli grater or grinder and stir into the flour.
3. Rub the margarine (if possible margarine which has been stored in a freezer) into the flour and hazelnuts.
4. Sprinkle the crumble topping over the raspberries. Cook in a preheated oven 375°F/190°C/Gas Mark 5 for 25 minutes.
5. Serve hot or warm with the yogurt.

Exchanges per serving: Bread 1, Fat 1½, Fruit 1, Milk ½, Protein 1, Optional Calories 30

INDEX